D1433968

A HISTORY OF BRITAIN VOLUME TWO
PART 1: THE BRITISH WARS

The British Wars is a compelling chronicle of the changes that transformed every strand and strata of British life, faith and thought from 1603 to 1776. Simon Schama explores the forces that tore Britain apart during two centuries of dynamic change—transforming outlooks, allegiances and boundaries.

The British wars began in 1637 with the Prayer Book riots. Over the next 200 years, other battles would rage on other battlegrounds. Most would be wars of faith—waged on wide-ranging grounds of political or religious conviction. The struggle to pull Britain together at first succeeded only in tearing our nations further apart. But as wars of religious passions gave way to campaigns for profit, the British people did come together in the imperial enterprise of 'Britannia Incorporated'.
The story of that great alteration—revolution and reaction, inspiration and disenchantment—is brought vividly, sometimes disturbingly, to life in Schama's rich and teeming tapestry of The British Wars

A HISTORY OF

BRITAIN

VOLUME 2 PART 1

THE BRITISH WARS
1603–1776

Simon Schama

BBC

**LARGE
PRINT**

First published 2000
by
BBC Worldwide Limited
This Large Print edition published 2004
by
BBC Audiobooks Ltd
a subsidiary of BBC Worldwide Limited

ISBN 0 7540 5669 4

British Library Cataloguing in Publication Data available

Printed and bound in Great Britain by
Antony Rowe Ltd., Chippenham, Wiltshire

CONTENTS

For Martin Davidson and Janice Hadlow—
history-makers.

Narrative is linear. Action is solid. Alas for our chains and chainlets of 'causes' and 'effects' which we so assiduously track through the countless handbreadths of years and square miles when the whole is a broad, deep immensity and each atom is 'chained' and complected with all . . .

THOMAS CARLYLE, 'History' from *Fraser's Magazine*

Vico's fantasia *is indispensable to his conception of historical knowledge; it is unlike the knowledge that Julius Caesar is dead or that Rome was not built in a day or that thirteen is a prime number, or that the week has seven days; nor yet is it like knowledge of how to ride a bicycle or engage in statistical research or win a battle. It is more like knowing what it is to be poor, to belong to a nation, to be a revolutionary, to fall in love, to be seized by nameless terror, to be delighted by a work of art . . .*

ISAIAH BERLIN, *Giambattista Vico and Cultural History*

Man is the only animal that laughs and weeps; for he is the only animal that is struck with the difference between what things are and what they ought to be.

WILLIAM HAZLITT, *Lectures on the English Comic Writers*

ACKNOWLEDGEMENTS

'Epic' is a word that suffers from over-use these days, but the history of *A History of Britain* certainly has a long roll-call of heroes—other than its author—without whose unflagging labours neither television programmes nor book could possibly have got made.

At BBC Worldwide Sally Potter and my excellent editor Belinda Wilkinson have remained heroically undaunted by the prospect of what had been commissioned as one short book turning into three. In every important sense this work has been a collaboration between myself and an exceptionally gifted and devoted group of colleagues at BBC Television, in particular Ian Bremner, Martin Davidson, Liz Hartford and Mike Ibeji. Melisa Akdogan, Ben Ledden and Ashley Gethin were exceptionally resourceful both in the libraries and on location. Had I not had the tireless and invariably considerate help of Sara Fletcher, I would have come unglued in locations throughout the British Isles. Tanya Hethorn, Tim Sutton and Mark Walden-Mills have, in crucial ways, helped the presenter present. Susan Harvey in Factual Publicity has been the gentlest and friendliest of promoters. It's been a source of great happiness to work closely with John Harle on the music for the series. Laurence Rees, Glenwyn Benson and Janice Hadlow have all cast a benevolently critical eye on our work when it most mattered and have been our most generous supporters. Alan Yentob and Greg Dyke have both given us the sense of how much *A History of Britain* matters to the BBC.

I'm deeply grateful to a number of colleagues who were kind enough to read both scripts and chapters for errors, in particular John Brewer, Ann Hughes, Holger Hoock, Peter Marshall, Steven Pincus and David Haycock. Any that remain are, of course, my own responsibility.

In a much larger and deeper sense, though, I owe an enormous debt of gratitude to the wisdom and erudition of teachers (including schoolteachers), from whom I first learned the great contentions of British and colonial history in the seventeenth and eighteenth centuries, and of friends and colleagues, whose scholarship and critical analysis is still a source of exhilarating illumination. Though they may well take exception to some (or many) of the views expressed in this book, I hope that the overdue thanks offered, in particular to David Armitage, Roy Avery, Robert Baynes, Mark Kishlansky, Sir John Plumb, Roy Porter, Kevin Sharpe and Quentin Skinner, will not go amiss.

My agents at PFD—Michael Sissons and Rosemary Scoular—have been, as ever, towers of strength on whom I lean, and occasionally collapse. My thanks, too, to James Gill, Sophie Laurimore and Carol Macarthur. Provost Jonathan Cole at Columbia University has been exceptionally kind in allowing me the necessary leave to work on the series and I'm delighted to have played a part in pioneering the on-line seminar, produced jointly by BBC Education and Columbia in partnership with Fathom.Com, about the eighteenth-century British Empire. Jennifer Scott was an extraordinary colleague in the production of that innovative departure in popular historical education.

Shifting back and forth between book and

script-writing is likely to make the head spin, and certain to make the writer-presenter generally impossible to be around. So I'm, as always, more grateful than I can say to my friends for submitting to recitations from the Schama book of lamentations —thank you, again—Clare Beavan, Lily Brett, John Brewer, Tina Brown, Jan Dalley, Alison Dominitz, Harry Evans, Amanda Foreman, Eliot Friedman, Mindy Engel Friedman, Andrew Motion, David Rankin, David Remnick, Anthony Silverstone, Beverly Silverstone, Jill Slotover, Stella Tillyard, Bing Taylor and Leon Wieseltier. To my nearest and dearest—Ginny, Chloe and Gabe—I give my heartfelt thanks for riding the storms of their unreasonably cranky Dad and husband, and for the calm waters and always-open harbour of their love.

PREFACE

If it's a truism that being British has never been a matter of straightforward allegiance, never was this more glaringly obvious than during the two centuries narrated by this book. Was this country an archipelago or an empire, a republic or a monarchy? 'Great Britain' began as a grandiose fantasy in the head of James VI of Scotland and I of England, and ended as a startling imperial reality on the bloodied ramparts of Seringapatam. The confident chroniclers of the mind-boggling transformation, from sub-insular realms to global empire, liked to imagine that this history was somehow pre-ordained, unfolding naturally from the imperatives of geography and from a shared sense of the inevitability of a parliamentary monarchy. But never was a nation's destiny less predictable, or *less* determined by the markers of topography, which said nothing about whether its bounds should be on the Tweed or the coast of Sligo, the Appalachians or the Bay of Bengal, nor whether those who decided such things should be thought of as the servants of the Crown or the representatives of the people.

It was these battles for allegiance—the British Wars, between and within the nations of our archipelago, and then beyond in the wider world, between different and fiercely argued ideas about our historical and political inheritance—that made us what we became. The creation of our identity was a baptism of blood.

But the slaughters were not always mindless.

xiii

Crucially, for our future, they were often, even excessively, mindful. The Victorian historians, especially Macaulay, who believed the good fortune of British birth to be a reward won by the sacrifices of ancestors, are habitually berated in much modern scholarship for their detestably insular smugness, their fatuous error of reading history 'backwards' and their habit of projecting on periods—entirely innocent of parliamentary civics— their own nineteenth-century preoccupations. Read those books, it's said, and you are in a world drained of historical free will, of the uncertainty of outcomes, a past ordered to march in lock-step to the drumbeat of the Protestant, parliamentary future. But a dip, or better yet, a prolonged immersion in the great narratives of the last century—Gardiner, Carlyle, and, to be sure, Macaulay—suggest, to this lay reader anyway, anything *but* imprisonment in a universe of self-fulfilling prophecies. At their most powerful, those wonderfully *complicated* texts deliver the reader into a world shaking with terror, chaos and cruelty.

But it is true, certainly, that many of the grand narratives assumed that the long story they told was one of a battle of beliefs, rather than a mere imbroglio of interests, and that the eventual, admittedly partial, success of the party of liberty represented a genuine turning point in the political history of the world. If to tell the story again, and yet insist that that much is true, is to reveal oneself as that most hopeless anachronism, a born-again Whig, so be it.

New York, 2001

xiv

CHAPTER ONE

RE-INVENTING BRITAIN

'Great Britain?' What was that? John Speed, tailor turned map-maker and historian, must have had some idea, for in 1611 he published an atlas of sixty-seven maps of the English counties, Wales, Scotland and Ireland, loftily entitled *The Theatre of the Empire of Great Britaine*. An energetic opportunist, Speed was taking advantage of King James's widely advertised desire to be known, not as the Sixth of Scotland and First of England, but as monarch of Britain. The fancy of a British history had been given fresh authority by William Camden's great compilation of geography, the antiquarian chronicle, *Britannia*, already in its sixth edition by 1607. On its frontispiece sat the helmeted personification of the island nation, flanked by Neptune and Ceres, together with an emblem of British antiquity—Stonehenge—thought to have been built by the Romano-British hero Aurelius.

But Camden's erudite work was originally in Latin, a volume for the shelves of a gentleman's library. Speed was after the public, sensing the excitement of even armchair travel, the need of the country to fix its place in the world, to contemplate, simultaneously, its past and its present. So the atlas, produced by John Sudbury and George Humble's print shop in Pope's Head Alley, London, was not just a compilation of topographic information but a busy, animated production, full

1

of comings and goings. Sites of historic interest, like the battlefields of the Wars of the Roses, were indicated by miniature sketches of horsemen and pikemen doing their worst; the colleges of Oxford and Cambridge by gowned scholars and coats of arms; royal palaces like Nonesuch and Windsor by elaborate pictorial illustration. On the map of Kent, ships, loaded with cargo, sailed up the Medway before Rochester Castle. Fifty towns were mapped for the first time, given their own insets, streets, markets and churches laid out for the prospective traveller or the proud resident. In this enterprising determination to be the first to provide a popular atlas for the new reign and the new century, the ex-tailor had no scruples about taking his shears to his predecessors. At least five of his maps of the English counties were pilfered more or less directly from the great Elizabethan cartographer Christopher Saxton (who had provided Burghley with his own pocket atlas) and another five from the English map-maker John Norden. For the single map of Scotland, which made good Speed's pretension of a British atlas, he relied on an earlier version by the Flemish cartographer and map-maker Gerardus Mercator, as well as on arcane information (Loch Ness never froze, horsemen speared salmon in the rivers) and on shameless flattery (the people being 'of good features, strong of body and courageous mien and in wars so virtuous that scarce any service of note hath been performed but they were the first and last in the field'). His eastern Ireland was so accurate that he may have gone there in person, but the west was obviously an exotic mystery, peopled by the medieval chronicler Gerard of

Wales's fantasy that off the coast 'lay islands, some full of angels, some full of devils'.

A roughly stitched thing of many odd cloths and fragments though it was, Speed's map of Great Britain was not entirely a fake. The comments he inscribes on the reverse of the maps may sometimes have been recycled platitudes about the cleanness or foulness of the air. But just as often they spoke of a real journey, of a man who had taken his theodolite to the shires. There were days when he must have trotted out from some damply shadowed valley and found himself surveying the panorama of England. The landscape before him would not have been so very different from our own: crookedly framed fields (with far fewer individual strips than a century before), copses of standing trees, a distant flock of sheep, a wisp of wood smoke. At one such place—the vale of the Red Horse in southeast Warwickshire—the prosaic Speed felt moved to reach for the hyperbole of the pastoral poets. The county was sharply divided by the river Avon. To the north was the semi-industrialized Forest of Arden, a country populated not by love-lorn Rosalinds and Celias but by impoverished charcoal-burners, woodland-gleaners, poachers and forge-workers on the verge of riot. But to the south was Feldon: 'champaign', rolling arable country, where the valley flats were planted with wheat and the gentle hills grazed by sheep. It was there, at just the point where the Cotswolds descend sharply, that Speed relates his rustic epiphany: 'The husbandman smileth in beholding his pains and the meadowing pastures with the green mantles so embroidered with flowers that from Edgehill we might behold

3

another Eden.'

John Speed died in 1629, leaving behind his *History of Great Britaine*, his pretty maps, eighteen children and (presumably) exhausted wife, Susanna. Thirteen years later, on 23 October 1642, Charles I arrived at the same Warwickshire ridge from which the map-maker had been given a glimpse of bucolic paradise, took out his prospective glass and peered down at the Roundhead troops below. By nightfall there were sixty bodies piled up where the king had stood on the top of Edgehill, and Charles was kept from his sleep by the vocal agonies of the thousands of wounded, groaning in the razor-sharp cold. Next morning, across Speed's flower-embroidered meadow lay the corpses of 3000 men, their allegiances indistinguishable in their nakedness, bodies stripped for loot, fingers broken to extract rings. Eden had become Golgotha.

By the time that the first round of the British wars was over—in 1660—at least a quarter of a million had perished in England, Wales and Scotland. They had been lost to disease and starvation as well as to battle and siege. Men had died of infected wounds more commonly than they had endured clean-cut deaths in combat. The scythe of mortality, always busy, never fussy, had swept up all kinds and conditions: officers and rank and file; troopers and musketeers; sutlers and camp whores; apprentices with helmets on their heads for the first time; hardened mercenaries who had grown rusty along with their cuirasses; soldiers who could not get enough to fill their stomachs or boots to put on their feet and peasants who had nothing left to give them; drummer boys and

4

buglers; captains and cooks. Even if the father of modern demography, Sir William Petty (Charles II's surveyor-general in Ireland), grossly over-counted another 600,000 dead in Ireland and his total is divided by three, the toll of life, expressed as a proportion of the 5 million population of the British archipelago, is still greater than our losses in the First World War (1914–18).

In any case, the raw body count fails to measure the enormity of the disaster that reached into every corner of the British isles from Cornwall to County Connacht, from York to the Hebrides. It tore apart the communities of the parish and the county, which through all the turmoil of the Reformation had managed to keep a consensus about who governed and how they went about their duties. Men who had judged together now judged each other. Men and women who had taken for granted the patriotic loyalty of even those with whom they disagreed in matters of Church and parliament now called each other traitor. Ultimately, what had been unthinkable was thought and acted on. Men and women, for whom the presence of a king was a condition for the well-being of the commonwealth, were asked to accept that the well-being of the commonwealth required that he be killed.

The wars divided nations, churches, families, father from son, brother from brother. Sir Bevil Grenville died at the battle of Lansdown knowing that his brother Richard was a parliamentary commander (who switched sides not long after). Private Hillsdeane, dying at the siege of Wardour Castle in Wiltshire, let it be known that it had been his own brother who had shot him, though he forgave him for 'only doing his duty'. During the most brutal year of the Scottish civil wars, 1645, Florence Campbell learned that her brother Duncan had been killed by the victorious leader of the MacDonalds after the battle of Inverlochy. While her brother had been a loser, her husband and son, royalist MacLeans, fought with the winners. But in her wrathful grief Florence was all Campbell. 'Were I at Inverlochy,' she wrote, 'with a two-edged sword in my hand and I would tear asunder the MacLeans and the MacDonalds and I would bring the Campbells back alive.'

The house of Britain was not just divided, it was demolished. The grandiose buildings that proclaimed the wealth and authority of the governing classes and that awed the common people to defer to their senatorial power were, in many cases, turned into blackened ruins by the relentless sieges that became the dominant form of assault. Many of those houses were converted into fortified strongholds and garrisons and, like Basing House in Hampshire and Corfe Castle on the Isle of Purbeck, held out to the bitter end. The defenders died, sword in hand, framed in burning doorways and windows, going down in hand-to-hand combat, or starved into surrender like the beleaguered defenders of Wardour Castle who had been subsisting on eight ounces of cereal each and their small share of half a horse. If anything much was left when the sieges were done, the houses were 'slighted'—one of the great euphemisms of the war—to make sure they would never again be a threat.

Epidemics of smallpox and typhus raged opportunistically through populations weakened by shortages of food. Perhaps the most successful army of all was the army of rats, which brought another great wave of plague to add to the bellyful of suffering. For a few years the worst affected regions of the four nations came perilously close to a total breakdown of custom, compassion and law. Towns like Bolton, subjected to a massacre in 1644, lost *half* their population. At Preston in 1643 'nothing was heard but "Kill dead, kill dead", horsemen pursuing the poor amazed people, killing and spoiling, nothing regarding the dolesful cries of women and children'. After Aberdeen fell to the army of the Marquis of Montrose and Alasdair MacColla, the better-off citizens were made to strip naked before being hacked to death so that the blood would not stain the valuable booty of their clothes. For some victims the trauma would never go away. The septuagenarian Lady Jordan, according to John Aubrey, 'being at Cirencester when it was besieged was so terrified with the shooting that her understanding was spoyled, that she became a tiny child that they made Babies for her to play withall'.

Why had the nations of Britain inflicted this ordeal on themselves? For what exactly had the hundreds of thousands perished? As often as this question has been asked, it can never be asked enough. As often as historians have failed to provide an answer, we can never give up trying to find one. We owe it to the casualties to ask if their misery had meaning. Or were the British wars just a meaningless cruelty? Did the Irish, Scots, English and Welsh of the seventeenth century suffer, as Victorian historians believed, so that their descendants might live in a parliamentary political nation, uniquely stable, free and just? Was their cause one of principle, an unavoidable collision between ultimately irreconcilable visions of Church and state? Or were the protagonists, high and low, the fools of history, jerked around by forces they only half-comprehended and whose outcomes they were blind to predict? Was the whole bloody mess an absurd misunderstanding that, by rights, ought never to have happened at all?

Victorian certainty about a providential purpose running through our histories has, it is safe to say, long been out of fashion, at least in the academic world. Reacting against the sententious, self-righteous view of the Victorians, some modern historical scholarship has argued that the bleaker, more complicated view happens to be the truth: that the British wars were eminently unpredictable, improbable and avoidable. Until the very last moment, late 1641 or 1642, the political class of England was united in a harmonious consensus that the country should be governed by a divinely appointed monarch assisted by a responsible parliament. If there were disputes they were containable. If there were matters that separated people they were as nothing compared to the interests and bedrock beliefs that bound them together. The king was no absolutist, the parliament no champion of liberty. They were all much of a muchness, and that muchness was Englishness: the sound, middling way. The Victorians, like the historian S. R. Gardiner, who blew up every petty squabble between the Stuarts and their parliaments into some great drama of political principle, were deluded by their two-party way of thought, their over-concentration on the sound and the fury of parliamentary debates and their need for a foundation epic. Thus, the argument goes, they read history backwards, so parliament, the beating heart of the nineteenth-century empire, would be thought always to have been the instrument of progress and the hallmark of the British 'difference', separating the nation from the absolutist states of continental Europe. It is this naively insular, nationalist, parliamentary narrative, with heroes like Pym and Hampden defending fortress England from sinking into European despotism, that has drawn the fire of scholars for the last half century. The very worst that can now be said of any account of the origins and unfolding of the civil wars is that it suffers from the delusions of 'Whig' history, in which the parties of 'progress' and 'reaction', of liberty and authority, are cleanly separated and programmed to clash. The truth was just the opposite, the critics insist. Crown and parliament, court and country, were not running on a collision course heading inevitably towards an immense constitutional train wreck. On the contrary, until the very last minute they were moving smoothly on parallel lines. The lights were green, the weather fair, the engine well oiled. When, in 1629, Charles I opted to govern without parliaments, no one, except a few self-righteous, self-appointed 'guardians' of English liberties, could have cared less.

But someone, somehow, seems to have thrown a switch. And, then, that utterly unpredictable, unlikely, what-shall-we-call-it?—a misfortune—took place. It was, I suppose, just about the biggest misfortune in our shared history. But there you are. Accidents happen.

Or do they?

For a time, it was rumoured that King James VI and I was about to change his name to Arthur. Well, why not? Hadn't Camden himself made it clear that 'Britain' was not some new invention at all but merely the *restoration* of an ancient unity, the realm of Brutus the Trojan and of King Lucius, who had been the first to be converted, and ultimately the heart of the great Arthurian-Christian British empire, which had extended from Iceland to Norway, from Ireland to Armorican Brittany. Certainly James himself believed that he was reuniting two realms that had been snapped apart, bringing about dreadful and unrelenting bloodshed. He was reminded by the court preacher John Hopkins of Ezekiel 37, in which the prophet had had a vision of two dry sticks, which he was commanded to put together; and when he did so, lo, they became one and a living thing too, a dream-parable of the reunion of the sundered Israel and Judah. John Gordon, a Scottish minister who had travelled down with James and who fancied himself a cabbalist, unlocked the esoteric significance of the Hebrew etymology of Britannia, in which Brit-an-Yah—translation: 'a covenant (*Brit*) was there'—encoded God's command to reconstitute Britain from its fractured halves. James was ready and eager to oblige, right from the moment he received the sapphire ring taken from Elizabeth's finger. By the time that he reached Newcastle upon Tyne in April 1603, the king had already redesigned the coinage, styling his kingdom 'Great Britain' and himself as its very Roman-looking, laurel-wreathed emperor. Throughout his reign, one of his adopted persona would be the new Constantine, the first Christian Caesar, born (as it was commonly thought) in north Britain.

Francis Bacon, the philosopher of science, essayist and politician, who would do his utmost to promote the union of realms, feared that the king 'hasteneth to a mixture of both kingdoms and nations faster perhaps than policy will conveniently bear'. But there was no stopping James. Union meant security, wholeness, peace. Everything, everyone, had to be enfolded within the inclusive embrace of his come-together kingdom. The Great Seal would incorporate all the coats of arms of his three kingdoms (four, if you count, as James certainly did, the lilies of France). A new flag, embodying the union, which James often and over-optimistically compared to a loving marriage, would fuse in connubial bliss the crosses of St George and St Andrew. Many trial designs were made, one with the Scottish saltire and the cross of St George side by side, another with the saltire merely quartered with the red and white. But in the end, the first Union flag, featuring the red and white imposed on the blue and white, was adopted in 1606. Scottish shipowners immediately complained that their saltire always seemed obscured by the cross of St George. It was not a good sign for the prospects of the union that any semblance of equity between the two kingdoms was defeated by the laws of optics, which dictated that a saturated red would always seem to project beyond the recessive blue, dooming St Andrew's cross to be read as 'background'.

But never mind the flags: bring on the players.

11

For those who offered themselves to be its publicists and showmen, the fantasy of the happy marriage of realms was a heaven-sent opportunity. Thomas Dekker, for example, East End slum-dweller, hack playwright, chronic debtor and jailbird, seized the moment as a godsend. Together with his much better placed colleague Ben Jonson, Dekker was charged with staging *The Magnificent Entertainment* for the city of London, by which the king would be formally greeted by his capital. Happy Britannia, of course, would be at the centre of it. 'St George and St Andrew, that many hundred years had defied one another, were now sworn brothers: England and Scotland being parted only with a narrow river.' Dekker knew exactly what to do. The two chevaliers, St Andrew and St George, would ride together, in brotherly amity, to greet the king: a real crowd pleaser, Dekker optimistically thought. And he would write a story of the nation in 1603, draped in mourning black and suffering from a melancholy ague, until a miraculous cure was effected by 'the wholesome receipt of a proclaimed king . . . FOR BEHOLD! Up rises a comfortable sun out of the north whose glorious beams like a fan dispersed all thick and contagious clouds.'

Unhappily for Dekker, the plague dashed the cup of success from his lips just as he was poised to taste it. ('But OH the short-lived felicity of man! O world, of what slight and thin stuff is thy happiness!') Between 30,000 and 40,000 died in the summer of 1603. The theatres were closed, the streets empty. So Dekker had to revert to plan B and squeeze some money out of misery rather than jubilation, making the most of the plague in a pamphlet, *The Wonderfull Yeare* (1603):

> What an unmatchable torment were it for a
> man to be bard up every night in a vast silent
> Charnel-house; hung (to make it more hideous)
> with lamps dimly & slowly burning, in hollow
> and glimmering corners: where all the
> pavement should in stead of greene rushes, be
> strewde with blasted Rosemary, withered
> Hyacinthes, fatal Cipresse and Ewe, thickly
> mingled with heapes of dead men's bones: the
> bare ribbes of a father that begat him, lying
> there: here, the Chaplesse hollow scull of a
> mother that bore him: round about him a
> thousand Coarses, some standing bolt upright
> in their knotted winding sheets, others half
> mouldred in rotten Coffins . . . that should
> suddenly yawne wide open, filling his nostrils
> with noysome stench, and his eyes with the sight
> of nothing but crawling wormes.

A year later, though, with the pestilence finally in
retreat, Dekker and Jonson got to stage their
pageant after all. If anything, the postponement had
only whetted London's appetite for the kind of
festivity not seen since the accession of Elizabeth a
half century earlier. Dekker was probably not
entirely self-serving when he reported 'the streets
seemed to be paved with men . . . stalles instead of
rich wares were set out with children, open
casements [the leaded glass windows having been
taken out] filled up with women'. With this king,
however, public enthusiasm created a problem
rather than an opportunity, since crowds made
James decidedly nervous, wanting to be off

13

somewhere else, preferably on horseback in the hills near Royston, energetically pursuing the stag. But the allegorical outdoor theatre, full of music and gaudy brilliance, disarmed, at least temporarily, the royal churlishness. In addition to the brotherly Andrew and George, Old Father 'Thamesis', with flowing whiskers taken from his emblem-book personification, offered a tribute in the form of 'an earthenware pot out of which live Fishes were seene to runne forth'. And it was hard not to be impressed by Stephen Harrison's immense wood-and-plaster triumphal arches, 90 feet high and 50 wide, punctuating the processional route. One of them was a three-tower trellis structure, thick with greenery, purporting to show James's realm as a perpetual 'Bower of Plenty' and featuring 'sheep browzing, lambes nibbling, Birds Flying in the Ayre, with other arguments of a serene and untroubled season'. On the arch, erected at Fenchurch, an immense panorama of London rose from a crenellated battlement (as though seen from a distant tower), with the pile of old St Paul's in its centre and looking a great deal more orderly than the chaotic, verminous metropolis of 200,000 souls it really was. Below this Augustan vision of New Troy was none other than Britannia herself, bearing the orb of empire on which was inscribed *Orbis Britannicus Ab Orbe Divisus Est* (a British world divided *from* the world). Sharp-eyed scholars of the classics—and perhaps there were some in the crowd—would have recognized an erudite allusion to Virgil, in particular to the pastoral poems of the *Fourth Eclogue*, in which the return of a new golden age was prophesied. Right at the beginning of *Britannia*, William Camden had already identified

14

Virgil's lines as a recognition of Britain's historic destiny as a place apart. And much, of course, had been made of the identification by some of the foggier classical geographers of the British archipelago as the legendary 'Fortunate Isles' of the western ocean. Until 1603 it was the English who had fancied themselves blessed by this priceless gift of insularity; Shakespeare's vision of 'This fortress built by Nature for herself/Against infection and the hand of war' confirmed the national faith in a divinely ordained immunity from the rest of the world's sorrows.

Now, however, this happy insulation was to be understood as *British*, extended to lucky Ireland and Scotland (notwithstanding the fact that, historically, Scotland had always enjoyed closer connections with Europe than England). In October 1604, to a deeply suspicious English parliament (which had already bridled at being informed by the king that its privileges were a grant from his majesty), James promised that 'the benefits which do arise of that union which is made in my blood do redound to the whole island'. When he spoke of his realm, he repeatedly referred to it, indivisibly, as 'the Ile'. His apologists conceded that there had been unfortunate disagreements, even bloodshed, between the neighbours on either side of the Tweed, but much of that could be attributed to the wicked Machiavellianism of interfering continentals (especially the French and the Spanish), who had deliberately set them at each other's throats. Now, in the person of James—in whom English, Welsh, French and Scots blood flowed and whom God had *already* blessed with two healthy sons—the long, miserable wars of succession were done with. 'The dismall discord,' Camden wrote, 'which hath set these nations (otherwise invincible) so long at debate, might [now] be stifled and crushed forever and sweet CONCORD triumph joyously with endless comfort.' Enter masquers, piping tunes of peace; roll on the Stuart Arcady.

As it turned out, the 'world divided from the world', the 'Britain apart' so cheerfully anticipated by Ben Jonson, Thomas Dekker, John Speed and William Camden, was the bringer not of concord and harmony but of havoc and destruction. The more strenuously that governments, both royal and republican, laboured to pull the pieces of Britain together, the more abysmally they fell apart. The obsession with 'union' and 'uniformity' that consumed both James and Charles I turned out to guarantee hatred and schism. In the first year of James I's reign no one (certainly not Jonson or Dekker) could have predicted this (although the high-handed remarks made by the king to parliament were not a good sign). It would take some time before the 'British problem' became dangerously apparent. The clearest warnings came from Charles I's Scottish friend and ally the Duke of Hamilton as late as 1637, when he counselled the king to back off from his obstinate plans to impose religious uniformity in Scotland as well as England, lest a violent backlash north of the border spread throughout his other two kingdoms.

Ironically, then, the business of building a harmonized Britain was auto-destructive, creating discord both between the three kingdoms and within them. The historians who want us to think of the Stuart realm as an essentially docile polity, bound together by consensus, have contended that arguments about religion and politics, such as they were, could always be contained within the conventions and habits of the settled order of government and society. Stuart England (in common with so much of British history) was, in this view, ruled by a gentlemen's agreement. The governing classes were agreed on the powers and limitations of the monarchy, agreed that parliament's job was to supply the king with money, agreed on the fixed hierarchy of society and, under James, agreed on a broadly Calvinist religious consensus. When differences of opinion arose between parliament and Crown, most people wished them to be resolved rather than further polarized. But then again, perhaps the impression given by scholars that there was nothing so seriously amiss about the country as to push it towards disaster results from a narrowly English focus: historians have asked not so much the wrong questions, as the right questions about the wrong country. If the country concerned is England and the questions are about the governing communities of its counties, a case for the containment of conflict can be made (though not, I think, clinched). But if the country in question is not England but Britain—Scotland and Ireland in particular—then very serious trouble did not suddenly pop up in the 1640s to disturb the calm of the English political landscape. It had been there for at least two generations. It was not as if, somehow, the English political commotions were suddenly and unaccountably aggravated by conflicts rumbling away somewhere remote on the storm-lashed Celtic fringe. The trouble *was*

17

Calvinist Scotland and Catholic Ireland and their deep religious appeal for some factions in Stuart England. Those religious entanglements, as we shall see, carried with them not just theological but also political and even foreign policy implications, which an imperially assertive England attempted to iron out through the imposition of a 'British' uniformity only at its own dire peril. The refusal of both Scotland and Ireland to do as they were ordered, except when coerced, brought about the British wars. Britain killed England. And it left Scotland and Ireland haemorrhaging in the field.

So if we return to those questions and put them to the *right* countries, a rather different accounting between long-term and short-term causes of the disaster becomes apparent. Ask yourself whether English Puritans were angry enough, or strong enough, by themselves, to bring down the Stuart monarchy and the answer is probably no, although they could certainly inflict punishing damage on its dignity and authority. Ask yourself whether Scottish Calvinists, in collusion with English Puritans (both of whom believed that kings were bound in a contract with their subjects), could bring down the Stuart monarchy and the answer is yes. When one of the militant Scottish Calvinist 'Covenanters', Archibald Johnston of Wariston, met Charles I at Berwick in the 1639 negotiations that ended the first Bishops' War, he interrupted the king so repeatedly and so offensively that the normally reserved Charles, unaccustomed to this kind of temerity, had to command Johnston, a common advocate, to hold his tongue. The Scots would inflict far worse indignities on Charles Stuart before they were through. Ask yourself whether an

Irish-Catholic insurrection could create a situation in which the king of England were suddenly revealed not as the defender but the subverter of Church and state, and the answer would again be yes. Had James been, say, Dutch or German (as kings were to be in the future), with no strong feelings about Scotland, would there have been a civil war?

But James was a Scottish king, and it mattered. James VI of Scotland, already in his late thirties, became James I of Great Britain with the heartfelt gratitude of a man who for many years has had to endure a stony couch and is at last offered a deep and welcoming featherbed. The stony couch had been James's painful and protracted education as the king of Scotland. With the unedifying and dangerous example of his mother, Mary Stuart, very much on their minds, the Calvinist nobility who deposed her made sure that her infant son received a stern Calvinist education. In 1570 they consigned James to the frightening tutelage of George Buchanan, beside whom the fulminations of John Knox seemed light as a spring breeze. Buchanan's briskly undeferential attitude to kingship is best summed up by the story of his response to the Countess of Mar when she protested at his rough handling of the royal child: 'Madam, I have whipt his arse, you may kiss it if you please.' No one was under any illusion that Buchanan was himself any sort of arse-kisser; quite the contrary. His view of monarchs, forthrightly expressed in *De juri regni apud Scotos* (1579), written to justify the deposition of James's mother, was that they were appointed to serve the people, who were entitled to remove them if they failed to

19

live up to the contract made with their subjects. It naturally followed from this theory of resistance that Kirk and Crown were separate and coeval powers and that royal meddling in the affairs of the Church would also be a warrant for removal. For the Presbyterian Kirk was inimical to any kind of royal governorship. It was a national Church with a single, uniform doctrine, but that doctrine was arrived at, and policed by, a general assembly constituted from delegates of its many congregations.

But James Stuart was, when all was said and done, his mother's son, and he was not about to spend the rest of his life as the doormat of Presbyterians. Unlike Mary, though, he would pave his road to sovereignty with arguments rather than adventures. His chosen tactics were more like Elizabeth's: subtlety, pragmatism and flexibility. From the time of his majority in 1587, James, whose intelligence and taste for learning were already evident, began to restore the authority of the Crown over both the general assembly (an institution created to govern the Kirk while a Catholic queen was on the throne) and the perennially factious nobility. Without any kind of standing army, his appeal was necessarily that of a Solomonic adjudicator, and James knew how to make his authority work through gestures heavy with symbolic meaning. To celebrate his majority, he made sure to provide liberal entertainment for the notoriously feud-prone Scottish nobility at Market Cross in Edinburgh. When the wine had them sufficiently relaxed, James asked them to walk hand-in-hand down the High Street to the royal residence, Holyroodhouse, where parliament sometimes met. They went like lambs, and did so dressed in the more formal costumes that the king had encouraged for parliamentary sessions. He also knew when division, as well as unity, might work in his favour. By making some small concessions to the Kirk, James managed to split his Presbyterian enemies into those who were prepared to work with him and hard-line Calvinists such as Andrew Melville, for whom any royal interference in the Kirk was a presumptuous abomination. Once strengthened by a 'royal party' inside the Kirk, he began to make further moves, determining, for example, the timing of general assemblies. By reinventing the episcopacy to look much less grandiose than its English counterpart James even managed, for five years at any rate, to reinsert bishops into the Kirk. In 1591 he felt strong enough to mint a gold piece bearing a Hebrew inscription referring to his Maker, 'Thee Alone Do I Fear'—a premature gesture, since the very next year Melville managed to get the Scottish parliament to do away with the bishoprics, and James was forced to consent. There was never a time when James would feel completely relaxed about his personal safety. Although he banned Buchanan's books, the old flogger continued to haunt his royal pupil, visiting his dreams as late as 1622 to inform James that 'he would fall into ice and then into fire' and that 'he would endure frequent pain and die soon after'. Not only Buchanan but the Ruthvens haunted him. It had been a Ruthven who had pointed a pistol at him *in utero*; a Ruthven descendant had held him hostage in 1582; and as recently as 1600 another of the family, the Earl of Gowrie, had abducted him, tied him up and threatened his life again. No wonder James was always a little jumpy.

For those who trade in thumbnail sketches of the British monarchy—blood-and-thunder Henry VIII, the Virgin Gloriana and the like—James I is bound to seem a baffling mixture of characteristics that have no business inhabiting the same personality: the hunt-mad scholar who would pursue Calvinist theologians and the stag with the same energetic determination; the slightly sloshed reveller, noisily demanding in the middle of an interminable masque and in his thick Scots accent to see the dancers, especially his queen 'Annie' (Anne of Denmark), who loved to perform in them; the long-winded, blustering master of disputation, battering preachers and parliamentarians over the head with his bibliography. But James's dominant characteristics (not least his sexual preferences) resist glib classification. Drunk or sober, shallow or deep, gay or straight, there certainly was no other prince who felt so repeatedly compelled to theorize about his sovereignty and to do so on paper. James, of whom it was accurately said 'he doth wondrously covet learned discourse', published no fewer than ten treatises dealing with various matters he considered weighty, including the evils of witchcraft and tobacco. Two of them, the *Basilikon Doron* (the 'Prince's Gift', written in 1598, but published in 1599, for his son Henry, and consisting for the most part, like its model, Charles V's advice to Philip II, of practical advice on the conduct of kingship) and *The True Law of Free Monarchies* (published in 1598), appeared in the immediate period before his arrival in England. At least until they attempted to read them (for neither work,

22

while succinct, could be fairly described as a page-turner), his new subjects must have been eager to see whether James's books provided any clues to the character of their king, because between 13,000 and 16,000 copies were sold in the first few months after his accession.

Both works have been misunderstood as the theoretical equivalent of a royal command to his subjects to begin practising their genuflections. It is certainly true James made no bones about the fact that his authority was based on appointment by God, to whom alone princes were ultimately and exclusively accountable. 'For Kings sit in the throne of God and thence all judgement is derived', as he would notoriously put it. This was the sort of utterance calculated to set parliamentary teeth on edge and persuade champions of the supremacy of common law, such as Sir Edwin Sandys, Nicholas Fuller and Sir Edward Coke, that James had been infected by despotic European attitudes to sovereignty and now needed a crash course of remedial instruction on just how things were in England.

Coke and those who thought like him believed that the 'ancient constitution of England', its origins lost in the remote mists of time (like other fundamental customs such as the age of majority and the size of a jury) but already established by the time of the Anglo-Saxon heptarchy, had been embodied in a common law that was prior to, and took precedence over, the person of any individual sovereign. Sovereignty was, and had always been, that of the indivisible king-in-parliament. Brutal conquests, such as that inflicted on England, might have temporarily set this aside, but the 'ancient constitution' embedded in the very marrow of Englishness was somehow preserved in custom, waiting its opportunity to assert itself again in, for example, Magna Carta. Going on about 'memory' to James (whose own memory was considered elephantine) did not, of course, help make the case, especially to someone who had been brought up in the very different and much more Romanized Scottish law tradition. And in his account of Scottish kingship James had already dealt briskly with the fable of primitive parliaments preceding the institution of monarchy. 'Parliaments . . . were not installed before them (as many have foolishly imagined) but long after that monarchies were established were they created.' None of this needs have been a serious issue, though, since in *The True Law of Free Monarchies* James had also taken pains to concede that the origins of a monarchy had little to do with the way it should govern in a 'settled' state, by which he obviously meant contemporary Scotland and England. As far as he was concerned, there was nothing at all contradictory about insisting on his contractual responsibility, first and foremost to God, his only superior, and accepting as a fact of life a 'mixed' and balanced monarchy, in which some matters of government were the exclusive prerogative of the king and many others were not. To ignore the 'fundamental laws' of a realm was precisely to cross the line between legitimate kingship and tyranny, to violate rather than respect the compact made with God. It was when responsible royal government degenerated into the tyranny of an arbitrary will that the king could be shown to have violated his contract with God as well as with his subjects. Although a 'king is preferred by God above all other ranks and degrees of men . . . the higher that his seate is above theirs: the greater is his obligation to his maker . . . And the highest benche is the sliddriest to sit upon.'

It would be misleading then to think of James arriving in England as completely impervious to the balance between king, lords and prelates, and Commons, which was endlessly touted as the peculiar genius of the nation's polity. But equally there was no mistaking his determination to uphold his 'regality and supreme prerogative' against any kind of impertinences, real or imagined, by the Commons. For the moment, though, putting aside self-appointed tribunes like Coke (who was perfectly willing to accept a government appointment himself when the opportunity arose), relatively few of the governing class, much less the common people, were apprehensive that an alien despotism was about to trample the liberties of England underfoot. They accepted the basic truism that order, both political and social, was the indispensable condition of the peace of the realm and that it was the office of the king and his councillors to provide it. They got much more upset about English wealth and offices being handed over on plates of gold to freebooters from Caledonia. James had actually been at pains to preserve the eminent Elizabethans on the Privy Council: the Lord High Admiral Howard of Effingham, hero of the Armada, and in particular the indispensable little hunchback Secretary of State, Robert Cecil, whom the king promoted to the earldom of Salisbury. Although six Scots had been appointed Privy Councillors, only two of them—Sir George Home (shortly to become the Earl of Dunbar) and Lord Kinloss—had any kind of high office. But because the king filled the more personal household staff of the Privy Chamber with Scottish friends and boyhood companions like the Duke of Lennox and the Earl of Mar (on whom he also showered lavish gifts and money), the impression was certainly given that access to the king could be gained only by way of these Scottish courtiers, especially the captain of the palace guard, Sir Thomas Erskine. More than one angry English suitor waiting for an audience with the king complained they had become 'lousy' sitting so long in Erskine's watchful presence. The Venetian ambassador reported in May 1603 that 'no Englishman, be his rank what it may, can enter the Presence Chamber without being summoned, whereas the Scottish lords have free entree of the privy chamber'. It was an exaggeration, but it was certainly a widely shared impression.

A Scottophobic backlash was inevitable. The ending of *Macbeth* (*c.* 1605-6) falsified Scottish history the better to suggest that Malcolm Canmore had won the throne only with English help. Stage comedies, like Jonson's *Eastward hoe* (1605) (for which he did a little time in the Tower with his co-authors George Chapman and John Marston), featured impecunious Scottish nobles freeloading at the expense of the English. In 1612 the sensational trial of the Scottish Lord Sanquhar for commissioning two assassins to shoot the English fencing master who had accidentally put out one of his eyes some years before produced a vitriolic outpouring of Scottophobic doggerel, not at all appeased by the conviction and hanging of

Sanquhar as if he were a common felon.

> They beg our Lands, our Goods, our Lives
> They switch our Nobles and lye with their Wives
> They pinch our Gentry and send for our
>   Benchers
> They stab our Sergeants and pistoll our Fencers.
> Leave off proud Scots thus to undo us
> Lest we make you as poor as when you came to
>   us.

Fights regularly broke out between Scots and English nobles at Croydon racetrack, and in the Inns of Court, where a Scot called Maxwell nearly started a riot by ripping out an Englishman's earring along with most of his ear. For a time the London Scots stayed close to their little colonies in Holborn and Charing Cross, especially avoiding the back alleys near theatres where they might be pounced on by 'swaggerers', who made roughing up Scotsmen their speciality. In more respectable theatres of opinion the hostility was just as fierce. Despite Francis Bacon's best propaganda, the king's project for a formal treaty of union ran into a storm of parliamentary protest that exchanging English for 'British' nationality would be the end of English law and the ancient constitution; would confuse foreigners when the English were abroad; and would open the country to hordes of impoverished, unwashed and greedy immigrants ('stinking' and 'lousy' were the usual insults of choice). By 1607 the union treaty had died the death of a thousand cuts, although James, bewildered and angry at the rebuff, continued to style himself 'King of Great Britain, France and

27

Ireland' and ordered (at public expense) a new 'Imperial Diadem and Crown' of sapphires, diamonds and rubies.

How did the abortive union look from the other direction? A ban imposed by James on *anti-English* ballads, poems and pamphlets suggests (not surprisingly) that the affronted Scots gave as good as they got in the abuse department. But wounded feelings aside, Scotland—or rather, Lowland, Protestant Scotland—had little reason to feel disadvantaged by the 'dual government' set up by James as long as its religious independence remained unthreatened. In this last, crucial department the king moved, as was his wont, slowly and cannily, waiting until his deputy governors (the earls of Dunbar and Dunfermline) had demonstrated the benefits of cooperation thoroughly enough to large sections of the Scottish nobility. With his base of support secure, he felt strong enough to move directly against the most uncompromising Presbyterians. Bishops were reinstated in 1610, and the fulminating Andrew Melville, incarcerated in the Tower of London since 1607, was finally banished in 1611. In 1618 a general assembly at Perth agreed (with some serious contention) on practices that not long before would have been denounced as Catholic idolatry: kneeling at communion, the celebration of five holy days and the administration of the sacraments.

James could get away with the 'Five Articles' of Perth, which, characteristically, he did not enforce very energetically, because the balance sheet of costs and benefits brought to Scotland by the union of crowns looked, from Edinburgh or Perth or

Stirling, fairly positive. Once a ferocious border policing commission (manned by both Scots and English) was in place and had started to catch, convict and hang the gangs of rustlers and brigands who had made the Borders their choice territory, cross-frontier trade took off. Fishermen, cattle-drivers and linen-makers all did well. Duty-free English beer became so popular in Scotland that the council in Edinburgh had to lower the price of the home product to make it competitive. The sections of Scots society, especially in the more densely settled areas of Midlothian and Fife, that had had enough of the rampages of feuding lords—small lairds, town burgesses, lawyers—all had little enough to complain of from a government that managed to be both distant and attentive. As for the great lords, with James handing over land and offices in England, Ireland and Scotland just as fast as he could, they knew better than to look a gift horse in the mouth.

But they were not all of Scotland. For as long as its histories had been written (starting with Tacitus), a profound division had been noticed between the lands south and north of the Forth and Tay: Lowland and Highland. In customs, language, faith and farming—everything that mattered—the two peoples were worlds apart. James himself made another distinction between the mainland Highlanders, who were 'barbarous for the most part and yet mixed with some show of civility', and the Hebridean islanders, who were 'utterly barbarous without any sort or show of civility'. Should the savages not avail themselves of the blessings of godly civilization, it was obvious that they should be uprooted, driven out and, if

29

necessary, killed off. Worst of all were the primitive clan leaders, scarcely better, the king and his officers of state thought, than cattle rustlers and brigands—like the MacGregors of the west, or the Gaelic chieftains of Ireland like Con O'Neill—who continued to mislead their followers into outlawry and plunder. James's plans for the colonization of the Western Isles, begun before he came to England, involved leasing land to Lowland nobles who were expected to 'develop' them for pacification and profit, if necessary deporting populations and replacing them with more pliable immigrants. When those schemes failed to overcome local resistance he turned to the big stick, in 1608 mobilizing a pan-British armada, raised from English troops in Ireland and ordered to do what was necessary in Lewis and Kintyre to teach the obstreperous natives a lesson they would never forget. Most of the draconian brutalities later inflicted on the Highlanders and islanders by William III and the Hanoverians—including the banning of the plaid and the Gaelic language— were all anticipated, at least in theory, by the Scottish James VI.

To their credit, James's own Scottish councillors balked at a punitive onslaught on the islands, for they knew it would be ruinously expensive and ineffective, and would create a permanently disaffected population for the Spanish or French to exploit. At the same time, they brought round the Highland clan leaders by inviting them to a meeting on board a ship, ostensibly to hear a sermon, and then holding them hostage on the island of Mull until they had seen reason. The result was the Statutes of Icolmkill, by which the solution of 'indirect empire', which Britain would use again and again (from southern India to northern Nigeria), was first unveiled. Instead of direct proconsular rule in the manner of a Roman conquest, the local chieftains and magnates were co-opted into a decentralized system of government and awarded status and land in return for being responsible for the conduct and taxation of their own clansmen. Made cooperative, they were organized around allegiances to grandees —the Campbells, Mackenzies and Gordons among others—who undertook to keep their huge territories quiet. Just as would be the case in the tropical empires, the deal came with all kinds of ostensible commitments to moral reformation: the regulation of alcohol, the suppression of feuds and the removal of native children to the metropolitan mainland, where they would be intensively re-educated for their own good and that of their homeland. The laboratory for the British empire turned out to be the Hebrides, and it was (as it would so often be in the future) entirely the enterprise of the Scots.

Now that the Highlands and islands were, for the time being, self-governing, James's grand design of settling impoverished but hardy Protestant farmers from the overpopulated Lowlands among the 'heathen' Catholics of the mountains had to be rethought. And the solution was staring at everyone right across the North Channel in Ireland. There were already some Scots in northern and eastern Ireland, but after the rebel nobles Hugh O'Neill, Earl of Tyrone, and Rory O'Donnell, Earl of Tyrconnel, fled to Rome in 1607, their huge estates, forfeit to the Crown, suddenly became available for James and his government to play British emperor.

And play it he did, on a massive scale. Up to 1641 close to 100,000 Scots, Welsh and English immigrants were 'planted' in Ireland, the vast majority in the nine counties of Ulster (six of which now form Northern Ireland), but with sizeable populations also in Munster (originally 'planted' in the 1580s). The seventeenth-century colonization of Ireland was, with the possible exception of Spanish Mexico, the biggest imperial settlement of any single European power to date, and it utterly dwarfed the related 'planting' on the Atlantic seaboard of North America. To such as Camden, of course, Hibernia was no more than the 'western enclosure of Britain'. Since an act of 1541, the status of Ireland had changed from a lordship to a kingdom, whose ruler had the 'name, style, title and honour' of a king, and all the prerogatives of a 'king imperial'. In effect, the throne of Ireland was 'united and knit to the imperial crown of England'. In Elizabeth's reign there had been wild-eyed schemes from the likes of Sir Thomas Smith, ambassador and privy councillor, to Protestantize and civilize the island by massive immigration and settlement. And such men imagined the land, as imperial dreamers generally do, either as conveniently vacant or populated by so many grunting Calibans who, once educated out of sloth, superstition and crime, would be impatient to acquire (in some necessarily menial way to begin with) the blessings of metropolitan culture. But Ireland, of course, was neither vacant nor inhabited purely by Gaelic-speaking peasants and cattle-rustling lords. In Leinster there were the 'Old

32

English' descendants of the original Anglo-Norman settlers who had come over with Richard de Clare (Strongbow), in the time of the Angevins and who had mostly remained faithful to the Catholic Church. And over the centuries the frontiers, once so sharp between native Gaels and English intruders, had softened to the point of there being many intermarriages and shared estates, especially in the southeast. Although many Old English defined themselves through their loyalty to the Crown, they shared with the native Gaels some basic common causes—a common religion and resentment of the threat of massive immigration from England.

Both communities were brushed aside in defeat—the Gaels, of course, with more contemptuous brutality than the Old English. James's attorney-general in Ireland, the poet Sir John Davies, became eloquent on the subject of the murdering natives 'little better than cannibals'. The confiscated estates of the Earl of Desmond in Munster had been handed over to thirty-five English landlords in large lots of between 4000 and 12,000 acres. Ulster, though, was subdivided into smaller parcels of between 1000 and 2000 acres to 'undertakers' and ex-military 'servitors' who, in return for their lucky prize of land, contracted to set aside sums for the endowment of the Protestant Church of Ireland and for the schools and colleges that would plant the Reformed religion so deep that no Papist could tear it up. In another unique transfer, Derry was handed over to syndicates of the City of London, which prefixed its name on the ancient city. When James ran out of forfeited and confiscated lands, he continued the process of

33

extraction by requiring all Irish landowners to prove title according to the rigorous standards of English law—a notoriously difficult if not impossible task for estates that had been granted countless generations before systematic records were made and preserved. But that, of course, was the point. Large tracts in Wexford, Longford, Waterford and Carlow were transferred by this route from Irish to planter ownership.

As far as the king was concerned, the whole project was a huge success, although regrettably slow to take root. When his 'undertakers' in Ireland seemed to be unconscionably timid about dispossessing the Irish, he threatened to seize back their land unless they carried out the evictions with greater speed and diligence. By 1620, large numbers of poor farmers had been transplanted from the over-populated, over-zealous Calvinist southwest of Scotland to a place where they could really get their teeth into a challenge, and James had found space and fortunes in Ireland for Scottish lords like James Hamilton, Earl of Abercorn, on whose loyalty he could now dependably count. Along with many of the planters themselves, James unquestionably believed in the socially and morally redemptive nature of the plantation. Free-wandering Irish herds and flocks would be rounded up inside winter stalls to provide heavy manure for the under-nitrogenated Irish pasture, milk yields would multiply, wheat would appear, markets would beckon, and farmers responding to them would be able to afford stone houses, glass windows, wooden floors. The picture-perfect landscapes of the Weald and the Wolds would magically become reproduced in Tyrone and

Fermanagh. Towns, those nurseries of civility, would grow and prosper. Literacy in the only language that counted—English—would spread like wildfire, and the unintelligible gibberish of the indigenes would recede into bogland. Such was the vision of the new Hibernia.

In fairness, it should be said that not all the Old English or even the Gaelic Irish were as uniformly hostile to the newcomers and their innovations as nationalist history needs to believe. Just as Old English and Gaelic cultures had become intermixed over the centuries, so too cities like Dublin and Derry were places where newcomers and natives shared all kinds of commercial, legal and social interests. Institutions like Trinity College, Dublin, turned into extraordinarily flourishing centres of learning. None the less, the plantation, especially in Ulster, was from the start deformed by its neurotically defensive character: Britain's frontier against Rome and Madrid. And the natives continued to be restless. Stone houses may have arrived with the planters, but beyond their walls and fences the country proved obstinately unwelcoming to Protestantism and that, in turn, perpetuated the insecurity of the planters, who were forever on the lookout lest the Catholic population invite in the Spanish and make Ireland the next major theatre of the ongoing British wars of religion. Seeds were planted in Jacobean Ireland all right, but they would not produce the kind of harvest the inventors of Jacobean Britain had imagined.

But if there were a strong note of Discord among the Music of British Harmony, one would never know it in Whitehall. Although Rubens' paintings decorating the ceiling of Inigo Jones's glorious new Palladian Banqueting House, celebrating the virtues of James as the British Solomon, were commissioned by his son Charles in 1630 and completed in 1634, nine years after James's death, they are none the less a perfect picture of Jacobean wishful thinking: an orgy of royal good intentions, with Peace and Plenty caught in a tight clinch while the new Augustus presides over Wisdom dispatching War. In view of what had actually happened (and what would happen to demolish the reign of Charles I) the nearest painting to the entrance was the most optimistic: the most famous Solomonic story of all, recycled as an allegory of the birth of a new Britain. The all-wise monarch leans forward to deliver judgement on two mothers who hold up a baby. But a proposal to chop it into two would hardly fit the mood or the message. Instead, James is all benevolence; the women are, of course, the two kingdoms, and the chubby Rubensian baby is none other than Britain itself.

This hyper-inflated expectation of the blessings to be conferred by the new reign was not just the fantasy of the Stuart court. From his gentleman's manor of Arbury in Warwickshire John Newdigate, one of the thousands of readers of the king's *Basilikon Doron,* decided to write to him personally—'my dear sovereign'—to express his pleasure that the country was now to be ruled by a Solomon and that his countrymen were rushing to witness for themselves, like the Queen of Sheba, the full measure of the king's wisdom and greatness. But, said Newdigate, warming to his subject, the king had a host of urgent matters to reform: the disgusting habit of men dressing in women's clothes, for example; gentlemen who spent their entire time in London being swallowed alive in costly lawsuits, while their estates and tenants languished in rustic decay; the loathsome parasites who bought monopolies from the Crown and proceeded to use them to fleece the defenceless; the heavy taxes and levies raised in his own county for foreign wars; and on and on. What Newdigate wanted from the king was not proclamations and legislation but reformation: a great cleansing of the country's impurities, not least at court itself. 'I hope your highness will . . . helpe many reform themselves to your couler,' wrote the optimistic Newdigate, adding, lest James was tempted to slack off, 'for all Solomon's wisdome and good beginning, perseverance was at sume times absent and the blessings of peace made him sinne.'

Grievously disappointed though they would be, there were many such as Newdigate who had the highest hopes of the new reign. Another godly gentleman who would become a parliamentary militant and survive into the Commonwealth, Robert Harley, of Brampton Bryan in Herefordshire, was happy enough to be included among the sixty-two gentlemen knighted by the king (as a Knight of the Bath, too) in his coronation honours. Such men as Harley and Newdigate had no idea, of course, just how much James despised Puritans, even while regarding them as a minority. Evangelicals, by contrast, James had a bit more sympathy for, even if they did sit 'Jack fellowlike with Christ at the Lord's Table'. Men like Harley and Newdigate looked at the godly Kirk in Scotland and thought

37

James was bound to carry its virtues to England, while the king was, in fact, overjoyed to be leaving it behind. 'Puritan' was still a term of abuse applied to the 'hotter' Christians. But of all the divisions that bedevilled the Stuarts, that which came between those who passionately believed that the Church had not yet been properly reformed and that Edward VI's godly evangelism had been put on hold for half a century by his sister, and those who were satisfied with the Anglican status quo, was perhaps the most dangerous, because it pre-supposed two utterly incompatible temperaments and ideologies about the duties of the state. The bugbears of the hot gospellers—the sign of the cross in baptism, the use of the ring in the marriage sacrament, the wearing of the surplice by priests—might seem so much trivia (and, to their fury were defined by James as *adiaphora* or things 'indifferent', which lay within the purview of the king to retain or discard as he saw fit), but to the godly they were relics of abominable Catholic idolatry. They wanted them purged and the Crown instead to promote godly preaching and teaching.

It is ironic that the only lasting accomplishment to survive the extended theological debates between James and the unsatisfied reformers was the imperishably beautiful Bible that bears his name. For a Church atomized into innumerable individual readers of scripture, engaged in obsessive self-interrogation or shut up with their own family in a hermetically sealed household of godly morality, was, to James's way of thinking and to that of those ministers he specially favoured, like George Abbot or Lancelot Andrewes, entirely destructive of the unity of Church and nation. To

Calvinists, for whom the world both now and hereafter was either black or white, Christ or Antichrist, appeals to 'unity' were at best a vain delusion, at worst a deliberate snare to inveigle the innocent into promiscuous communion with the sinful. Was it not obvious that the Almighty himself had no interest in the subject of 'union'? As Calvin and St Paul had both well understood, God had decreed that mankind was irremediably *divided* into the damned and the saved, or, as the rector of Holy Trinity Church in Dorchester, John White, forthrightly put it, according to a startled member of his congregation: 'Christ was not the Saviour of the whole world but of his elected and chosen people only.' They assumed that James's refusal of a more 'thorough' reformation was amoral spinelessness, when in fact it was a carefully thought-out theology, heavily rehearsed by him at the Hampton Court conference, convened in 1604 to consider these matters. James's preference for ceremony, sacrament and the 'decencies' of the Church was not just some middle way, arrived at by default to position himself between Catholicism and Puritanism. It embodied his active wish for the incorporation of Christians within a big-tent Church—attracting both loyal Puritans and loyal Catholics, separating them from their more extreme elements and offering the possibility (not the certainty) that sinful man might still achieve salvation through good works and observances. And there was the matter of rank and order, which James took very seriously indeed, and which he believed was properly embodied in the hierarchy of the Church, with himself, prince temporal and spiritual, at the top, the archbishops and bishops

39

immediately below. Through his entire reign, in both Scotland and England, James never swerved from his conviction (not unlike Henry VIII's or Elizabeth's) that the combination of the royal supremacy and bishops was the strongest way to *resist* Rome. And he passed that belief on to his son, with, as it turned out, fatal consequences.

All this was incomprehensible to the evangelicals, for whom any fudging of predestination, any suggestion that good works might to the slightest degree affect the prospects of salvation, was the purest papism. In fact, many *Catholics* also (and happily) misunderstood such views as the expression of a secret wish to return home to the old Church. When James made peace with Spain in 1604, the rumours about the king's conversion and his restoration of England to Roman obedience seemed miraculously imminent. The fact that the queen, Anne of Denmark, had already converted to Catholicism, did nothing to dampen these expectations. Had they read James's wonderful account of his own baptism they might have been better informed about his potential for conversion. 'At my Baptism I was baptised by a Popish Archbishop [his mother, Mary] sent word to forbear to use spittle . . . which was obeyed being indeed a filthy apish trick . . . And her very own words were "that she would not want a pocky priest to spit into her child's mouth".' Like his mother (but from the other confessional stance) James saw no reason why his queen should not practise a different private religion from the official Church, but at no time did he ever think of himself as anything other than an unequivocal Protestant. Blinded though they may have been to James's true position, it is understandable that loyal Catholics like Sir Thomas Tresham, out of prison and able to give his attention once more to his Northamptonshire house, Lyveden New Bield, designed to symbolize his faith, could now imagine that their days of persecution and recusant impoverishment were at last over.

Very soon they realized just how wrong they had been. Instead of offering them relief, James's regime, enthusiastically enforced by Robert Cecil and Archbishop Richard Bancroft, cracked down even harder on recusants and hidden Jesuits. Predictions of plots became self-fulfilling. It was from the bitterness of having been so thoroughly deceived that conspiracies to eliminate the king and his heretical ministers were born. George Buchanan's Calvinist teaching of the legitimacy of resistance to an ungodly king was matched on the Catholic side by the Jesuit Juán de Mariana's doctrine of lawful insurrection against the tyranny of a heretical prince. That absolution fed the ardour and optimism of Catholic conspirators and assassins. Even before the gunpowder plotters had designed their own coup, at least two violent plots had been exposed in 1604, one (a real stroke of genius, this) meaning to abduct the king and hold him hostage until parliament had agreed to demands to tolerate Catholicism in England. But the plan launched by Robert Catesby together with Tresham's son, Francis, Sir Everard Digby, Thomas Percy, Thomas Winter and Guido Fawkes, a soldier who had served the Spanish armies in the Netherlands, and blessed by a Jesuit, Father Thomas Garnet, was much the most dramatic. The idea was not just to destroy parliament on the

41

opening day of its session, along with the king, Prince Henry and possibly even the four-year-old Charles, but to set their sister, Princess Elizabeth, on the throne in their place, since they supposed that she had been most influenced by her mother, the Catholic Queen Anne, and would at the very least be more inclined to tolerate them. How close it came to success was entirely another matter, since it seems possible that even before Lord Monteagle was advised by an anonymous letter (which probably came from Lady Monteagle's brother) not to attend the opening of parliament on 5 November 1605, Robert Cecil's intelligence network had penetrated the conspiracy. A search was made of the cellars beneath the Westminster house whose premises had been rented by one of the plotters, Thomas Percy. There they found Fawkes together with thirty-six barrels of gunpowder, enough to destroy the entire House of Lords immediately above the cellar.

The confederates came to famously gruesome ends: Catesby and Thomas Percy were tracked down to their safe house in Staffordshire and killed in the assault, Catesby dying holding a picture of the Virgin. Their bodies were exhumed from their graves so that their heads could be removed for proper display at the corners of the parliament building they had planned to detonate. Tresham died in the Tower of some monstrous urethral infection after a copious confession, his excruciating condition presumably making the customary rack redundant. Fawkes and the rest were hanged very briefly, then, still living, had their hearts cut out and displayed to the appreciative public.

More important than the plot itself were the

effects it had on the prospects of the Stuart monarchy, which were all positive. Even though he always suffered from the conspiracy jitters (his father, Darnley, had, after all, also been the victim of a gunpowder plot), the king was careful not to go on an anti-Catholic rampage. In fact, he and his government were at pains to separate the 'fanatics' like Fawkes from loyal Catholics like the senior Tresham and to hope that they had been scared into settling for private ways of exercising their conscience. But 5 November became the Protestant holy-day *par excellence*, the new 'birth-day of the nation', with bonfires and bells celebrating the deliverance of not only the king himself but also the entirety of the English constitution. James had never seemed so English, so parliamentary as when he had come close to sharing a terrible incineration with the Lords and Commons. Catesby, Percy and Guy Fawkes had achieved something that James could never have done by himself: they had made him a popular hero. Declaring the Gunpowder Treason day a holiday, parliament outdid itself in eulogizing James as 'our most gracious sovereign . . . the most great learned and religious king that ever reigned'.

This did not mean, of course, that the next twenty years were a prolonged honeymoon. If anything, the longer the reign went on, the more out of love with each other James and the British became. Godfrey Goodman, Bishop of Gloucester, was just one of many contemporaries who noticed nostalgia for Elizabeth grow ever rosier as the lustre of the Jacobean court became tarnished by outlandish extravagance and scandal. The dimming of reputation, though, was not necessarily a prelude to constitutional crisis, not least because parliament met for only thirty-six months in total out of the twenty-two years of James I's reign, and this intermittent record seemed no more controversial than it had been in the reign of Elizabeth. Parliament did not yet think of itself as an 'opposition' nor even as an institutional 'partner' in government. The majority of its members, in both the Lords and Commons, accepted the king's view that their presence was required principally to provide him with the money needed to conduct the business of state. But—and it was an enormous qualification—they shared the inherited truism that they had a responsibility to offer the king counsel and to see that this revenue was not raised in a way that damaged the 'liberties' or the security of the people. This meant that, when the king did come to them for money, they felt duty bound to present him with a list of grievances. The litany of complaints had become a ritual, and the king was expected to respond, after cavilling about the infringement of his prerogatives, with concessionary gestures, such as the impeachment of some disposable officer of state or a few generalized expressions of love for the worthy representatives of the nation. Sometimes James could be relied on to make those gestures, but most often he had to be pushed. Not infrequently he behaved like a sulky adolescent forced to come home and ask his parents to bale him out from the creditors, gritting his teeth and rolling his eyes while they berated him for his wickedly irresponsible behaviour.

But then James's problems of the purse were self-inflicted. Compared with the famously tight-fisted Elizabeth he was a bottomless well of prodigality. From the very beginning of his reign he threw money at his Scottish companions and courtiers, provoking one parliamentarian to characterize the treasury as a 'royal cistern wherein his Majesty's largesse to the Scots caused a continual and remediless leak'. But James had come from a relatively poor country with limited resources (which had not, however, stopped him from piling up debts), and in England he obviously felt himself to be in hog heaven. Lands, monopolies, offices, jewels, houses were all showered on favourites, who then took their cue from the king by themselves spending colossally more than they could afford. The entire court culture was drunk on spending, and there was plenty to spend it on: elaborate masques (average cost £1400 a year) devised by Ben Jonson and Inigo Jones, in which mechanical contraptions were constructed to make men appear to be flying through the air or swallowed by the oceans; fantastic costumes, encrusted with carbuncle gems; immense dresses for the ladies, pseudo-Persian, billowing beneath the waist, or breasts revealed above, covered only with the most transparently gauzy lawn (a fashion that, to the horror of godly ministers, became ubiquitous at court). Feasting was Lucullan. In 1621—a rocky year for Crown–country relations—one such banquet costing more than £3000 needed a hundred cooks for eight days to produce 1600 dishes including 240 pheasants. The Jacobean court's devotion to futile excess was perfectly epitomized by the novelty of the 'ante-supper' invented by the Scots lord James Hay, later Earl of Carlisle. Guests would arrive to ogle a vast table magnificently set with food, the only point of which was to be inspected, tickling the saliva glands into action before the whole thing was removed, thrown away and replaced by identical food that had just come from the kitchens.

The craze for conspicuous waste was contagious. Anyone within the wide circle of the court (which James made a lot wider by creating no fewer than thirty-two earls, nineteen viscounts and fifty-six knight baronets, the last a wholly new invention) who wanted to be taken seriously needed to build on the spectacular scale demanded by fashionable taste and by a king who was constantly on the hoof between hunting lodges and who, even more than Elizabeth, expected to be entertained in palatial style. James made himself so much at home in his courtiers' houses that one desperate host wrote a letter to his bulldog, Mr Jowler, asking him, since he had the royal attention, if he would not mind urging departure on the king. Inevitably, the 'prodigy houses' that had been going up in the last decades of Elizabeth's reign became even more prodigious in James's time. With Britain at peace, its aristocrats travelled more freely and widely in Europe and brought back with them exuberantly Mannerist designs for stone-clad façades and intricately carved interior panelling. The show places of the Jacobean grandees, like Robert Cecil's Hatfield (the Hertfordshire estate given by the king in exchange for Cecil's sumptuous Theobalds), the Earl of Pembroke's Wilton in Wiltshire or the most prodigious monster of them all, the Earl of Suffolk's Audley End in Essex (on which James passed his famous backhand compliment, 'too big for a king but might do well enough for a Lord Treasurer'), boasted galleries as long as football pitches, and, now that the English glass industry had been properly established, great ranges of windows to light them. Even the furniture of the houses—beds, desks and cabinets—sprouted putti and sphinxes, obelisks and miniature temples. Draperies were required to be especially stunning and often renewed. Some £14,000 were spent just to furnish the Countess of Salisbury's (by definition temporary) lying-in chamber with white satin, embroidered with gold and ornamented with pearls. Nothing was too fantastic not to be diverting, especially the stunning gardens, which, since they now featured complicated riddles and allusions to the classics, embedded in statuary, fountains and grottoes, now required specialized hydraulic engineers, like the de Caus family, to design and maintain them.

All this was, of course, ruinously expensive, and many of the most ambitious builders were duly ruined. The most prodigal of all, the king (whose spending was at twice the rate of Elizabeth), drove successive treasurers to distraction attempting to find ways to support his extravagances. There were old ways and there were new ways, but none of them ever came up with enough money and all of them created resentment. The old ways featured the exploitation of 'Crown rights' like the 'purveyances', the right granted to the Crown to set prices for goods and services, ostensibly for the household, at well below market rates. Over time it seemed easier, especially to the Crown, to settle for money sums that represented the difference between purveyance prices and market prices, instead of the goods themselves. What had begun as something necessary to the dignity of the Crown had degenerated into a racket. That the honour of the Crown—still an important element in its authority—was shabbily compromised by James's creation of more than 800 new knights at £30 a head was obvious from all the jokes showing up in libels and ballads featuring figures like 'Sir Fabian Scarecrow', whose landlady coughed up the necessary for his knighthood.

None of these expedients was likely to endear the Crown to its subjects, especially out in the country, where knighthood and aristocratic hierarchy were still treated with reverence. Likewise, when the government sold tax 'farms' (the right, in return for an up-front sum, to run a tax-collection or customs operation as a private business), it seemed to be delivering the helpless consumer to a private individual who had an interest in maximizing his take in a period of continuing low wages and high prices. In many respects it was no worse than their experience in the last decade of Elizabeth's reign. But then there had been hope, by now gone, that James's government would be an improvement. By 1610 it was clear to Robert Cecil, now given the thankless job of Lord Treasurer in addition to being Secretary of State, that something had to be done to find a more dependable source of income for the Crown. In that year he did his best to sell a 'Great Contract' to parliament, in which the Crown would relinquish its feudal rackets, like purveyances and 'wardships' (the right to manage the property of a feudal minor), in return for a guaranteed annual revenue of £200,000. The deal came to grief when, simultaneously, James decided to demand compensation for the abolition of wardship officers and parliament came to the conclusion that it had overpaid. In the general bitterness, the row over money turned constitutional. Dissolving the uncooperative parliament, James denounced the Commons who had 'perilled and annoyed our health, wounded our reputation, embouldened an ill-natur'd people, encroached on many of our privileges and plagued our purse'. Lord Ellesmere believed that the Commons' presumption in denying the king adequate funds had encroached on the 'regality supreme' of the Crown by parading a concern for 'liberty' that, if not checked hard and fast, 'will not cease until it break out into democracy'.

Without its life-line, the government staggered on, although Robert Cecil did not, dying of stomach cancer in 1612. He was hardly gone before the predictable attacks on 'Deformity', including one very pointed polemic by Francis Bacon, appeared. With Cecil collapsed both the moral and actual credit of the Crown. London brewers (hitting the king where it hurt) refused to supply any more ale without advance payment. A Dutch goldsmith, from whom James asked for a £20,000 loan on security of jewels he had bought from him, turned James down on the grounds that others had contributed to the purchase price! It did not help that the king now entrusted the Treasury to one of the Howard clan, the Earl of Suffolk, whose reckless prodigality at Audley End ought to have been an immediate disqualification. But the bigger the debt the more impressive the player, the king seems to have felt.

Little went right in the years ahead. In 1612 Henry, the Prince of Wales, the paragon of Protestant patriots, lauded as virtuous, intelligent, handsome on a horse and (compared to his father, old *Rex Pacificus*) refreshingly interested in bloodshed, died. The outpouring of sorrow at his huge funeral was genuine. In contrast to the defunct Protestant hero, his replacement as Prince of Wales, Charles, had been such a puny child that no one expected him to survive infancy, and even at the age of five he needed to be carried around in people's arms. He was tongue-tied (in glaring contrast to his father), solemn and very short. After Prince Henry died the golden suit of parade armour that had been made for him was passed down to the new Prince of Wales. It was too big for him. Much of his subsequent life would be spent trying to grow into its imperial measurements.

To compensate for a death, two great weddings were celebrated the following year, 1613. At the time there seemed reason only for rejoicing, but both unions turned out to be extremely bad news for the peace and good order of James's realm. The more auspicious of the two matches was the marriage of Princess Elizabeth to Frederick, the prince-elector of the Rhineland Palatinate. If the court had had to suffer the loss of its own native Protestant son in Henry, the son-in-law, Frederick, seemed a reasonable replacement. The festivities, held in mid-February, were, as usual, rowdy and excessive, culminating in an elaborately staged mock naval battle on the Thames between 'Turks' and 'Venetians', during which the paper and paste-board port of Algiers went up prematurely in flames.

50

The second marriage crashed and burned even more spectacularly. The match was between Frances Howard, the daughter of the spendthrift Lord Treasurer, the Earl of Suffolk, and James's current favourite, Robert Carr (Scottish page of Lord Hay, the great party thrower), whose shapely length of leg caught James's eye when Carr was injured in the tilts. Carr, whom the Earl of Suffolk described as 'straight-limbed, well-favoured, strong-shouldered and smooth-faced with some sort of cunning and show of modsty, tho, God wot, he well knoweth when to show his impudence', had been promoted at dizzy speed, first in 1611 to the Viscountcy of Rochester, where he had been endowed with Henry II's immense pile of a castle, and then in November 1613 to the even grander earldom of Somerset. For the nuptials Ben Jonson produced a masque called *Hymenaei*, designed, in its rapturous extolling of marriage, to draw a veil over the unsavoury circumstances in which the union had come about. For Frances Howard had been married before, in 1606, at the age of thirteen, to the second Earl of Essex, then fourteen. But—so it was later claimed in the proceedings for annulment—the marriage had not gone well, at least not in bed. Not much was kept private in the world of the Jacobean court, especially since this kind of gossip was meat and drink for the printed *courants* or news-sheets, which, much as tabloids today, lived off stories of spooky astral occurrences and the juicy adulteries of the rich and famous. In Frances Howard they had a story beyond their wildest dreams.

Even before she had met Carr, stories of Essex's impotence were doing the rounds, along with rumours that Frances had obligingly unburdened Prince Henry of his virginity. In 1613, to the horror of his friend and political adviser Sir Thomas Overbury, Carr made it clear that he wanted to convert their affair into a marriage. It was a period when the power of the Howard clan was at its peak, and when the king found it virtually impossible to deny Carr anything, not even a wife, for even if the king were a sexually active gay, he seemed completely without jealousy where the heterosexual needs of his young protégés were concerned. And once she had made her mind up, Frances was simply unstoppable. Her marriage to Essex, she insisted, had never been consummated and not for want of her trying her best. (She was later accused of feeding Essex drugs to guarantee his impotence.) A commission of the Church was appointed to judge whether there was a case for divorce based on the claim of non-consummation, which (to the consternation of the Archbishop of Canterbury, who begged the king to be excused) involved the prelates of England solemnly listening to detailed evidence concerning the failure of the noble earl to introduce his member satisfactorily into the well-disposed orifice of the countess. A physical examination found that she was indeed virgo intacta (although it was later said that Frances had insisted on veiling her face during the inspection and had actually substituted a virgin hired for the imposture, which in light of her subsequent inventiveness cannot be entirely ruled out). When the reluctant Archbishop of Canterbury demurred over supplying the correct result, the king stacked the jury by adding bishops who were less exacting in their judgement. The

Essex–Howard union was declared no union at all, and the new marriage sanctioned.

There was, however, one obstacle to the realization of marital bliss between Frances Howard and Robert Carr, and that was Sir Thomas Overbury, who annoyingly continued to refer to her as 'that base woman' and to counsel Carr to break off the alliance with someone he thought little better than a whore. To shut him up, Overbury was offered a foreign embassy, which, to general consternation, he declined. Declared an affront to the king's majesty, he was locked away in the Tower, where he died in September 1613.

For a while Frances and Somerset enjoyed a prolonged honeymoon. But about eighteen months after the wedding, in the summer of 1615, it emerged that Overbury had not simply died in the Tower but had been murdered, by the unusual method of a poisoned enema. The lowdown on Overbury's death had come from an apothecary's assistant, who, before dying, had confessed that he had been paid £20 by the Countess of Essex to do the deed. An investigation produced an extraordinary story that the Lieutenant of the Tower had noticed that tarts and jellies and the like, delivered from the Countess for the prisoner, looked and smelled suspicious, especially when one of his own men had already confessed to attempting a poisoning. Scared of offending the most powerful woman in the country after the queen, the poor Lieutenant did what he could to protect the target of her fury by intercepting the lethal provisions and replacing them with food prepared by his own cook. But there was no intercepting (or even suspecting) an enema filled with mercury sublimate. Although Somerset himself had known nothing of the murder scheme, once confronted with the *fait accompli*, he made feverish attempts to cover up the traces of the crime, bribing where necessary, destroying documents where essential. With the appalled king pressing the investigation, going in person to the council and 'kneeling down there desired God to lay a Curse upon him and his posterity if ever he were consenting to Overbury's death', the plot unravelled. Once exposed, the sinister cast of plotters—a crook-back apothecary from Yorkshire who had supplied Frances with a whole range of poisons, including 'Powder of Diamonds', white arsenic, and something called 'Great Spider', and Anne Turner, dress-designer-cum-procuress, famous for popularizing yellow-starched fabrics, who passed the poisons to Overbury's gaoler—made the most lurid productions of John Webster seem understated by comparison. Confronted with the damning evidence, Frances broke down and pleaded guilty. Somerset, able with some conscience to plead not guilty of advance knowledge, was none the less convicted of having been at the very least an accessory after the deed. The commoners were, needless to say, given the horrible deaths reserved for poisoners; the nobles, of course, were spared by James and kept confined in the Tower, where Somerset contented himself with periodic exercises in interior redesign.

To those out in the shires whose theology divided the world into the legions of Christ and the battalions of Antichrist, the Howard–Somerset affair, featuring as it did all the prime transgressions —fornication, murder, criminal suppression of the truth, perhaps even witchcraft—was the clearest evidence that the court was indeed a Stuart Sodom, an unspeakable sink of iniquity. Puritan manuals on the right ordering of the commonwealth never tired of stressing the patriarchal family as the building block of a just and godly state. It was surely not accidental that the chief mover in bringing the king's attention to the likelihood of a hideous plot was himself an evangelical Protestant, Sir Ralph Winwood, the Secretary of State. To men like Winwood, the decency and integrity of the social and political order were at stake, for everything about that social order seemed to have been perverted in the Howard plot, involving as it did protagonists at the apex of the social and political pyramid. The proper deference of wife to husband had been demonstrably violated by the subjection of the pathetic Somerset to his frightening wife. Frances and her confederate Anne Turner seemed the incarnation of all the misogynist nightmares that haunted Jacobean culture: the insatiable, demonically possessed succubus, the fiend who destroyed through carnal congress. Could there be any doubt that the manner of poor Overbury's death must have been devised by the anally obsessed Devil? James himself seems to have concluded that Turner was, indeed, a sorceress.

Seen in this light, the grip that the Howards appeared to have on the government of England seemed evidence of a Satanic conspiracy to subvert the godliness and manliness of the aristocracy, whose privileges were still conditional on its status as an exemplary warrior caste. To soldiers like Barnaby Rich, writing in 1617, the atrophy had gone devilishly far, as it had with the Romans. No wonder the evil genius behind the Howard–Somerset plot had been the fashion queen, Mrs Turner, since 'our minds are effeminated, our martial exercises and disciplines of war are turned into womanish pleasures and delights . . . we are fitter for the coach than the camp'. As for the bishops, they too had also demonstrated the criminal worthlessness of their office by becoming party to infamy. (This was no surprise to Puritans, who made much of Mrs Overall, the notorious wife of the future Bishop of Coventry and Lichfield, who had run off with one of her many lovers in 1608.) The king won some credit from the critics of the court for his evidently sincere determination to get to the bottom of the crime. But the fact that he had forborne from punishing the principal malefactors with the full severity of the law while condemning their minions to death seemed further proof that James was impotent to prevent the descent of England into a pit of pagan immorality.

In the last thirty years of the twentieth century, it became a received wisdom that the Puritans were, especially by the 1620s, no more than a small if very vocal minority in England. (It is much harder to minimize the significance of ardent Calvinism in Scotland, which, of course, knew as much about the Howard affair as England.) And it is not to be imagined that episodes like the Howard scandal suddenly brought a majority round to thinking of the court as somehow irreversibly corrupt. But what it did do was reinforce the conviction of those who were already committed to the cause of moral cleansing (and who were doing something about it in their own households and local towns and villages) that the band of the Elect would, by definition, be a select but zealous troop. For the moment, the godly had to concentrate on local purifications, beginning, as always, with themselves and their immediate family and extending outwards into their community. A few would come to the conclusion that England was so far gone in abomination that to create a Zion apart required putting the distance of the Atlantic between them and Albion-Gomorrah. There was, to be sure, no strategy about any of this. It was not 'stage one' of some sort of timetable to create a true Jerusalem in England, but equally only the most myopic focus on the immediate circumstances of the outbreak of the civil war in 1641–2 could possibly write off the strength and spiritual intensity of the godly as of no consequence at all to the fate of Britain. Of course, the Puritans had no inkling whatsoever that the path ahead would involve an overthrow of the monarchy. But the agents of all such upheavals—in eighteenth-century France and early twentieth-century Russia, for example—are invariably zealous sects who believe themselves moved by some higher calling to a great and general scouring.

In the early years of the seventeenth century, the construction of Zion was a local business. But what the godly might achieve in places like the Dorset cloth town of Dorchester must have supplied for some, at least, practical evidence that with God's help his Faithful might yet prevail against the hosts of darkness. In 1613—the year of the Howard –Somerset marriage—Dorchester, then a town of only 2000 souls, was ravaged by a terrifying fire, which destroyed 170 of its houses, miraculously taking just one life. To the Puritan rector of the

Church of Holy Trinity, John White, who had been appointed to Dorchester in 1606, it was a communiqué from Sodom: a clear sign of God's wrath at the stiff-necked sinfulness of the people and their wickedly complaisant magistrates. Together with recent immigrants to the town of like-minded godliness, White set about, through preaching and teaching, to make a great and holy alteration. His targets were the usual suspects: fornication in general; adultery in particular; drunkenness; cursing, sports and pastimes (like bear-baiting and street theatre), which were especially vile when profaning the Sabbath but reprehensible at all times; chronic absenteeism from church; and casual rowdiness and violence. His enforcers were the constables (three of them), the part-time night-watchmen, the daytime beadles and the local justices, who were to send offenders to the stocks or, if necessary, to gaol. But White and his zealot friends also meant to make a positive change in the habits of the community by exhorting the flock to charity, even or especially at times of economic distress. The funds gathered from church collections were to be used to refashion the town: to create new schools and a house of learning and industry for children of the poor, and to care for the sick and old. Dorchester became a veritable fount of charity, not just for its own distressed, but also for any causes identifiable as morally deserving: victims of the plague in Cambridge and Shaftesbury, and victims of a fire (with which the locals had special sympathy) in Taunton, Somerset.

The fact that White and his fellow Puritans, a majority of whom came to dominate the town corporation, correctly believed themselves to be contending with a county society that was far from sympathetic to their goal of conducting a new godly reformation, only strengthened their passionate conviction that God's work had to be done. And between the year of the fire and 1640 they did accomplish an amazing change in the little town. Their moral police bore down on offenders with tireless zeal. Landlords who took advantage of their tenants' or their debtors' wives by forcing themselves on them were exposed, fined or pilloried. Compulsive swearers like Henry Gollop, who was presented to the magistrates for unleashing an awesome string of forty curses in a row, had their mouths stopped. Women who kept houses of assignation and alehouse-keepers, whose taverns were a place of constant riot, had their premises shut down or were evicted. Traditional festivals, which were notorious for promoting drunkenness and licentiousness, were expunged from the local calendar. Notorious absentees from church (especially among the young) were driven back there and sternly awaited every Sunday. Theatre disappeared. In 1615 an actor manager called Gilbert Reason came to town armed with a licence from the Master of the Revels in London entitling him to play before the townspeople. Dorchester's bailiff refused him in no uncertain terms, and when Reason replied that, since he was disregarding a royally authorized document, the bailiff was no better than a traitor, he found himself spending two days in gaol before being sent on his way. More sadly, a 'Frenchwoman' without hands, who had taught herself to do tricks with her feet (like writing and sewing) for a livelihood, was likewise sent packing.

In 1617 the killjoys were dealt an unexpected blow by the king's *Book of Sports*, which expressly allowed certain pastimes (like music) on Sunday evenings, while upholding the ban on bear- and bull-baiting and bowling. James's demand for a relaxation on censoriousness had been provoked by a stay in Lancashire en route back from Scotland, where he discovered that a particularly ferocious moral regime had been inflicted on innocent games and pastimes. But in Dorchester, the *Book of Sports* was heeded less than the vigilance of the local magistracy. The number of pregnant brides fell dramatically, as did the packs of beggars and unlicensed transients. Children were taken into the new schools and a 'hospital' established for the encouragement of sound work habits and piety. There were two new almshouses and a municipally funded brewhouse to employ the 'deserving' (that is non-begging) indigent. A house of correction was built with a homily carved over the door summing up the prevailing ethos in Dorset's little Jerusalem: 'Look in yourselves, this is the scope/Sin brings prison, prison the rope.'

In 1620 there was a new and urgent cause for which the godly in Dorchester were asked to empty their purses: Protestant refugees fleeing from an invasion of the Rhineland Palatinate by Catholic troops of the king of Spain. Some of the fugitives even came to settle in Dorchester, such was the international reputation of White, whose German assistant made sure the town was in close touch with events in continental Europe. Those events in the Rhineland, apparently remote from English and British concerns, became immediately a topic of supreme importance in the country's political and religious life, the subject of innumerable tracts, sermons and pamphlets, to the point where they changed Britain. By marrying his daughter Elizabeth to the apparently dull but safe Protestant Elector Frederick, James had unwittingly put his entire reputation as the king of peace in terrible jeopardy. The consequences of that marriage and the predicament in which it put the Crown would dog James until his death in March 1625 and would cast a long shadow over the beginning of his son's reign.

The problem could hardly have been anticipated, happening in the same place that even three centuries later Neville Chamberlain would notoriously describe as a 'far away country of which we know little': Bohemia. In 1618 the Protestant Estates rejected the Catholic nominee for their crown (the archduke who would become the Emperor Ferdinand) and made their point by throwing the envoys sent from the Emperor Matthias out of the windows of Hradčany Castle in Prague on to the substantial dung-heap below. Invitations went out to eligible Protestant candidates, and Frederick, certainly to his father-in-law's consternation, accepted the throne in August 1619. In November 1620 his army suffered a disastrous defeat at the hands of the Catholic Holy Roman Emperor at the battle of the White Mountain, and at the same time Spanish troops invaded his Rhineland home territory of the Palatinate. Frederick and Elizabeth—the Winter King and Queen, from their short stay in Prague— became the most famous and fashionable refugees of their age, travelling between England and France and finally settling in The Hague, where they established their own court in exile.

In the more Protestant centres of Britain, from London to Edinburgh (and certainly in Dorchester), a hue and cry went up for war against Spain and the Catholic powers. To the godly this was the battle of the Last Days, heralding the coming of the kingdom of the saints. Sides had to be taken. And the king, it was clear, would have to be pushed. But James's deep reluctance to turn warrior was not just a matter of ending his long and successful career as a pacifist; it was also a matter of bankrupting the realm. His trusted adviser, and later, from 1622, his Treasurer, Lionel Cranfield, who knew what he was talking about, coming as he did from a commercial and financial background, and who by dint of painstaking economies had managed to contain, if not reverse, the damage to the Exchequer from years of profligate spending, now warned of the fiscally catastrophic consequences of a war. But James was equally aware that to do nothing about the humiliating predicament of his daughter and son-in-law, to say nothing of the standing of the Protestant states of Europe, was to compromise beyond any possibility of recovery the authority of his government.

James felt personally betrayed by the Catholic offensive because for some time before 1620 he had been making overtures to Madrid for a marriage alliance between his son, Charles, and the daughter of King Philip III of Spain. In return for expressions of his own sincerity in seeking the match, James had been told not to worry about the Palatinate itself. Even after the occupation, the Spanish disingenuously claimed that their presence in the Rhineland was merely pressure to dislodge

Frederick from Bohemia. Such was his aversion to conflict that, given this straw to grasp at, James was prepared to believe the transparent lie. He was abetted in this pathetic self-deception by his new favourite, George Villiers (the son of an impoverished Leicestershire knight), whose star had risen when those of Somerset and the Howards had crashed. In rapid succession Villiers had been promoted to become Knight of the Garter, privy councillor, baron, earl, marquis and, finally, especially shocking since there had been no dukes in England since the execution of Norfolk in the reign of Elizabeth, Duke of Buckingham.

The last Spanish marriage—between Mary Tudor and Philip II—had not turned out well for anyone, so the gambit was from the beginning fraught with controversies that went to the heart of national and religious sensibilities. There were those, like the Puritan Sir Robert Harley in Herefordshire, who were old enough to remember the Spanish Armada. And Camden's immensely popular history of the reign of Elizabeth ensured that the epic of the wars against Spain was very much alive in Jacobean England. The Spanish court and government simply sat back and enjoyed the inexplicable desperation of the English, delighted that they were so keen to rule themselves out as adversaries in the wider European war. Their terms were aggressive. As a condition of the marriage they insisted (pushed by an equally overjoyed Rome) that the Infanta Maria be allowed not just a private chapel but a church that would be open to the public as well. Until they were into their adolescence, the responsibility for educating the children of the union would fall to the infanta, not the prince. And, most daring of all, they stipulated that English Catholics should now be allowed open freedom of worship. James must have known that to accept these terms would be to light a wildfire in both England and Scotland, but he was in absurd thrall to the beauteous Duke of Buckingham. In letters James addressed him as 'Steenie', a Scots endearment referring to his supposed resemblance to an image of St Stephen. In return Buckingham wrote back to his 'deare dade', knowing that no flattery would be too cloying for the besotted king, thus: 'I naturallie so love your person and upon so good experience and knowledge adore all your other parts which are more than ever one man had that were not onelie all your people but all the worlds besids sett together on one side and you alone on the other I should, to obey and pleas you, displeas, nay despise them.' Gouty old men should, of course, be wise enough in the ways of the world to discount sycophancy on this scale. But evidently James needed someone to lean on, both metaphorically and literally, and Buckingham, who had been entirely 'made' by the king as much as if he had fathered him, was obviously assigned the role of the perfect son: virile, clever and dynamic. He could do no wrong, especially when expanding on the wonderfulness of King James.

Charles might have been a tougher nut for Buckingham to crack, being so reserved in his demeanour and alienated from the unbuttoned bonhomie of his father, but a special feast that Buckingham gave for him took care of that. Together, Charles and Buckingham managed to persuade James—over what was left of his better judgement—that a way to nail the match was for them to go to Madrid, woo the infanta in person and confront the court there with a *fait accompli*. James was so anxious to avoid a war that he agreed to the hare-brained plan. In 1621 he had come through the fiercest political conflict of his whole reign when he had summoned parliament to provide a subsidy in the event of a war. The initial session in early 1621, with the prospect of doing damage to Spain in the offing, had turned into a virtual love fest, with parliament offering funds and James offering up the usual sacrifice of a minister for them to impeach (in this case, Lord Chancellor Bacon, who was accused of taking bribes) and conceding that he had brought some of the ruin on himself by being 'too bountiful' when he first came into the kingdom. By the end of the year, however, news of the serious consideration being given not to a war but to a Spanish marriage had soured relations. Parliament now adamantly refused to grant monies in advance of a commitment to go to war. In response, James turned furiously on them, denying their right to discuss matters such as a royal marriage and affairs of war and peace. 'You usurp upon our prerogative royal and meddle with things far above your reach.' This was, in fact, virtually the same position that Elizabeth had taken when she, too, had turned on parliament in 1566. But in the intervening period, History had happened, in particular, a richly developed historical discourse, which held that parliaments had, since time immemorial, been able to discuss such things and that their right to speak freely on matters of state was, in the words of their 'Protestation' of 1621: 'the ancient and undoubted

65

birthright and inheritance of the subjects of England; and that the arduous and urgent affairs concerning the King, state and defence of the realm and of the Church of England, and the maintenance and making of laws and redress of mischiefs and grievances which daily happen in this realm are proper subjects and matters of counsel and debate in parliament.' James, who continued to insist that any such 'privileges' were a grant, not a right, may have been on more accurate historical ground, but he was, as his son also would be, the ideological loser of the argument. And losers turn petulant, especially Stuarts. The king's response was to have the offending page torn from the Journal of the House of Commons and the most offensive speakers locked up.

So perhaps it was the need to bring about an evacuation of the Palatinate without having to go to parliament for war funds that moved James to allow Buckingham and Charles to proceed with their adventure. Or perhaps James was just losing his grip, as an extraordinary letter to 'Steenie' and 'babie Charles' suggests, when he addressed them as 'my sweete boyes and deare ventrouse Knights worthy to be putt in a new romanse'. From the beginning, from when they chose the persuasive incognitos of 'Tom and Jack Smith' complete with false whiskers (which fell off en route), to Charles's adolescent determination to climb the garden wall in Madrid to get a better view of the object of his adoration, the entire enterprise began to resemble one of the more puerile products of the Jacobean stage. The Spanish, at any rate, were hugely amused at the pit of embarrassment that Smith and Smith had so boyishly dug for themselves. For while Buckingham and Charles naïvely imagined that they were hastening a conclusion, the Spanish realized that they had been handed, in effect, two diplomatic hostages. If James had allowed such a thing, their reasoning went, he must be desperate for the marriage. And if he were desperate, then they would extract the most extortionate terms they could from his predicament. Not only would there now be a royally protected public Catholic church created for the infanta, but Prince Charles would also have to agree to take instruction from her chaplain. To their amazement this, too, was accepted by the prince, along with more or less anything else the Spanish could think of. Testing the limits of English tolerance, they now went one step too far. The marriage, they stipulated, was to be considered made on paper but strictly subject (for its actual realization and consummation) to the satisfactory completion of a one-year probationary period, to be served not just by Charles himself at Madrid but also by his father's government and kingdom. If during that period the terms of the treaty had been properly fulfilled, the infanta and her husband would be free to travel back to England; if not, well then not.

This last demand appalled King James, who now became genuinely (and rather touchingly) distraught at the possibility of not seeing his beloved 'Steenie' and his 'babie' for at least a year, during which time, God alone only knew, his aching old bones might have to be put in their tomb. Fortunately for James, Charles and Buckingham had also been affronted by the notion of their probation, and the heady romance of the Spanish affair had cooled. One of

Charles's companions, the young Buckinghamshire gentleman Sir Edmund Verney, had struck a priest in the face when he attempted to administer the Catholic last rites to a dying page in the prince's retinue. The indignity of being captives rather than suitors began to seem like the humiliation it was. To secure their freedom Charles and Buckingham pretended to go along with the treaty, only to make it clear even before landing in England that they would repudiate it. By the time the party had got home, livid at the indignities, Buckingham had completely recast the prince's role (and his own) not as Spanish bridegroom but as Protestant hero. Instead of a wedding there would now be a war. There is nothing like a bad pre-nuptial agreement, it seems, to bring on an attack of belligerence.

When Charles returned home in October 1623, still a Protestant bachelor, the country exploded in relief, the likes of which had not been seen since the unmasking of the Gunpowder Treason. Once more, there were bonfires and bells. The spring session of parliament, summoned in February 1624 to provide a subsidy for the king, immediately turned into a concord between king and nation. Another minister (this time the relatively blameless and tireless, if well-rewarded, Lord Treasurer Cranfield) was duly served up for disgrace and ruin, and, now that the country was going to get its patriotic-Protestant war, parliament was prepared to give the king his money.

It was not quite the war they had bargained for. Memories of Elizabethan strikes against the Don, much glamorized by the passage of time and the embellishments of history, must have led many to assume that there would be swift and lethal raids and the capture on the high seas of Spanish treasure. But apparently there was to be a land campaign too, waged in the Rhineland by the mercenary general, Count Ernst von Mansfield, using troops impressed—that is to say coerced—from England. No one was chafing at the bit to sign up for this doubtful enterprise. Men sawed their fingers off or blinded themselves in one eye to avoid impressment, but 12,000 poor souls, digits and eyes intact, were plucked by the constables from alehouses and street corners and marched to Dover. By the time they could find a port willing to land them on the other side, at Flushing in Zeeland, the entire force had been so badly hit by the plague that bodies had to be thrown into the harbour every day, until just 3000 troops remained, scarcely enough to make any kind of military impact. So the Mansfield expedition ignominiously collapsed before it ever got under way.

It was to have been the last great campaign of the peacemaker king. But in March 1625, the king, who had become so stricken with gout that he could barely move at all, made his own peace with the Almighty. 'And Solomon sleeps with his fathers,' was the text of the funeral sermon preached by John Williams, Bishop of Lincoln, invoking the dusty cliché of Jacobean eulogies. But this time it was literal, since the great tomb of Henry VII in Westminster was opened and James's own remains were placed next to the founder of the Tudor dynasty. If he had had trouble making a union of his two realms in his life, at least he would manage one particular peaceful cohabitation in death. For although James was hidden from view, the tombs of his mother and his predecessor, Mary and Elizabeth, the one brilliantly coloured, the other virginally white, were made, by his order, to share the same space. Magna Britannia: R.I.P.

If James had been Britain's Solomon, could his son aspire to be its imperial Charlemagne? *Carolus Rex Magnae Britanniae* appears on a shield hung over an ancient oak in the most imposing of all of Van Dyck's equestrian portraits, in which the golden-spurred king rides forth in a pose unmistakably reminiscent of Titian's great equestrian portrait of the armoured Habsburg emperor, *Charles V on Horseback*, of 1548. Behind him is the sylvan glade of England, before him the cerulean sky of the new golden age over which he will preside, Roman Emperor and *miles Christianum*, Christian knight. Because he was so little, Van Dyck had to take liberties with the relative proportions of king and horse, so that Charles would seem a naturally commanding Caesar. Riding and ruling were supposed to be one and the same. Antoine de Pluvinel, the most famous riding instructor in all Europe, had published a widely read treatise that not only compared the stoical, perfectly calm control of a fiery charger to the ruler's government of his realm but actually argued as well for equestrian education in this style as a precondition of establishing proper princely authority. To command the great horse— impassive, fearless and still—as the statue of Marcus Aurelius on the Campidoglio in Rome made clear, was the mark of a true Caesar.

It is a certainty that Charles would have read deeply in the classics as part of his humanist education, and that the Stoics, Seneca in particular, would have been at the heart of such instruction.

70

From an early stage the new king cultivated an aura of stoical self-possession, which made a startling contrast with the garrulous, expansive, disconcertingly unbuttoned informality of his father. Perhaps Charles, like so many others, had been impressed with the gravitas that ruled the Spanish court. At the Escorial sobriety ruled, and the king's presence was closed off from the common mob of courtiers by a solemn and elaborate fence of ritual. Sir Edmund Verney, who had not shown himself overly decorous by attacking a Jesuit, was now repaid by being awarded the office of Knight Marshal of the Palace, saddling him with the unenviable task of policing the court and its environs. It was Verney who had to see to the yards and corridors of the royal palaces, especially Whitehall, clearing them of the innumerable over-dressed louts, dunning tradesmen, doubtful men-at-arms and sundry petitioners who hung around the premises. There was, in any case, much in Charles's own reserved (not to say secretive) and rather prim manner that predisposed him towards solemnity. Of course, the more demure atmosphere he brought to the court could hardly have been thought a liability. A thorough cleansing of the Augean stables was, after all, what polite (not just Puritan) opinion had been clamouring for. And the substance of Charles's policies was not, in principle, so very different from that of his father, who had also refused to acknowledge the illegality of extra-parliamentary taxation, or the right of parliament to debate what it saw fit. When he bore down on parliament for presuming such things, he was doing no more than reiterating what he could be

71

forgiven for thinking an accepted article of the Jacobean creed about sovereignty.

It was not so much what Charles said that got him and England into trouble as the way he said it. The violent ups and downs of James's political apprenticeship had educated him early and well in the need for timely, pragmatic concessions, and he was capable of alternating Caledonian wrath with equal bursts of ingratiating charm. Charles, though, set great store by consistency. Perhaps he had overdosed a little on Seneca and his seventeenth-century neo-Stoic admirers for whom there was no greater virtue in public men than constancy, for Charles was constitutionally incapable of seeing two (or more) sides to any matter. More seriously for the government of the realm, he was even more incapable of acting against his own decided convictions.

Charles would not, for example, do what kings of England had done since the days of Edward III and the 'Good Parliament' of 1376 and jettison a royal favourite for the sake of an improved working relationship between Crown and parliament. Cynicism and disloyalty shocked him deeply. Instead, Charles insisted on looking at the individual merits of the case. This was a terrible mistake. You will not find any chapters in constitutional histories devoted to the rituals of therapeutic disgrace, but creative scapegoating had, none the less, long been an integral element of English politics. Concentrating odium for unpopular policies on the head of a politician (which, of course, might fall as a result) preserved the fiction that the 'king could do no wrong'. By insisting from an honourable but obtuse loyalty (in the case of Buckingham and, later, Laud and Strafford) that there was no difference between the king's view and his servant's, he wrecked the convenience of impeachment. Blame had nowhere to go but back to HM himself.

None of this, of course, would occur or could be explained to Charles himself even when, as in Buckingham's case, the favourite had reserved most of his energies for the accumulation of an immense empire of patronage rather than for the prosecution of the war he said he was so impatient to fight. In 1625 the doomed Spanish marriage project had been replaced by a successful French match (to Henrietta Maria, sister of Louis XIII), and, as part of the alliance, English ships and troops were supposed to join a French attack on Spain. But Cardinal Richelieu proved not much less manipulative than the Spanish and absorbed the English force into an attack on the Huguenot enclave of La Rochelle. When, in addition, it became apparent that Henrietta Maria was to enjoy the same conditions of freedom for Catholic worship that would have been guaranteed to the Spanish infanta and, even worse, that the recusancy laws were to be suspended as a condition of the marriage, it suddenly seemed that England was fighting a war *against*, rather than on behalf of, the Protestant cause.

The suspicion that the country had somehow been turned aside from a godly Protestant crusade to a sinister quasi-Catholic war, designed to insinuate popery back into the Church, was shared by the Puritans both in parliament and in the shires. Sir Robert Harley's letters to his third wife, Lady Brilliana (whose wonderful name had been taken from the seaport of Brielle or Brill, where the Dutch revolt had had its first success against Philip II, and where Brilliana's father had been commander), are heavy with mistrust and anxiety. What capped it for Harley was the appointment by Charles of Richard Montague as court chaplain. To men such as Harley, Montague was a notorious 'Arminian', which was little better than an outright Papist, perhaps even worse because of his pretence of remaining within the Church of England. In fact, Montague's brand of theology was no different from that preached and practised by ministers favoured by James, like Lancelot Andrewes and his successor, John Buckeridge. But the Puritans knew that in the cockpit of theological combat in the Dutch Republic the struggle (which had degenerated into a real civil war in 1618) between 'Arminians' and their more militant late sixteenth-century Calvinist adversaries was precisely over the crucial issue of predestination. The followers of the Dutch theologian Jacobus Arminius believed that salvation was not exclusively predetermined and that God might (not necessarily, but possibly) be persuaded to relent by the penitent good works of the sinner, and that therefore the boundaries between the saved and the damned were not hard and fast after all. Rightly or wrongly, they had been anathematized in Holland as little better than Catholics, and the same was true of their counterparts in England, including Montague and William Laud, whom Charles would appoint to be Bishop of London and then Archbishop of Canterbury. Like his father before him, Charles saw the anti-Calvinist theology as broadening the Church, conceivably even managing to bind up the wounds that had hurt it since the Reformation. To the godly, though, this was nothing but a counter-Reformation by the back door.

When Charles's first parliament convened in June 1625, summoned to provide funds for the war, it made clear—from the niggardly sums voted and the deliberately insulting grant of the usual customs duties, 'tonnage and poundage', not for life but for one year—that religious issues were going to be linked to the supply of revenue. A parliamentary commission of inquiry was appointed to investigate Montague, and the next on the list of targets was bound to be Buckingham, who had botched a raid on Cadiz so badly that suspicions were being voiced that his heart had never been in it. To persuade parliament otherwise, Buckingham abruptly switched tack to give them a war they might like—against, rather than on behalf of, the French and in support of the beleaguered Huguenots.

By the standards of past liability, Buckingham had already done enough to earn himself impeachment thrice over, but during Charles's second parliament, in June 1626, the king made it clear he would never countenance proceedings against his favourite. On 12 June, a tornado cut a path through southern England, opening the graves of plague victims who had been buried the previous year. The godly knew what this portended, but apparently the king did not. Faced with parliamentary refusal to vote subsidies for the new war unless Buckingham was impeached, Charles decided to levy a forced loan. This was bound to be inflammatory. The medieval tradition of 'benevolences'—money required without parliamentary sanction for the defence of the realm —had been outlawed in 1484 and abandoned since 1546, as it invariably raised serious constitutional questions about the king's exclusive right to judge when a war constituted an emergency or not. In 1614, however, James had revived benevolences, though they remained bitterly controversial. It was predictable that those whom Charles believed to be conspiratorial rabble-rousers, the orchestrators of 'popularity', should misrepresent the loan (as he thought) as an illegal confiscation. But the scale and breadth of outraged resistance must have startled him. Had not William Laud preached that since no power but God could judge the king, obedience to God extended, without demur, to obeying the king? The point, however, was not well taken. It was not just Puritans who denounced the loan as unlawful. The heart of the resistance came from sections of the political community on whom the king relied for stable government: the nobility and the gentry of the counties. Even so, not all the shires were equally incensed. It helped that the administrative arrangements for the loan were left to the counties themselves to organize, and the fact that £240,000 was raised, despite the hue and cry, suggests that by no means all of England and Wales was up in arms.

But some sections of the country were, indeed, belligerent in defence of the 'liberties' and property of the subject as never before. In Cornwall, for example, often thought of as loyal and royal, the MP William Coryton made it clear to the commissioners for the loan that he had consulted God, his conscience and historical precedent and had been instructed by all three that the loan was emphatically illegal. Coryton was imprisoned in the Fleet prison in London for his resistance. Some of the greatest and most powerful figures in the country became resisters: the Earls of Warwick, Essex, Huntingdon and Arundel. The twenty-seven-year-old Theophilus Clinton, Earl of Lincoln, an unlikely opposition hero, none the less mobilized resistance among seventy prominent gentry in the county and, when deposited in the Tower for his presumption, made sure his steward carried on the work of frustrating the commissioners. The spectacle of the mighty leading the charge in counties like Essex, Suffolk, Oxfordshire, Warwickshire, Northamptonshire and Buckinghamshire gave heart to godly preachers and men who would normally be thought of as pillars of stability. And the crisis provoked statements of shocking defiance and militancy. 'If it [the loan] goes forward,' wrote one Lincolnshire knight, 'we make ourselves and our posteritye subject to perpetual slavery without any recovery to be taxed at pleasure without any limits.' And in Yorkshire Sir John Jackson warned that 'if any of his men had give anie they should never hold land of him and iff anie of my tenants shall give, God's wounds I could or would hange them with my owne hands'.

The sound and fury did not die away once the money was collected. In the thirty-two contested elections for the parliament of 1628, opposition or submission to the forced loan became a critical issue in mobilizing the freeholders to defeat court-approved incumbents. Coryton and his friend, Sir John Eliot, who had also been jailed for resistance, were pressured by the government not to stand in Cornwall. But stand they did, turning their incarceration into a badge of honour and, more significantly, organizing like-minded gentry in a region supposedly warmly loyalist to ensure their triumphant return to parliament. Even more ominously for Crown control of politics, some of the more fiercely contested elections saw feisty mob scenes. At Cambridge Joseph Mead, the collector of political intelligence for his news 'separates', reported that in London not only had a linen draper, who had been in prison for resisting the loan, been elected, but the crowds had also been 'very unruly'. At Westminster supporters of the court-sponsored candidate, Sir Robert Pye, attempted to cry up his chances by parading the streets shouting, 'A Pye! A Pye! A Pye!', but were met with derisive counter-cries of 'A pudding! A pudding! A pudding!' and 'A lie! A lie! A lie!' Many of the names that would become a fixture of parliamentary ideology and local political organization in the early 1640s—Francis Rous in Cornwall, John Pym at Tavistock—had their first political blooding in these elections, which were unlike anything that had yet been seen in English political life.

Of course, England was not yet on the verge of revolution, or even approaching it, but moments like the forced loan crisis were, unquestionably, politically transformative. Rightly or wrongly, they fixed in the minds of an active, nationally educated political community the suspicion that this king was bent on breaching parliamentary defences of their property and their common law. It was an explosive apprehension, and from the most anxious it produced statements of unprecedented militancy about the limits of royal power. In Canterbury, for example, the city's MP Thomas Scott responded to the dean's sermon demanding unconditional obedience to the king with the statement that 'conscientious Puritans' (the word now self-attached as a badge of pride) were required to resist the abuses of unjust rulers: 'subjects may disobey and refuse an unworthy kinge his command or request if it be more than of duty we owe unto him.'

Standing firm in their belief in the supreme rationality of the English common law, the resisters were now taking to the courts to test both the legality of non-parliamentary taxation and the right of the government to imprison without showing due cause, something a Marlborough lawyer, Oliver St John, had said in 1614 violated the Magna Carta. In this case, the courts upheld the legality of the loan and thus the right of the Crown to confine resisters. And once the furore abated, the king should still have been able to contain the political fall-out, fierce though it was. But two events, both of them disastrous, made sure the book was not yet closed on the debate about taxation.

In October 1627 Buckingham turned in yet another hideous fiasco by failing—at huge expense —to take the French Atlantic fort of the Ile de Ré, not least because the organizational genius of the navy had failed to notice that the scaling ladders supplied for the siege were 15 feet too short to do the job. This single débâcle ate up £200,000 of the £267,000 collected by the loan. The duke was mercilessly pilloried by ballad-mongers and newsletter-writers. But even worse was to come. In March 1628 it was revealed that the terms of the judgement handed down in the challenge to the legality of the loan had been deliberately falsified by the attorney-general with the express knowledge and encouragement of the king. What the judges had ruled was that a forced loan was legitimate in this particular military emergency. What was published was a ruling that the king was entitled to make extra-parliamentary levies whenever he judged them to be appropriate to the kingdom's needs. It was a bombshell. Those who had believed the king found their trust badly shaken. Those who had taken the worst possible view of Charles's intentions, on the other hand, had a field day with the revelation. With the wind at their backs the guardians of the 'immemorial constitution' turned an argument over a specific measure into an all-out battle of constitutional principles. As a precondition of any further grants, they demanded a Bill of Rights declaring the illegality of non-parliamentary taxes, the prohibition of any imprisonment without trial by the king for unspecified 'reasons of state', and the unlawfulness of martial law and forced billets. The warriors for parliamentary liberties were, however, still in a minority in both the Commons and the Lords. The crisis was, in effect, a three-way showdown, with the party of moderate criticism in the middle, calling the tune. In the House of Lords the Earl of Warwick and Viscount Saye and Sele (both serious Puritans in their personal and religious life) decided, with a large measure of support, on the less confrontational form of a Petition of Right. A petition embodied the same points of substance as a bill, but crucially allowed Charles to save face and protect James's compulsively reiterated principle (restated as recently as 1621) that such rights were granted by grace, not acceded to as of right.

This should have been the end of the crisis. The assassination of Buckingham in August 1628 was a body blow to Charles, but it neatly took the vexed question of what to do about the widely detested favourite out of the political equation. In shocked mourning, Charles was convinced that the parliamentary demonization of the duke had contributed directly to his death. (The assassin, John Felton, had, in fact, imagined that he was ridding the country, and his king, of a diabolical monster.) Smarting at being deprived of his effective power to wage war, Charles mounted a counterattack, asserting his control over matters not expressly specified in the Petition of Right. It's hard not to imagine the king burning the candle at both ends as he pored over the petition to find loopholes to exploit, a legitimate but politically foolhardy impulse. He pounced on two significant omissions. First, he now claimed the right to go ahead and impose those 'tonnage and poundage' customs duties without waiting for parliamentary permission. Still more controversially, his appointment of Montague to the bishopric of Chichester and Laud to that of London said as loudly as possible that the king had no intention of conceding anything about his monopoly of wisdom and power in matters spiritual. Like his father, he thought of himself as God's 'lieutenant on earth'.

But the norms of politics and what could or could not be legitimately accepted as sovereign authority were changing under him even as Charles reiterated what he assumed to be the self-evident truths of his sovereignty. Yet even if he were incapable of compromising those principles, the arts of political management called for something other than noble obstinacy. The parliamentary moderates, who had cobbled together an artful resolution of conflict the previous year, were prepared to try again and were called to a negotiation with the king, however bleak the prospects. In the meantime, though, Charles had ordered a suspension of parliamentary proceedings to allow discussions to proceed without further public polarization. The order, of course, was construed as an enforced shut-down, and the militants in the House of Commons loudly advertised it as an infringement of their rights to debate. On 2 March 1629 the Speaker, Sir John Finch, attempted to adjourn proceedings in compliance with the king's order but was told that he was the Commons' servant, not the king's, and would not be allowed to suspend debates until a resolution attacking and condemning 'innovations in religion' and extra-parliamentary taxes had been read. In an awkward bind, Speaker Finch replied, rather pathetically: 'I am not the less the king's servant for being yours. I will not say I will not put it to the question but I must say I dare not.' He had no choice. Sir Miles Hobart had locked the door of the House and kept the key. With the king's officer hammering on the door and Denzil Holles, the member for godly Dorchester (and a big man), pushing the Speaker down in his chair and making sure he stayed there, the most eloquent leader of the radicals, Sir John Eliot, held the floor, warning that 'none had gone about to break parliaments but in the end parliaments have broken them'. Resolutions of startling fierceness were then read, declaring 'whoever should bring innovation of religion . . . . advise the taking and levying of subsidies not granted by parliament' to be 'a capital enemy of the kingdom and Commonwealth and every subject voluntarily complying with illegal exactions a betrayer of the liberties of England and an enemy to the same'. Shouts of acclamation, 'Aye, Aye, Aye', rang through the battle-hot House. Two days later Hobart, Holles, Eliot and six others were arrested and sent to the Tower. Parliament dissolved on 10 March.

It is not much, is it, this shift from speaking to shoving and shouting? On the other hand, it's everything: a startling violation of decorum in an age when body language spoke volumes about authority and its vulnerability. Holles's roughness and his evident contempt for polite procedure presuppose a collapse of deference that was genuinely ominous for the status quo. And along with it came something equally pregnant with consequences for the future—the creation of a public sphere of politics, the birth, in fact, of English public opinion. Although debates in parliament were still largely supposed to be confidential, lengthy, detailed reports were being written by specialist scriveners, sometimes on commission, sometimes for a news-hungry market, and reproduced in multiple copies. Thus the great theatre of debate inside parliament became news, and for the first time it was possible to make a living from selling it. John Pory, who was also a geographer and foreign adventurer, had a network of correspondents through the country, and he collated their information into a newsletter, which he sold to subscribers for £20 a year. Ralph Starkey, another of these pioneers of the mail-order news business, offered a range of products and services, from '20 shillings a quire' for parliamentary reports to £10 a copy for the Black Book Proceedings of the Order of the Garter. The newsmongers recognized the importance of keeping it hot and juicily divisive. By hiring a team of copyists it took just a few days for a vendor of 'separates' to get the word out (on paper) of the latest debates. So the news business, in a recognizably modern guise, first saw the light of day during the battles between Crown and parliament in 1628–9. Its emphasis on conflict may not, as the revisionist historians reasonably insist, reflect any kind of actual polarization in the country at large, but it has always been the mischievous genius of news to shape politics even while pretending to report it. And the marked preference of the newsmen of early seventeenth-century England for offering a theatre of the bad and the good, the court and the country, may well have had the effect of making it happen by virtue of saying it was so. The circulation of newsletters did something else, too, of fundamental significance for the future: it connected events in London to a provincial public (and on occasion local events could be turned into 'national' news). Reports of speeches would not be printed until the Long Parliament in 1642, but the sixpenny 'separates' travelled along the king's highway, taking all kinds of liberties with his sovereign prerogatives.

News always needs heroes, and the heavy hand of royal government made sure it got them. For bad things had happened to the militant critics of the Crown. Denzil Holles, Sir Miles Hobart and Sir John Eliot were all in the Tower, and Eliot died there in 1632. In the circles of parliamentary opposition to Stuart absolutism, Eliot's fate made him the proto-martyr of their resistance. John Hampden, a Buckinghamshire gentleman and MP, was one of those who kept the torch burning by corresponding with Eliot, visiting him in the Tower and acting as guardian to his two teenage sons. Whether the opposition was dormant or secretly indignant made no difference to the king. Parliament would not be called again until 1640.

In the 1950s, the textbook assumption was still that this long period of non-parliamentary government was a bandage applied so tightly over an open wound as to ensure that the wound would fester, not heal, and that the body politic would become quietly but morbidly infected. The condition of England was said to be one of sullen acquiescence in 'ship money' and the quasi-Catholicization of the Church, while the gagged and bound champions of parliamentary freedom waited for the great day when they could recover the liberties of the nation. Not much of this story has survived drastic revision. A recent history of the personal rule goes so far as to argue that the 1630s were the 'halcyon days' of disinterested royal government, when an energetic administration responded to the wishes of an austere but public-spirited king.

Perhaps somewhere between these two poles (though not, I think, at the mid-point) lies the truth. The suspension of parliamentary government was certainly not thought of as some sort of royal *coup d'état* heralding the introduction of a Habsburg–Bourbon Catholic despotism. Long periods without parliament were not unknown in the English system, and Charles made it quite clear that he did not see this one as signifying the end of the 'king-in-parliament' tradition. Should parliament itself wish to return to what he called its 'ancient' and reasonable way of conducting business, especially the business of providing him with money to secure the nation's defence, it would be back in business. And, of course, the Jacobean and Caroline parliaments were not yet thought of as the elected tribunes of the people. Most of the members of the Commons had taken their seats as a result of consensual and uncontested selection in the counties and boroughs. Some of the most radical of their number, like John Pym, owed their place to a not merely exiguous but virtually non-existent electorate in a pocket borough owned by the Earl of Bedford. By and large, members of parliament were the same kind of people who were the natural governors of the county community as magistrates, deputy lord-lieutenants and sheriffs, and whatever their misgivings about the misuse of Crown prerogatives they still had no problem accepting its offices. It was thus perfectly possible for upright Puritans, like Sir Robert Harley, who had been incensed by the forced loan and by Arminian appointments in the Church, to fill the lucrative position of Master of the Mint, from 1626 to 1635 when he lost office.

On the other hand, neither was England between 1629 and 1640 quite the land of sleepy contentment and harmony that has lately come to dominate the revised histories. What had happened in 1628 and 1629 had happened. Barriers of politeness had been breached. Unforgivable and unforgettable things had been said on both sides.

86

There had been excitement, agitation. Matters had turned physical. And even if those who had been exercised by the theatre of the extreme played out in those stormy years were only a tiny minority, they were a tiny minority with a long memory and access to the newsletters. If there was no sense of 'biding their time' (though this surely was the case for John Pym), neither would the deep grievances and arguments that had been aired at the end of the 1620s completely evaporate in some sort of cloud of resignation and goodwill. It's often said that had there been no furore in Scotland in 1637, the Long Parliament might never have happened. But that Scottish furore was not simply something that happened out of the blue, from causes utterly unrelated to Charles I's vision in the 1630s of a docile Britannia. On the contrary, what happened in Scotland, as we shall see, was, root and branch, sturdily connected to the royal trunk.

The problem with Charles Stuart was not his authoritarianism, his deviousness nor his political tin-ear, all of which have been overstated in the understandable interests of making the civil war seem more likely than it actually was. The problem with Charles Stuart was his good intentions, and the stubborn literalness with which he meant them to take effect. Conversely, in retrospect one can see quite clearly what enormous political assets his father's natural laziness and low threshold of distraction really were. (Uncannily, the same would be true of Louis XV and Louis XVI. Benign torpor should perhaps have been on the list of recommended virtues for successful princes.) James I's tendency to leave government to others, both in the Privy Council and in the shires, so that he could get off after the hare at Royston, was, since those others happened to be of the calibre of Robert Cecil and Francis Bacon and Lionel Cranfield, the best thing he could have done for the country. Charles I, on the other hand, was positively driven by the itch to govern. To be fair, since he inherited James's gargantuan debts and a war to boot, he did not have much choice in the matter. But once England and Scotland settled back into a peace imposed on the king by fiscal stringency and political opposition, Charles was not one to spend the rest of his life hunting or posing for Van Dyck (though he was, in his way, partial to both). Just as it had for Augustus, for Constantine and, especially, for Alfred the Great, whose biography was commissioned by the king, Duty Called!

And that duty was to make a harmonious realm of Magna Britannia whether it liked it or not, especially in religion, where it seemed most divided. Charles conceived of his kingship in terms not so much of a political office and high judgeship (as James theorized) as of a triple calling: knight-commander-cum-Caesar, spiritual governor and father of the nation. In the first department he made St George something of a fetish, turning the saint's day into a national holiday and investing the Order of the Garter with immense significance. The badge itself, which he wore every single day, was personally redesigned to feature the enormous silver aureole (borrowed from the French order of Saint Esprit), which gave it the appearance of a numinous sacred emblem. Beyond this sense of chivalric Christian appointment, Charles (like many of his contemporaries in baroque Europe) evidently understood his place in the scheme of things as a Platonist. Plato's vision of a celestially ordered unity of the universe, governed by ineffable ideas and truths, which were beyond the reach or the earthly articulation of mere men but which could be apprehended through beauty by a discerning few, the guardians, had been grafted on to Christian theology to create a fresh justification for the priesthood. Charles undoubtedly thought himself to be guardian-in-chief of Great Britain, and the exacting self-discipline of the Platonic guardian—personal austerity, tireless dedication, emotional and sensual self-denial (not qualities for which his late lamented dad was famous)—was what he tried at all times to uphold and personify. What better aim could there be, given the unhappy experience of his first years on the throne, than to bring Harmony to England and Scotland—whether they damned well liked it or not?

In the Dutch and Flemish paintings Charles loved to collect (and for which he had stupendously good taste), Harmony was symbolically represented by the family, often playing music. It was a truism that the family was a commonwealth in miniature and at the same time a pattern for its proper rule. And, again in contrast to the rather slatternly chaos of his father's household, Charles meant his family to be an exemplary image of firm but benevolent government. After a rough start, relations between king and queen became genuinely and reciprocally warm, and Charles's devotion to Henrietta Maria was passionate enough to blind him later to its very serious costs. Van Dyck's portraits of the royal family would be unique in the history of dynastic, even if they were just documents of private, sentiment. But as their prominent display in public spaces at Whitehall and Hampton Court makes clear, they were also a faithful visual translation of Charles's own ideology: that in the patriarchal family, with its strict but affectionate regulation of the relations between husband and wife, parents and children lay the foundation of all good order. In this, as in many other respects, his views were surprisingly close to those of the Puritans, and one of the reasons why Puritan nobles like Warwick were at such pains not to break with the king is because they saw in him someone as deeply committed to a moral vision of family and commonwealth as themselves.

But needs must, and needs could, disrupt the Caroline quest for Harmony, especially when it was the perennial want of money that was at issue. 'Ship money' would become reviled as one of the most notorious impositions ever laid on the country, a classic case of arbitrary and over-bearing government, but it was originally introduced as a response to the widely acknowledged neglect of the navy, painfully exposed in the Spanish and French wars, which had left English shipping vulnerable to Dutch privateers and pirates. Initially, only the coastal counties were required either to supply a ship or (as was more practical for most of them) pay the equivalent sum. So Charles was able to defend his imposition of ship money without parliamentary consent as legitimate, since it had been levied in defence of the realm. But an on-going need for naval rearmament was not the same as if the country were facing a second armada, so there were some who thought this merely another edition of the forced loan. It was, though, only when the levy was extended to the inland counties in 1635 that concerted opposition started to gather momentum.

Money was raised. The wheels of local government cooperated with the Crown. The men who ran England and Wales—from lord –lieutenants, through their deputies, to sheriffs, justices of the peace and constables and beadles—even if they had been critics in the stormy days of the 1620s, settled back into the role of political and social leaders of their communities, presiding at quarter sessions, leading the hunt, dominating the pews. But what does this resumption of local leadership really mean? That their criticisms had now been put to sleep by their self-interest or that they could without much difficulty administer justice and government without necessarily abandoning their strong reservations about the court?

Some of them, it is true, became partners in Charles's agenda of modernizing reform and renewal, which often resembles nothing so much as the Puritan programme in towns like Dorchester: extended poor relief, the suppression of unlicensed alehouses, the foundation of schools and colleges, and projects designed to improve agriculture like the Earl of Bedford's famous drainage of the Fens in the 1630s. But the intense hostility to the Dutch drainage programme on the part of the affected Fenland population is a good instance of the reaction of some local communities to the obsessive intervention of government in their own backyard, however well-intentioned. And the manner in which those 'improvements' were carried out was not always calculated to allay suspicions that, beneath grandiose declarations about the government promoting the welfare of the commonwealth, there lurked something that smelled of a scam. In the Fens the medieval Court of Sewers had been absurdly revived to move local populations off boggy land. Once conveniently vacated, the land could be transferred to the drainage syndicates, which profited from the enormous capital appreciation of the drained land.

To avoid this kind of odium, Charles's administration did its best to co-opt the county gentry and nobility in its projects. But there were still some schemes in which the intrusiveness of government was bound to be felt much more keenly than its good intentions, never more so perhaps than in the notorious project for the production and conservation of a strategic supply of gunpowder. This was not a trivial issue. The gunpowder shortage was a Europe-wide problem in an age of constant warfare, and a stockpile could make the difference between victory and defeat. What, then, could be a more laudable or necessary patriotic enterprise? In practice, though, what the scheme entailed was the creation of a national store of saltpetre. And the cheapest and most readily available source of nitrous saltpetre was the excreta of animals and humans. Only a monarch as solemnly bereft of a sense of humour as Charles I could possibly have asked his subjects, in all seriousness, to preserve a year's supply of their own urine as a major contribution to the national defence. (This would not, in fact, be the most outrageous attempt to turn body waste into munitions. During the Irish rebellion and wars of the Confederacy in the 1640s and 1650s, the remains of corpses were recycled into gunpowder—the most perfect example, I suppose, of a self-sustaining industry.) But the very energy of Charles's 'petre-men' quickly turned them into enemies of liberty and private property, as armed with warrants they entered barnyards and private households, digging up floors if necessary to get their hands on the precious and strategically important deposits of dove-droppings or sheep shit. Given the unusual working conditions of this assignment, it seems unlikely that, when confronted by householders understandably displeased at having their floors dug up without a by-your-leave, the petre-men would have made much of an effort to appease them.

Likewise, Charles's support for Archbishop Laud's programme for the Church was, while perfectly well intentioned, easily open to misinterpretation. The heart of Laudian doctrine was nothing more than the endorsement of ceremony and sacrament that had certainly been upheld by James I and his own favoured ministers and bishops, including Lancelot Andrewes. But James's Scottish apprenticeship had made him in practice, if not in principle, a grudging pluralist. He had spoken for uniformity (and in Scotland pushed it through in 1618), but in England he was more judicious and circumspect. Charles, on the other hand, saw in Laudian theology a way to bring the congregation of Christians together within an orderly hierarchy of the Church. The obsession with sermons and preaching, the privileging of individual reading of the scripture, the harping on the unbridgeable chasm between the saved and the damned he felt to be profoundly divisive. With the débâcle of Laudianism in 1640–1 came the assumption that somehow it was, indeed, an alien growth on the body of the native Church. But there were plenty of adherents in the 1630s who saw as a national duty, for example, Laud's levy for the repair and restoration of the ruinously neglected and profaned St Paul's Cathedral.

Herefordshire may have been home to the Harleys of Brampton Bryan, who turned their castle into a magnet for Puritan teachers and preachers and an asylum for those suffering from the enforcers of the Laudian Church. But it was also home to the Scudamores of Holme Lacy. The Scudamores had been in the business of supplying knights for the royal tilts right into the reign of James, and they took special pride in their horses, kept not just for the hunt but to be at the disposal of the king. As deputy-lieutenant for Herefordshire, the first Viscount Scudamore made public exhortations to the Herefordshire gentry to improve the quality and quantity of the horses they could bring to the service of the king. Arthurian chivalry was not, it seems, quite dead on the Welsh borderlands. But Scudamore was not just a loyal *preux chevalier*; he was also a genuinely learned country gentleman with an Oxford education. And like so many of the post-Baconian generation, he was an enthusiastic amateur scientist, a manipulator of nature. Scudamore's pride and joy was the Red Streak apple, said to produce the best and most commercially sought-after cider in England. All of Scudamore's passions—his veneration of the past, his vision of a Christian monarchy, his instinctive feeling for beauty—came together in a project that must have seemed as though it were the very justification for his authority in the Herefordshire countryside: the restoration of Abbey Dore.

The abbey was a Cistercian ruin. The Scudamores had acquired it along with its land in the mid-sixteenth century and had it reconsecrated, but by the time the viscount came to its rescue it was, like so many monastic wrecks all over Britain, at the point of collapse. The roof was so badly fallen in that the curate was forced to read the service from the shelter of an arch to avoid rain falling on the prayer book. And when Scudamore went looking for the old stone altar slab he found it being used to salt meat and press cheese.

Scudamore, doubtless encouraged by Matthew Wren, Bishop of Hereford and one of the most ardent Laudians, evidently thought of himself as the Hezekiah of Herefordshire: the patron who would rebuild the ruined temple to the greater glory of God. The restoration of decayed churches and abbeys seems to have been a passion among the antiquarian community of the counties, so much so that the earliest date of the 'Gothic revival' might well be pushed back to the 1640s, when the antiquary and genealogist William Dugdale, in the depths of Puritan Warwickshire, began his monumental work of describing and chronicling all the church monuments of the country. Dugdale also produced the first great illustrated history of St Paul's Cathedral, a crucial weapon in Laud's campaign to cleanse and restore the polluted building and churchyard (freely used as a latrine) and to have the church thought of, as much as Westminster Abbey, as a national temple.

Scudamore busied himself locally much as Laud busied himself nationally. The desecrated altar was returned to Abbey Dore (according to a local story,

95

crushing a servant who tried to make off with it, its surface running with blood). The beautiful green-glazed tiles of the medieval church scattered around farms and hamlets were reused where possible, replaced where not. And from the surviving *in situ* remnant of the crossing of the old abbey church, Scudamore had the Herefordshire craftsman John Abel (who had also designed a gloriously ornamental town hall at Leominster) carve a spectacular chancel screen in the authentic style of the Palladian revival, complete with Ionic columns. On Palm Sunday 1635, the date chosen not just for its place in the sacred calendar but as the anniversary of Scudamore's baptism, Dore was reconsecrated with a full day of prayers and processions, and much kneeling and bowing, the congregation commanded to remember that henceforth Dore was to be considered a 'Holie Habitation'.

Just across the county at Brampton Bryan Sir Robert and Lady Brilliana Harley would have seen the reconsecration of the Cistercian abbey as the most horrifying and damning evidence that the Popish Antichrist had already made a successful conquest of England, and that his Laudian minions were abusing their office to re-institute the full monstrous servitude of Rome. But to the Laudians, their work was not in any sense an act of spiritual or ecclesiastical subjugation. On the contrary, they saw the restoration of spectacle and mystery as a way of bringing back to the Church those who had been alienated by its obsession with the Word. To feast the eye rather than tire the ear was a way of appealing to all those whom the Calvinists had told were either damned or saved, a way of giving hope to sinners that they might yet be among the flock of those who would see salvation. So the restoration of propriety was not, in their minds, an affectation but a genuine mission. How could the flock be properly reminded of the redeeming sacrifice of the Saviour at a mean little table on which worshippers were accustomed to deposit their hats and from which dogs made off with the communion wafers? Reverence, order and obedience would make the congregation of the faithful whole again.

The Laudian emphasis on inclusiveness fitted neatly with Charles's own innocent concept of his monarchy as an office for the entirety of his subjects. The trouble, though, was that by entirety he meant Scotland as well as England. For if the object of the Laudian reforms was to create an orderly harmony within the Church of England, any kind of exceptions to its uniformity would, by definition, sabotage the whole project. Thus, thoroughly convinced of the rightness of his convictions, Charles planned to introduce the Laudian prayer book to Scotland. In 1634, a year after his coronation in Edinburgh, it must have seemed a good, a necessary project. How was he supposed to know that it was the beginning of his end?

CHAPTER TWO

GIVE CAESAR HIS DUE?

The British wars began on the morning of 23 July 1637, and the first missiles launched were foot stools. They flew down the nave of St Giles's Cathedral in Edinburgh (the kirk of St Giles until the east and west walls had been removed to enlarge the church to proportions compatible with its new dignity), and their targets were the dean and the Bishop of Edinburgh. The reverend gentlemen had just begun to read from a new royally authorized Prayer Book. Even before the hurling of the stools, the attempt to read the liturgy had triggered a deafening outburst of shouting and wailing, especially from the many women gathered in the church. The minister John Row, who called the detestable object 'this Popish-English-Scottish-Mass-Service-Book', described keening cries of 'Woe, woe' and 'Sorrow, sorrow, for this doleful day, that they are bringing in Popery among us' ringing round the church. Terrified, the dean and bishop beat a swift retreat, but not before hands reached out in an attempt to strip the white surplices from their backs. In other churches in the city, such as the Old Kirk close by St Giles, the minister was barracked into silence; at Greyfriars the Bishop-designate of Argyll surrendered to a storm of abuse. In the afternoon the appearance of bishops and clergy was a sign for crowds to appear from nowhere, surrounding the nervous ministers, jostling and yelling their undying hatred of the

'Popish' liturgy.

The Prayer Book riots were not, of course, a spontaneous protest by the outraged common people of Scotland. The royal council had conveniently let it be known, months in advance, that the Prayer Book would be introduced by Easter 1637, which gave its opponents—Calvinist preachers and lords—time to organize their demonstration. Printing delays had postponed the date further, so that by July the trap was well set, and Archbishop Laud, his bishops, the council and the king innocently fell right in. They were caught completely off guard. As far as Charles I could see, Scotland was likely to be perfectly obedient to his ambition to create a single Arminian Church throughout Britain. Had not the Scottish parliament obliged him, if reluctantly, in 1633 when he had come to Edinburgh for his coronation (eight years after being crowned in Westminster)? To be sure, there had been some fuss in 1626 when he had revoked the land titles and grants of the Scottish nobility, but it was customary to do this every twenty-five years, before regranting them on terms spelled out by the new sovereign. What Charles had failed to notice was the intense resentment caused when it was made clear that some of those land grants transferred by the Reformation from Church to lay hands were now to be given back to establish endowments for the bishops. And the king had been much too complacent about the apparent lack of resistance to his 'book of canons', introduced in 1636, restricting preaching and giving dominant authority to the bishoprics.

But then Charles talked to all the wrong people

in all the wrong places, to deracinated silk-coated London-Scottish noblemen like the Duke of Hamilton, or to his tough-minded treasurer in Edinburgh, the Earl of Traquair, who for the most part told him what he wanted to hear. The king had been born in the ancient royal abbey town of Dunfermline, but he was an absentee monarch who knew virtually nothing about the reality of Scotland and fatally misjudged the depth and breadth of its impassioned Calvinism. What he ought to have done was go to one of the little granite-grey towns of the southwest, such as Irvine, on a Monday marketday, and hear the full trumpet blast of preachers like Robert Blair or David Dickson thundering against the iniquitous destruction of the godly Church by such as Archbishop Laud and his corrupt and tyrannical lackeys, the bishops. The mere notion that the Church of Rome (as the Arminians argued) was a 'true', if misguided, Church and not actually the abominable institution of Antichrist, sent them into a paroxysm of wrath. Hard-pressed by the official Church, often stripped of their livings, such men had become itinerant preachers, taking refuge with their equally fierce Presbyterian Scots brethren in Ulster, across the North Channel. There, they were embraced into like-minded communities of psalm-singers and scripture-readers. Despairing of the realm of the Stuarts, some of the godly ministers had even decided to build their Jerusalem in Massachusetts and had got as far as Newfoundland before being blown back by a tempest, which, needless to say, they interpreted as God's design that they should, after all, do his work at home. Back in Scotland they turned into so many Jeremiahs and

Ezekiels, calling on God's children to resist such abominations as surplices and kneeling and stone altars as if they were the desecrations of Sodom.

Charles, however, was incapable of appreciating the power of Scottish Calvinism's clarion call for a great purification. As far as the king was concerned, Scotland was not all that different from England, and if the one had been bent to the royal will by well-intentioned firmness, so might the other. But the Scottish Reformation, of course, had been nothing at all like the slow, staccato progress of England's conversion to Protestantism. Its Calvinism had struck in great electrifying bursts of charismatic conversion, backed up by teachers, lecturers and ministers, and only forced into reluctant and periodic retreat by James I, who, unlike his son, had known when to stop. It was an irony in the great holy shouting match of 1637–8, that *both* sides imagined they represented continuity not change. Charles and Laud thought they were building on the Five Articles of Perth of 1618 and that the protesters were Presbyterian rebels who sought to overthrow the whole royal supremacy of the Church. But ministers like Samuel Rutherford, whose preaching at Anwoth had been so offensive that Bishop Sydserf of Galloway had him banished to the safely conservative confines of Aberdeen, believed that they were merely upholding a much more ancient covenant between Scotland and God. That covenant was in every respect like the one made between God and Israel but had specific roots in the (fictitious but immensely influential) history of Scotland's conversion in the third century AD. According to those histories, the Church had been received by the *community* before ever the first king, Fergus, had begun his reign in the year 310. His sovereignty, then, had been conditional on acceptance of the covenant made between God and Scotland, the *original* godly nation—before England and even before Rome.

This is what the likes of Blair and Dickson and Rutherford and countless other ministers preached, and this is what their flock fervently believed. Laud and the bishops were the filthy priests of Baal, who presumed to come between them and their covenant with the Almighty. For the moment, the king himself was given the benefit of the doubt, being led astray by 'evil counsel'. The Prayer Book riots in July 1637 and the still more startling events that followed were not meant to herald the overthrow of the house of Stuart. On the contrary, they were intended to reaffirm its sovereignty in Scotland but only on the understanding that that kingdom could not, and would not, be treated as a mere appendage of England. The hope, especially among the more moderate nobility, was that the unenforceability of the Prayer Book would persuade the king to listen to wise advice and retreat from his policy of 'innovations'. In fact, the Duke of Hamilton, who replaced Traquair as the king's principal commissioner in Scotland, warned the king in June 1638 to back away from further confrontation. Hamilton even had the prescience to predict to Charles that if he persisted trouble would not be confined to Scotland but would inevitably spread to all three of his kingdoms.

What Hamilton had witnessed since arriving in Scotland was the first revolutionary upheaval of seventeenth-century Britain. Even the organizers of the Prayer Book riots had been taken aback at the force and overwhelming popularity of the protests. Town officers did nothing about apprehending the rioters, other than briefly detaining a few of the serving women and apprentices who had made the loudest noise. But through the winter of 1637–8, the moment was seized to mobilize a great petitioning movement against the bishops, which caught up ministers, nobles, lairds and townsmen in its crusading fervour. A dissident group on the royal council in Scotland produced a 'Supplication' to the king, urging him to abandon the Laudian Church and replace it with a godly Presbyterian order. Charles's response was to assume that only some sort of foreign, probably French, influence could explain this temerity, to order the council out of the continuously riotous Edinburgh and to threaten to treat as traitors those who persisted in their opposition.

Instead of cowing the resistance, this response turned it into a revolution. On 28 February 1638 a 'National Covenant' was signed in a solemn, four-hour ceremony at Greyfriars Church, Edinburgh, full of prayers, psalms and sermons exhorting the godly to be the new Israel. Later that day it was exhibited at the Tailors' Hall on Cowgate, where it was signed by ministers and representatives from the towns. The next day the common people, including a substantial number of women, added their signatures, and copies were made to be sent throughout Scotland. Although the covenant at first sight seems to be written in the language of conservatism, claiming to protect the king's peace, it had been drafted in part by the uncompromising

Calvinist lawyer Archibald Johnston. Johnston was the kind of dyspeptic, self-mortifying zealot who lay awake at night, tortured by the possibility that he might have one grain of impurity too many to qualify for the Elect, and who, on getting into bed with his teenage wife Jean, immediately assured God (out loud) that he preferred His face to hers. For Johnston, the covenant was 'the glorious marriage day of the kingdom with God', and he, like Samuel Rutherford, had no hesitation in assuming that kings could be lawfully called to account and if necessary removed if ever they should violate *that* marriage bed.

For countless thousands of Scots, signing the covenant was just an extension of the vows they took 'banding' them with God in the Kirk, but the document itself rapidly assumed the status of a kind of patriotic scripture, a way of determining who was truly Christian and who not, who was a true Scot and who not. Belatedly, Hamilton attempted to organize a 'King's Covenant' as a moderate riposte, and he managed to secure some 28,000 signatures, proof that, as in so many other crucial turning points in Scotland's history, the country was divided rather than united in its response. But it seems extremely unlikely that Charles himself ever thought of the 'King's Covenant' as anything more than a tactical manoeuvre while he mobilized enough force to bring the Scots to heel. And by late 1638, most of Scotland was already borne aloft in the whirlwind. A righteously intoxicated general assembly in Glasgow, where Johnston served as chief clerk, went the whole distance, effectively severing all connections between the English government and the Scottish Church: it abolished bishops and the rest of the Laudian establishment. Then the Scottish parliament, which first met in August 1639 and reconvened without royal permission in June 1640, introduced three-yearly parliaments, whether or not they were called by the king.

None of the Covenanters could have been under much illusion about what Charles I's response to the Glasgow assembly would be. Their own view was that they threatened nothing, presumed no interference in the affairs of England (although, as part of the international Calvinist defence against the Counter-Reformation, they could not but hope that they might set an example for Presbyterians south of the border). If, on the other hand, the king of England came in arms to undo their godly Reformation, they would, of course, defend it with their lives. And proper precautionary measures were quickly taken through the winter and spring of 1638–9 to see to this defence. The veteran soldier of the religious wars in Europe, General Alexander Leslie, was made commander of their forces; money was borrowed from the banker William Dick to buy munitions and powder from the Dutch; castles and strongholds were transferred from royal to Covenanter authority; and the local networks that had produced signatures for the petitions and covenant—the towns and villages of Scotland—were now mined to produce money and men. Charles and Laud had really managed something quite unique: they had contrived to unite two parties, the Kirk and the lords, who were more naturally accustomed to quarrelling. And two sets of loyalties, the Church and the clan, could be used to produce a godly army. By the spring of 1639 that army numbered at least 25,000 and perhaps as many as 30,000 men.

On the other side of the border it proved much harder to get an army together, let alone a force that could be relied on to strike terror into the hearts of the Scots (or at least persuade them to abandon the Covenant). Sir Edmund Verney, who by now was much more the country gentleman than the courtier, enjoyed nothing more than to tend his estate at Claydon in Buckinghamshire, and to keep company with his wife Mary and their rapidly expanding family. But he was still officially Knight Marshal, a member of the Privy Chamber, and therefore duty bound, however reluctantly, to answer the royal summons to attend the king at York, 'as a cuirassier in russett armes, with guilded studds or nayles, and befittingly horsed', despite his deep misgivings about the wisdom and propriety of the king's and Laud's policies. His eldest son, Ralph, was even less happy about his father (who was, in any case, in poor health) risking his life to enforce contentious doctrines of which he himself rather disapproved and which were best left to the divines to thrash out. Ralph could hardly have been reassured by his father making his will before leaving Claydon, nor by letters, which his father worried might be opened before reaching him, describing military disaster in the making: 'Our Army is butt weake; our Purce is butt weaker; and if wee fight with thes foarces and early in the yeare wee shall have our throats cutt.' The learned Thomas Howard, Earl Marshal Arundel, seemed to be better equipped to collect art and antiquities than to lead an army, for he led the king on to fight without warning him of the dire condition of the troops. 'I dare saye ther was never soe Raw, soe unskilfull and soe unwilling an Army brought to fight,' wrote Sir Edmund witheringly of Arundel.

My lord marshall himselfe will, I dare saye, bee safe, and then he cares not what becomes of the rest; trewly here are manny brave Gentlemen that for poynt of honor must runn such a hazard as trewly would greeve any heart but his that does it purposely to ruine them. For my owne parte I have lived till paine and trouble has made mee weary to doe soe; and the woarst that can come shall not bee unwellcome to mee; but it is a pitty to see what men are like to be slaughterd here unless it shall pleas god to putt it in the king's Hearte to increase his Army or staye till thes may knowe what they doe; for as yett they are like to kill theyr fellows as the enemye.

Verney was not exaggerating. The machinery of mustering the trained bands in the Midlands and northern counties to make up the English army was showing signs of imminent breakdown. It was proving difficult, and in some cases impossible, to raise the ship money that had been extended into the inland counties. County commissioners for troops and sheriffs for ship money were disappearing or protesting the impossibility of delivering funds. The men themselves—trained bands of literate artisans, such as clothiers—often failed to show up at the mustering places, and replacements had to be rounded up from wherever the impressment officers could find them. They, too, failed to understand why they were being called on to fight this 'bishops' war'. The trained bands were supposed to be called out strictly in defence of the realm against invasion, and it was known, not least from the propaganda the Covenanters were already circulating south of the border, that the Scots had explicitly disavowed any such aim. The reluctance of the trained bands was shared by many of their social superiors and officers. The king sensed this strained loyalty but only made matters worse by demanding of his officers an oath of loyalty, which the Puritan nobles, Viscount Saye and Sele and Lord Brooke (of Oxfordshire and Warwickshire respectively), point blank refused. The dissident nobles were immediately imprisoned in York for their shocking rejection of the royal command, thus covering themselves with glory among the godly. As for the rank and file, it was, as Sir Edmund Verney noted, a surly, underpaid (in many cases unpaid), poorly armed, wretchedly led force that trudged north from York towards the border.

At Kelso, just inside Scottish territory, all of Verney's pessimism seemed borne out. A small force of cavalry, led by the Earl of Holland and including Sir Edmund himself, was confronted by what seemed at first a manageably modest Scots army. But as Holland got his men into battle order the Scots army seemed to grow before their eyes, pikemen and dragoons and horse becoming more and more numerous until it was appallingly obvious that any kind of engagement would end in a calamitous rout. Hastily, Holland withdrew his troops to camp where they (necessarily) exaggerated the size of the waiting enemy. Charles, whose own mood had gone from supercilious complacency to grim irritation at the news of discontent and desertion, now thought better of an impetuous campaign. The Scots' request to clarify their own position (for they did not at any time consider themselves rebels) was accepted, and a meeting of delegations organized at Berwick-on-Tweed in June 1639. Charles himself appeared at this meeting, where he had his first chance to encounter the full, glaring Calvinist hostility of Archibald Johnston. As usual, the king's idea of diplomacy was to chide the Scots for their 'pretended' assembly and to concede nothing, except that the issues might be aired and, it was hoped, resolved by the calling of a Scottish parliament rather than on the field of battle. Pending that resolution, both armies were to be disbanded. Johnston suspected that this was merely a ploy on the part of the king to play for time, and he had the bad manners to say so, more or less to his face. But suspicious or not, a 'Pacification' was duly signed. The ink was hardly dry before Johnston's scepticism was vindicated as Charles made it known that he would expect a new general assembly to be called that would nullify all the reforms of Glasgow.

In Scotland in July that year there were near-riots when the terms of the Pacification became known, since it was felt not unreasonably that an opportunity to defeat the king had been frittered away and that the Scots were now locked into a truce, pending the onset of a round of more serious warfare. And perhaps, for a time, Charles may have been smilingly deluded, imagining that he had got the better of the Scots tactically and would shortly get the better of them militarily, too. For he was now listening to the counsellor he thought would without question bring him victory, vindication and retribution against the Covenanters: Thomas Wentworth, his Lord Deputy in Ireland. Wentworth had been a kind of miracle for the king. From being one of his most aggressive critics in parliament, he had become the most unflagging and uncompromising upholder of the absolutism of the Crown. Psychologically, Charles must have felt that the flinty, saturnine Wentworth was truly one of his own: a man who understood that the destiny of the Crown was to apply the balm of royal adjudication to nations hurting from confessional wounds. Except that the Wentworth medicine invariably had a nasty sting to it. Those who begged to differ with the Lord Deputy found themselves smartly disadvantaged: their land title investigated, their property taken, themselves in prison. But the policy of 'thorough' had kept Ireland quiet, and that in itself was a recommendation for his understanding of the obscure and irate war of the sects—Old English Catholics, Ulster Presbyterians, Gaelic Irish. As far as Charles could see, Wentworth had kept the royal ship of state sailing high above the fray like some celestial galleon in a court masque. So when he gave the king advice about the Scottish crisis, Charles paid attention. Call a parliament, Wentworth advised. Without it, your army will never be well supplied nor the country truly disposed to fight the war. And fear not. Parliaments, however truculent they might seem, are manageable, especially when the defence of the realm can be legitimately invoked. To show the king what could be done, in March 1640 Wentworth called an Irish parliament at Dublin, which behaved like a lamb, the Old English voting with enough New English to produce solid majorities and fat little subsidies for the Crown. Strategy two was admittedly a little trickier. Wentworth was proposing to use an Irish army to deal with the Scottish rebellion. The only problem was how disciplined troops in numbers sufficient to make any impact on the Scottish war could be expeditiously raised. Needless to say, they could hardly be drawn from the New English and Scottish Presbyterians of the Ulster plantation, whose sympathies were all with the Covenant.

A solution was at Charles's right hand in the shape of Randal Macdonnell, the Marquis of Antrim. He was a unique figure in northern Ireland, a native Irish Catholic, but one who had profited from Wentworth's bargain, by which his own fortunes were expanded to the degree to which he made room for planters on his enormous estates. At the same time, Antrim had become a familiar, if not entirely trusted, figure in the inner circles of Charles's court. So when he offered to raise his own native Irish army to be put at the king's disposal Charles was tempted to take the proposal very seriously, even though Wentworth had deep misgivings about what he considered to be a low, barbarian Catholic force, 'with as many "Os" and "Macs" as would startle a whole council board', claiming to do the work of the king. Should the gamble not pay off, he had an all too clear vision of how the idea of a semi-private Catholic army deployed against the godly Covenanters would play in England!

From the beginning then, even Wentworth could see that the two arms of the king's strategy—

111

a parliament and a native, predominantly Catholic –Irish army—might turn out to be in glaring contradiction to each other. But the king was not thinking logically. In fact, he was not thinking at all, just dreaming dreams of vindication and victory: the Grand Harmonization of Britannia virtually within reach.

Step one was the calling of a parliament in April 1640. Encouraged by Wentworth and Laud, Charles was confident that the interrupted but unresolved crisis with Scotland would ensure an assembly that, as in Ireland, would discuss only the matters proposed by the king and, after such discussion, produce adequate supplies for his armies. He also seems to have felt that his eleven years of personal rule had actually made this docility more, rather than less, likely, since the country had been exposed to the wisdom, energy, benevolence and disinterested justice of his sovereignty. And since he believed that the Covenanters had been in touch with the king of France, all he would have to do would be to flourish evidence of this revival of the notorious 'auld alliance' and the country would rise to the defence of the realm. Shades of the Plantagenets and the Bruces (albeit with the odd outcome of the Stuarts fighting against, rather than for, the independence of Scotland)!

It must have come as an unpleasant shock, then, when this new parliament, far from putting old, imagined grievances aside, immediately resurrected them. Virtually the first order of the day was their summoning of the records of the proceedings against Sir John Eliot, whose death in the Tower of London had not been forgotten but had been religiously remembered as a martyrdom suffered for the people's liberty. However extreme, this was precisely the way in which the fate of Eliot and a whole pantheon of victims of Laud's Court of High Commission and of Star Chamber appeared in the newsletters and 'separates' that were distributed around the provinces. For the newsmongers Eliot made wonderful copy, and there was a steady supply of victims and heroes to join him, men whose stories were celebrated in the newsletters as chapters in a scripture of godly liberty. Some of them like the obdurate, steely lawyer, William Prynne, had done everything they could to court persecution. Prynne's *Histrio-Mastix* had been a scathing attack on the court and in particular on the masques in which the king and queen liked to appear as dancers. More dangerously, in the course of the polemic Prynne had asserted a doctrine of resistance (shared by both ultra-Catholic and Calvinist theorists) by which a prince plainly resolved to violate God's laws might be set aside. For his sedition Prynne was sentenced in 1634 to have his ears sliced off, pay a fine of £5000 and spend the rest of his life in the Tower of London. In London and in strongly Puritan communities like Dorchester the irascible, unstoppable Prynne became an immediate saint, his epistle broadcast through the network of the godly from Ulster to Scotland. In 1637 the government blunderingly reinforced and perpetuated his popularity by dragging Prynne out of the Tower to stand in the pillory along with Dr Henry Burton—the Puritan rector of St Matthew, Friday Street, London—who had preached sermons on a popish plot and the evils of the Church, and John Bastwick, another

113

active sympathizer, who likewise refused to remain silent. Both the new malefactors had their ears cut off—no deterrent to Burton who defiantly continued to preach while profusely bleeding, or so the Puritan Apocrypha had it.

Nehemiah Wallington, a devout wood-turner living in the parish of St Andrew's Hubbard, Eastcheap, believed every word of the gospel according to Prynne and began a 2000-page account of the sins and events of his times, including an encomium to the earless martyrs, Burton and Bastwick. In Wallington's tight little universe nothing could possibly happen without some sort of providential meaning. A boating accident was God's punishment for the profanation of the Sabbath; a storm that broke the stained-glass windows of a church His judgement on gaudy idolatry. Prynne, Burton and Bastwick had obviously been called to preach against the uncleanness of the times, and their torments were a sign that great days of reckoning were nigh. In this fevered world miracles, portents and signs abounded. A conversation set down in Wallington's book suggests just how intensely he and his fellow Puritan artisans felt the coming of the battle between the children of God and the legions of Antichrist. No sooner had one of these heretics finished denouncing the three as 'base schismatical jacks' who deserved hanging for troubling the kingdom, than he suddenly fell into a terrible sweat with blood pouring from his ears. Wallington's sense that Prynne, Burton and Bastwick were fighting the good fight, *his* fight, was brought home all too directly when he was named, along with the three others, in a charge of seditious libel and ordered to answer for it before the court of Star Chamber in 1639. But his own ears survived the ordeal, and he lived to join the triumphal celebrations in the streets of London that greeted the liberation of Bastwick, ordered by parliament at the end of 1640.

The gallery of resistance heroes took in all social types and conditions, from dissident minor clergy like Peter Smart, who had lost his position as prebend at Durham Cathedral and had been fined £500 for attacking Bishop Neile's innovations in ceremony, to the Buckinghamshire gentleman and MP John Hampden (the guardian of Eliot's children) who had refused to pay the 20 shilling ship-money assessment on one of his estates and had gone to court to test its legality. Although the King's Bench had found against Hampden in 1638, it had done so by only seven votes to five, and both the impassioned arguments of his lawyer, Oliver St John, and the dissenting judgement of Judge George Croke added to what was rapidly becoming a canon of virtue: men who exemplified the counsel given in one of John White's sermons at Holy Trinity, Dorchester, that 'obedience to the will of God discharges a man from performing the will of the ruler'.

Unlike Prynne or White, John Hampden was not some abrasive and unworldly hothead but a well-respected county figure whose strength and clarity of opinion about the illegality of non-parliamentary taxes made essentially moderate gentlemen from the same county, like the Verneys, think very seriously about the constitutional price to be paid for obedience to the king. The Buckinghamshire members elected to parliament

115

in 1640 no longer looked like a bunch of backwoods provincial knights and burgesses concerned first and foremost with parish-pump affairs and loyally willing to do the king's business. From militant Puritans, like Bulstrode Whitelocke, to Hampden himself and the Verneys, there was at the group's core a highly literate and politically articulate group, intensely tuned to national politics—indeed, who made no distinction at all between the affairs of the county and those of the nation. There were, of course, shades of opinion between them. While he felt the times did call for reform, Sir Edmund was less impatient for it than his son, Ralph, who would make a chronicle of the doings of the Long Parliament and who evidently felt that one of the great moments in the country's history was at hand. But father and son were not (yet) estranged. Hampden's case may have changed nothing on the law books in respect of the legality of non-parliamentary taxes, but it had changed a lot of minds. The very conditions of the personal rule had ensured that the king and his councillors would keep themselves ignorant of the many ways in which a genuine public opinion in England was in the process of being formed. And like so much of the radicalization of English politics, the catalyst travelled south in the form of broadsheets printed in Scotland by the busily righteous Covenanter press. Occasionally, there are documentary glimpses of just how quickly a politicized reading public was forming. At Radwinter in Essex an unknown man marched up to the curate in a Laudian church and threw a Puritan pamphlet on his desk, saying, 'There is reading work for you, read that.' In Stepney in 1640 another minister found a man reading the printed proceedings of parliament in his churchyard. But until it was much too late, in the winter of 1641–2, the royal government thought no more of these 'ephemera' than of the vulgar gossip of the impotent common people.

They were fatally deluded. The talk-filled, rumour-ridden, preachy, preternaturally suspicious, gossipy world of news was already giving the rough kiss of life to institutions that had been politically inert for generations. For the first time in living memory, elections for knights of the shire were being contested in the counties, sometimes hotly. The government did everything it could to influence the poll to produce members who would be as tractable as Wentworth's Irish parliament in Dublin, but where it faced money and local power from a determined opposition it almost invariably lost. In Dorset, for example, a great campaign was waged to elect Dudley Carleton, son of the English ambassador to the Dutch court at The Hague, in place of Denzil Holles, but it failed, and Holles was returned, more determined than ever to bring court and council to a reckoning before the representatives of the 'country'. The regime fared no better in the boroughs. In Cornwall, where loyalty to the king was usually thought fierce, government support was the kiss of death to all eight candidates recommended by it. And the elections in 1640, for both the April and November parliaments, began to turn up men from a much broader social circle (and much more strongly partisan religious colouring) than the usual gentlemanly MP. In counties like Warwickshire and Oxfordshire the Puritan nobles—Brooke, and Saye and Sele—spent money and knocked heads together to secure the election of godly members, many of them famous local resisters of ship money. In December 1639 Brooke apparently even had the audacity to try to bring to Warwick Samuel Rutherford, the Covenanter preacher, whose *Lex rex*, published just five years later, made it clear that he thought political authority was 'a birthright of the people, borrowed from them; they may let it out for their own good and resume it when a man is drunk with it'.

By the 1630s Puritanism was not just a manner of worship. It was an entire sub-culture, which began in the cradle of the family hearth, embraced and enclosed men, women and children within its godly vision and conditioned the way they saw the political world. Crucially, for the future of Britain, that unity of vision cut across the old lines of social rank and deferential hierarchies. Puritan aristocrats like Brooke felt themselves to have far more in common with humble preachers and teachers than with their fellow nobles. These families raised their children on a common literature, sent them to the same kind of schools and to exemplary godly colleges like Emmanuel and Sidney Sussex in Cambridge, and ensured that they made godly marriages, perpetuating the cohesion of their tight little world and sealing it off, they hoped, from infection by worldly pragmatism and temptation. And, most important, they did business together, not exclusively to be sure, but often decisively, and those businesses could sometimes germinate something other than just money. In fact, they could lose money and still be profoundly fruitful for the common enterprises of the children of God. Throughout the 1630s, for example, virtually all those who would shape the destinies of political Puritanism in parliament— John Pym, John Hampden, his lawyer Oliver St John, Sir Arthur Haselrig, Lord Brooke, Viscount Saye and Sele, the earls of Bedford and Essex and, ubiquitously, Robert Rich, the colossally important and powerful Earl of Warwick—were all involved in ventures to create settlements in the Caribbean and New England. The Providence Island Company in the Caribbean, which was eventually destroyed by the Spanish (thus confirming the Puritan view of the world as a crusade between Christ and Antichrist), was the most intensively organized of their ventures. But the two lords/nobles also created the Saye-Brooke settlement on Long Island Sound, and most of them (especially Warwick) were in regular correspondence with the most promising colony of all, planted on Massachusetts Bay and including at least a dozen of the Dorchester godly in its complement of emigrants in March 1630. It had been John White who had preached the farewell sermon at Plymouth's 'New Hospital'. The deliberation on the government of those settlements in New England was, for the founding fathers back home, akin to a seminar on political theory, a learned speculation on the possibility of the shared Christian life. Across the Atlantic, in a cleaner, godlier world, schools and colleges would thrive, a true Zion would plant its seed. And those days and years of long-distance stewardship could only have encouraged them to think in like manner of making in England itself, should God so will it, a new Jerusalem.

These men were very much a minority, but

being of the Elect they expected to be a minority: the redemption caucus. They gloried in their slightness of numbers as if they were the self-purifying troop of Gideon's army. (The analogy was often invoked.) Modern history is full of such intensely motivated minorities with a self-conscious martyr complex and a talent for collective self-promotion. With the right independent historical conditions, where their adversarial regimes have been weakened, such little legions of the righteous can move mountains. And that was precisely what happened in the astounding unravelling of the Stuart monarchy between 1640 and 1642.

Right from the opening of the 'Short Parliament', from 13 April to 5 May 1640, it was apparent that those who saw themselves appointed by God to deliver the country from the Antichrist had managed to persuade a much larger and more moderate phalanx of members, both in the Lords and in the Commons, that their view of the endangered liberties of the subject was historically accurate. The diaries and correspondence of peers and gentry, by no means all of them hot Presbyterians, are full of commonplace remarks to the effect that thorns had to be removed from the feet of the kingdom before it could walk; that ulcerous veins needed cleansing before the body (politic) could be healed. Edward Hyde, later the die-hard royalist Clarendon, along with his friend and patron, Viscount Falkland of Great Tew, and the legal scholar John Selden, were at this time, like so many of their fellows, convinced of the imperative necessity of reform and of a government that could rest securely on the confidence of parliament. And although the notion

120

of the outright abolition of the episcopacy, following the Covenanters, was still a shockingly radical proposal in England, there was a surprising degree of agreement that they needed taking down a peg from their Laudian loftiness. Bishops like John Williams of Lincoln, who, in the tradition of George Abbot, Laud's predecessor at Canterbury, had always seen Rome rather than Geneva as the enemy, who claimed to be the true custodians of the Tudor Reformation and had been prosecuted and imprisoned for their outspokenness, were now very much listened to.

The likelihood, then, that parliament would tamely hand over to the king the money he needed to resume the Scottish war and crush the impertinent and rebellious Covenanters was precisely nil. Charles grandly offered to forgo ship money (no hardship since by 1639 it had proved virtually impossible to collect) if parliament voted him twelve subsidies (later reduced to four). This was immediately treated as a bad joke. Relatively moderate members of the Commons, like Sir Harbottle Grimston, a great friend of the Verneys, insisted on the redress of grievances (not least the status of the courts of Star Chamber and High Commission), before any thought of a money bill could be entertained. On 17 April John Pym embarked on a lengthy frontal attack on the infamies he said had been perpetrated by the administration during the eleven years of personal rule, concentrating especially on the affronts done to religion by the Laudian 'innovations'. It was Pym, more than any other of the Commons' tribunes, who would contribute to the sense, both in April and in November 1640, when another parliament was called, that something like a national emergency was at hand, with the allied forces of popery and despotism planning an assault on the liberties of the English subject. And increasingly, inside the House and on the streets of London, where men like Nehemiah Wallington were all ears, John Pym was believed.

Fuming with frustration, the king dissolved parliament barely three weeks after it had been called. This was a tactical blunder of monumental proportions, since nothing is quite so inflammatory as the abrupt interruption of raised expectations. Both Wentworth (whose idea the parliament had been) and Edward Hyde immediately understood the decision as the political disaster it undoubtedly was: a priceless opportunity to settle problems within the traditional framework of king-in-parliament carelessly thrown away. But Charles had heard all the ranting and raving in 1629, and it had gone away when parliament did. He still blindly assumed that his real problem was Edinburgh, not Westminster, and that unless he destroyed the Covenanters—and swiftly, too—the contagion of their Calvinism and their apparently contractual notions of monarchy would spread like the plague south to England. He was, in fact, quite right (Pym was in treasonable correspondence with the Covenanter leaders, as were also Saye and Sele). But he chose the worst of all possible options: to fight the Scots without any idea of whether his army (which had looked so shaky the year before) was in any condition to follow him. At the back of Charles's mind, of course, was Wentworth's contingency plan to use the Irish to do the job for him, and in the course of the summer campaign against the Scots he appointed Wentworth Commander-in-Chief, having already raised him, in January 1640, to the earldom of Strafford, an honour that turned out to be a poisoned chalice. To discount the effect that Strafford's Irish strategy would have on the anti-Catholic propaganda fast spreading through London, presupposed a truly breathtaking obtuseness on the king's part. He had not listened to the sensible people in Scotland in 1638, and he was not listening to the sensible people now. The only person he was listening to, other than himself, was his Catholic queen.

What immediately followed in the summer of 1640 was a breakdown of deference of frightening magnitude. With no pay and none in the offing, the soldiers who were mustered in the Midlands and north imposed themselves on their billets in a bad temper and with growling bellies. In a number of towns, such as Hereford, the citizens rose in indignation and ran them out of town. Looking for someone to blame for their real distress, the rank-and-file soldiers turned on their own officers, especially any of them tainted as Catholics or Irish. Ugly scenes became commonplace. In Wellington, Somerset, a lieutenant suspected of being a Catholic was cut to pieces and the dead body robbed. In Faringdon, Oxfordshire, another officer was beaten senseless by soldiers from Dorset (including a number from Dorchester), and when he was found to be receiving medical attention was pulled through the streets and beaten again, this time fatally. What was left of the mangled corpse was set in the stocks for posthumous abuse. As for their religious dependability as an anti-Calvinist army, the soldiery showed exactly what they thought of that by smashing communion table rails, altars and stained-glass windows and ripping surplices off clergy when they found them. Young Edmund Verney wrote to his father that he had to go to church three times in a day to assure his men that he was no papist, 'But once that day I a little nodded at church and had it been a minute longer truely I doe thinke I had been pulled by the nose, for the souldyers pointed extreamely at me.' To any foreign observer it must have seemed for all the world that the English troopers were the allies, not the enemies, of the Covenanters. 'Whereas before our soldiers would go against Scotland,' noted Nehemiah Wallington, 'now not any that I know of in this land would go.'

The disorder was rapidly spiralling out of control. The trained bands opened the gaols where men who had refused to pay the 'coat and conduct' money for their supply had been incarcerated. Other sections of society, equally alienated by the government, took the opportunity to make their point violently against those who enclosed common land or had chased them out of the forests. None of these aggrieved populations was logically connected, but it didn't matter—they were all hunting for someone to blame—and together they persuaded the men responsible for keeping law and order intact, the justices of the peace and the constables, that royal government as it had been constituted over the past eleven years was a broken reed.

In the circumstances it was hardly surprising that the war was a humiliating fiasco for the English. The commander of the Covenanters, General Leslie, knew exactly what he was doing, crossing the Tweed into England on 20 August and aiming for Newcastle to cut off the coal supply to the metropolitan heart of England. Leslie had now given the lie to the Scots' claims of fighting a defensive war, a nicety swept aside in the reality of the conflict. At Newburn, where the English army attempted to make a stand on the banks of the Tyne, Leslie's army, commanding the higher northern bank, raked the English with fire, sending the survivors reeling back to York, while the Scots occupied Newcastle and then Durham. The day after the ignominious defeat at Newburn, a group of inner-core parliamentarians—Oliver St John, Pym, Saye and Sele, Warwick and Brooke—and the earls of Essex and Bedford met at Bedford House in London to draft a petition, in the name of the twelve peers, calling for a new parliament. Manuscript copies were widely circulated around the city and provinces. Charles attempted to find some other way, any other way, to finance another campaign without calling a parliament, but a meeting of nobles made him understand that the war was lost and, since the Scots were demanding an indemnity as the price for evacuating England and releasing the coal supply, only a parliament could possibly supply those funds. On 24 September 1640, pre-empting another grand meeting of the lords, which would certainly have reiterated the demand for a parliament, the king conceded. It would meet on 3 November and would remain in session, in one form and another, until it had ended the life of Charles I and the monarchy along with it.

For Nehemiah Wallington the autumn of 1640 was the time of rosemary. Bunches of the grey-green herb, together with conquerors' garlands of bay, showered down on the heads of Burton, Prynne, Bastwick and Bishop Williams, who had been liberated—Bastwick from Scilly, the rest from the Tower—and paraded triumphantly through the packed streets of London. Rosemary was for remembrance, and how this parliament remembered! Almost immediately it continued the note struck in April by establishing forty committees of investigation into those responsible for illegal and arbitrary acts: ship money, the prerogative courts of Star Chamber and the Church's High Commission. But there were two designated villains on whom parliament concentrated its prosecutorial wrath: Strafford and Laud. Attacking the king by proxy, through his chosen counsellors, was of course a time-honoured way of making the Crown reverse course while still preserving intact the dignity and independence of its sovereignty. In both houses of parliament in 1640 there was a substantial majority for impeaching both men as well as the next rank of councillors, such as Lord Keeper Finch, and courtiers, such as Bishop Wren of Ely, as a way of marking the irreversible end of the Laudian Church and the years of personal rule. But beyond that, there was a serious division about what the impeachment, especially of Strafford, was supposed to accomplish. For men like Viscount Falkland and Edward Hyde the impeachment was essentially therapeutic and restorative. By concentrating the odium for unpopular government, the king had been given a chance to embrace a reformed version of his government, one that would rule together with a responsible parliament and through councillors who enjoyed the confidence of parliament. Their reform programme was corrective: the elimination of what they considered to be either imprudent and alien innovations (the Laudian Church regime and extra-parliamentary taxation) or obsolete institutions that had been shamelessly abused for power and gain (the prerogative courts, the forest regime and the knighthood fines). Clear them away, and you gave the monarchy a fresh start.

But for the most visible, audible and energetic group—Pym, Oliver St John, Sir Arthur Haselrig from Leicestershire, Brooke, Saye and Sele—who took control of the parliamentary agenda from the beginning, this was not, and would never be, enough. Only Zion sufficed. The destruction of Laud would be a pyrrhic victory unless it got rid of the institution of the episcopacy altogether and replaced it by a godly Presbyterian Church, much as the Scots, whom they now treated openly as allies, had done. (When the king at the opening of parliament rashly referred to them as 'rebels' he was forced to retract the forbidden word a week later.) On 11 December a petition (petitioning having become a major weapon in the mobilization of opinion) on behalf of the City of London demanding the abolition of the episcopacy, 'root and branch', was presented to parliament. Pym was much too astute to press the issue on the Commons, knowing how divisive it would be and wanting to protect a tactical majority for Strafford's impeachment. The radical controlling minority also had something much more far reaching in mind when they considered the restructuring of the constitutional relationship between Crown and parliament, in effect, a Scottish programme for England—beginning with a triennial act, requiring the summoning of parliament every three years. When Charles signed the triennial act on 15 February 1641, he completed a circle of pure political futility. The war he had launched to suppress the Covenant and its works had succeeded only in transplanting it to England. Pym and his like-minded colleagues also wanted to make membership of the government not merely subject to parliamentary veto but directly *accountable* before the Lords and Commons and incapable of acting contrary to the expressed will of its majority. No longer would parliament be little more than a tax-sanctioning or denying body. Henceforth the Lords and Commons, as much as the king, would set the agenda. Henceforth it would be a legislator. No one was pretending yet that it could legislate without the king, but no one imagined that the king could legislate or choose his councillors in defiance of parliament. Pym was being spoken of (if Charles had any sense) as a possible future member of the Privy Council.

Huge amounts of ink and paper have been used to insist that this kind of alteration was no revolution at all. But to treat it as a mere adjustment absurdly short-changes its overwhelming novelty. It's quite possible, as a fresh generation of historians has bravely reminded us, to be so frightened of committing Whiggery, of reading history backwards that we fail to give disruption its due. The fact that the authors and instruments of these profound changes had, until the last minute, little inkling of their long-term consequences does not for a minute dilute their significance. Revolutions invariably begin by sounding conservative and nostalgic, their protagonists convinced that they are suppressing, not unloosing, innovation. There's nothing so inflammatory as a call for the return of an imagined realm of virtue and justice.

To look at the doings and utterances of the Long Parliament, and at the immense political upheaval unfolding in the streets of London and on its printing presses, is to be convinced that its protagonists were correct in their belief that they were engaged in a battle of principles over both Church and state and that the outcome would be as momentous as the crisis that produced Magna Carta, a document often on their lips. This was not, of course, the birth of parliamentary democracy (not even the most Whiggish of the Victorian historians ever supposed so), but it was, unquestionably, the demolition of absolute monarchy in Britain. And it was the prospect of this that filled the hearts of men such as the Earl of Warwick, Sir Robert Harley, Oliver St John and Oliver Cromwell MP with racing excitement.

This revolution had no manifesto until the Grand Remonstrance of November 1641. Instead, it had a trial. Almost invariably great political upheavals require an arch-malefactor against whom the righteous can define themselves in the new community, and the Scottish peace negotiators, received warmly by the parliamentary leaders even though their armies were occupying much of northern England, made it quite clear that they wanted Strafford's head for threatening their own revolution with an invasion of Irish Catholics. Robert Baillie, a relatively moderate Scots Calvinist, had no hesitation in referring to Laud and Strafford as 'incendiaries' who, if left at liberty or even alive, would never stop until they had reduced the country to a papist despotism. And Pym himself had enough respect for Strafford's formidable abilities to know that his own reconstruction of English politics could move safely ahead only when the earl was permanently out of the way. Moreover, Strafford's peculiar success in impartially alienating each of the three Irish communities (something he was rather proud of) now left him with no friends.

All the same, he would not be an obliging scapegoat. To stereotype Strafford as 'Black Tom Tyrant', the thuggish bully of the personal rule, was to make a terrible mistake. This was, after all, still the Thomas Wentworth who in the late 1620s had mounted a passionate attack against the forced loan, a man who had at least as deep an understanding of the law as the barrister John Pym. Strafford knew that Pym needed a full public show trial, duly observant of the procedures of the law, to uphold the superiority of justice over force, and he also knew that his prosecutors would have the greatest difficulty in turning criticisms of his administration in Ireland into acts of treason. Alone in the Tower, pondering his chances, Strafford nursed precisely the touching faith in the impartiality of the law and of English justice that his vilifiers claimed he had so consistently abused. How could he possibly be condemned, he must have asked himself, for violations of laws not yet passed when the alleged violations were committed, for acts of state that, at the time, were perfectly in keeping with the king's expressed will?

Through the seven weeks of the trial in the

House of Lords, from March to April 1641, Strafford, not looking at all the part of Tom Tyrant, grey-whiskered and obviously sick, his head covered in a fur-lined cap, conducted his own defence with compelling logic, tearing apart all the inconsistencies and weaknesses in the evidence presented by his prosecutors. It was easy enough to demonstrate that he had walked roughshod over all kinds of persons and interests in Ireland—the Irish Catholics, by continuing to dispossess their lands (not that anyone in the English parliament minded that); the Old English, by seeking to expand the plantations into Connacht and trespass on the Pale; most damagingly, the Ulster-Presbyterian Scots and English, by strengthening the episcopal Church of Ireland and regulating their trade—but none of it amounted to treason. On the contrary, it had all been done to maintain the king's authority as loyally, impartially and firmly as was within his legitimate power as Lord Deputy. The only count among the twenty-eight charges remotely capable of making the case for treason was number twenty-three, which rested on a remark, said to have been uttered by Strafford, that he would send an Irish army to 'reduce this kingdom'. It had never been a secret that this had been part of the strategy to achieve victory over the Scots, and Strafford reasonably argued that at the time, in the spring and summer of 1640, the two nations had still been at war. The gravamen of the charge, suggested by the New English planter from Antrim, Sir John Clotworthy, was that by 'this kingdom' Strafford had actually meant England, not Scotland, and that he had sought to destroy parliament and the liberties of the people through an armed *coup d'état*. That would, indeed, have constituted treason. Strafford continued to deny that he had ever intended such a thing for England and to attack the credibility of verbal testimony, at which point a written note containing the same ominous phrase was introduced in evidence by Harry Vane the younger, who had discovered in the papers of his father, the Secretary to the Council, the records of the meeting in which Strafford had suggested bringing over the Irish army. But it was not in Strafford's hand, merely a note claimed to be a verbatim, contemporary record, and by mid-April it was far from clear that the Vane note, by itself, would be enough to convict as long as the trial continued to be conducted according to the regular conventions of impeachment.

But Strafford's trial was, of course, not at all a normal judicial event, more a public theatre of disgrace and retribution. Every day the House of Lords and the streets and courtyards around it in Westminster were packed with huge crowds, hungry for news of the day's events. Handbills, broadsides and improvised petitions created a sea of paper for the crowd to wade through. Ballads were sung; sermons were preached against the pope-friendly Strafford. Nehemiah Wallington, who was among an immense throng flocking to the House of Lords at the beginning of May to petition for the death of the earl, said he had never seen so many people in all his life, 'and when they did see any lord coming they all cried with one voice, "Justice! Justice!" ' What Wallington was witnessing, again without knowing it, was another element of modern politics, the fever of the crowd, beginning to make itself felt.

Without any precocious understanding of the concept, Pym, St John, Haselrig and the rest intuitively understood the need for 'revolutionary justice', that baleful euphemism for crowd-pleasing demonstrations of political annihilation. So in mid-April, Pym changed the form of prosecution from an impeachment, a judicial process that required a decisive burden of proof, to an act of attainder, which was passed in a legislative process and needed no more than a body of suspicious evidence to constitute a presumption of guilt. Attainder effectively converted a trial into a hearing on the security of the state. Oddly enough, an act of attainder actually solved the problem of conscience for some like Viscount Falkland who, while unable to agree that the evidence against Strafford rose to the severe standards required for a conviction for treason, was prepared to vote for attainder by the weight of suspicion. Falkland and those like him believed that Strafford had, in fact, become a conspirator against the liberties of the country, and they were happy to be relieved of the bother of worrying precisely how this came to happen.

The only problem with an act of attainder was that it required the king to sign it. A day after it went through the Commons by 204 to 59 votes, Charles had written to Strafford, promising that he would not abandon him or repay his loyalty by allowing his loss of life, honour and fortune. And on 1 May 1641 Charles, who had been ostentatiously cordial and friendly towards Strafford throughout the proceedings, told the Lords that his conscience would not allow him to sign. Once again the king had managed to act directly against his own best interests. The whole point of the proceedings had been to deflect popular hatred and rage from the king himself (and from the queen, whose Catholic circle was becoming a daily target for the anti-popery lobby) and to safeguard the constitutional possibility of a new beginning. But Charles, and especially Henrietta Maria, believed they had other cards to play: a soft-line strategy, suggested by the Earl of Bedford, which involved bringing Pym in to the Privy Council, and a hard-line strategy, which involved getting his own loyal troops to the Tower and encouraging a move by some officers in the army to free Strafford, if necessary by force. In the end, it was Strafford himself who saw clearly where this was heading—towards chaos and bloodshed— and who decided on an extraordinary act of pre-emptive self-sacrifice. On 4 May he wrote to the king asking him to sign the act.

> May it please your Sacred Majesty . . . I understand the minds of Men are more and more incensed against me, notwithstanding Your Majesty hath Declared that in Your Princely opinion I am not Guilty of Treason, and that You are not satisfied in Your Conscience, to pass the Bill.
>
> This bringeth me in a very great streight, there is before me the ruine of my Children and Family, hitherto untouch'd . . . with any foul crime: Here before me are the many ills, which may befall Your Sacred Person and the whole Kingdom, should Your Self and parliament part less satisfied one with the other, than is necessary for the preservation both of King and People; Here are before me the things most

valued, most feared by mortal men, Life and Death.

To say Sir, that there hath not been strife in me, were to make me less man, than, God knoweth, my Infirmities make me; and to call a destruction upon my self and my young Children . . . will find no easy consent from Flesh and Blood . . . So now to set Your Majesties Conscience at liberty, I do most humbly beseech Your Majesty for prevention of evils, which may happen by Your refusal, to pass this Bill.

On 10 May Charles signed the act, it's said with teary eyes, and almost without noticing what he was doing signed another, much more revolutionary bill presented to him, which prohibited the dissolution of parliament without its own consent. At the same time he wrote a letter to the House of Lords urging clemency, 'mercy being as inherent and inseparable to a King as Justice', and for Strafford to remain in prison for the rest of his life. 'This if it may be done without the discontentment of my People, would be an unspeakable contentment to me.' The Prince of Wales delivered the letter the following day, and on the day after that, 12 May, Strafford went to the block, protesting: 'In all the honour I had to serve His Majesty, I had not any intention in my heart, but what did aim at the joint and individual prosperity of the King and his People.' From his window in the Tower, Laud watched the execution. He never forgave Charles the betrayal, noting in his diary that the king 'knew not how to be, or to be made, great'. But then Charles never forgave himself. He truly believed that his own execution, eight years later, was God's proper judgement on him for consenting to the death of a loyal servant.

Strafford was right to think that his death would be a national catharsis: a chance for the country to vent its anger on a convenient scapegoat but also an opportunity for the king, if he was shrewd, to cut his losses and stabilize his position. There was no doubt that the brutal business of the attainder had made some who were originally among the government's fiercest critics profoundly uneasy. Was one kind of arbitrary power to be exchanged for another?

Once both the earl and the institutional symbols of the old regime—the prerogative courts, ship money, communion rails—had been swept away in the summer of 1641, many on the benches of both the Lords and the Commons, and many more among the county communities of gentry and justices, began to ask themselves why the self-appointed tribunes like Pym continued to bang on relentlessly about tyranny and conspiracy. Although the Root and Branch Petition to abolish the episcopacy was steered through two readings in the Commons by Sir Robert Harley (to the proud delight of Lady Brilliana), it stalled badly in the Lords. Harley had to content himself with becoming the new *Thomas* Cromwell, overseeing a survey of the condition of parish churches (an ominous inquiry) and in Herefordshire pulling down the cross at the local Wigmore church in September 1641, causing it 'to be beaten to pieces, even in the dust, with a sledge and then laid . . . in the footpath to be trodden on in the churchyard'. To overcome the opposition of the Lords, compromises were made, disappointing the more intensely Calvinist Scots. If this were Presbyterianism, it was a very English kind: committees of nine laymen to replace the bishops, Church government by the hunting classes. Even so, there were many among the hunting classes who wanted none of it, who were prepared to see an end to the surplices and kneeling, and perhaps even see crucifixes trodden in the churchyard, but who thought bishops—plain and modest bishops, not the lofty, over-ornamental, theologically obscure, philosophically grandiose, Laudian bishops—were a proper part of the Church of England.

Others reacted to the outbreak of iconoclasm with deep horror. It was in the summer of 1641 that William Dugdale, the Warwickshire antiquary and genealogist, became convinced that there would shortly be a great and terrible obliteration. As he wrote in the introduction to his wonderful history of St Paul's Cathedral: 'Prudently foreseeing the sad effects thereof which by woeful experience were soon after miserably felt often and earnestly incited me to a speedy view of what Monuments I could find—the Principal Churches of the Realm, to the end that by Ink and Paper, the Shadows of them with their Inscriptions might be preserved for Posterity, the Things themselves being so near to Destruction.' And off Dugdale went, sketching and transcribing, poring through muniments and cartularies, spending furtive mornings in front of tomb effigies and stained-glass windows, working just as fast as he could to outpace the image-breakers, haunted by Lord Brooke's threat to St Paul's that he hoped 'to see no one stone left upon another of that building'.

Not everyone was quite so frantic. Noticing the backlash against the anti-bishop campaign, which by December included a decision to impeach twelve of them, a group of more moderate reformers, among them Edward Hyde, saw that Charles had a precious opportunity to exploit the divisions. It was their instinct (borne out by events twenty years later) that a non-absolutist but non-emasculated monarchy, the governor of the Church and the army, still possessed of legitimate prerogatives, including the right to choose its own government and to summon and dismiss parliaments, truly represented the wishes of the majority of the political nation. And it was from the clarity and strength of their convictions that constitutional royalism—hitherto a Stuart oxymoron—was born.

But Charles was not thinking with either clarity or strength of purpose about how the monarchy could best be renewed. He was thinking, when he was thinking at all, about how its full sovereignty might be restored. His most trusted advisers had been taken from him or had departed in the interests of self-preservation. Strafford was dead. Laud was in the Tower and most likely would follow him. Lord Keeper Finch (who had been Speaker during the stormy debates of 1629) and Secretary of State Windebanke had both fled to Europe to escape arrest. More than ever Charles depended on the queen for counsel, and her instincts were militantly against compromise. Any show of moderation that Charles now affected was just that. Not for a moment had he abandoned his deeply held conviction that the divine appointment of kingship required him to be faithful to the plenitude of its power. A mean little kingship seemed to him unworthy of the name, a kingship that said yea to whatever a parliament might propose was not the crown he had received from his father, nor one he could pass on to his son without the deepest sense of shame and betrayal. So when he travelled to Scotland in August 1641, ostensibly to conclude a peace settlement with the Covenanters, Charles was actually casting about for some way to use the Scots against the English as he had once hoped to use the English against the Scots. Even there, though, Charles was incapable of deciding between persuasion and plotting, between a campaign to win over aristocratic generals, like James Graham, Earl of Montrose, and the physical seizure of Covenanter leaders, like Archibald Campbell, eighth Earl of Argyll. It was, in any case, all moot. For while Charles imagined that he might order the affairs of one of his kingdoms to settle the disorder of a second, a third, Ireland, now exploded in violent rebellion.

It was as much of a jolt as the Covenanter rebellion had been four years earlier. The fall of Strafford's 'thorough' government, both Charles and the English parliament must have imagined, had probably removed most of the grievances of which those who counted in Ireland had complained. But as usual in the politics of Stuart Britain, everyone was looking the wrong way, addressing the problems of the last crisis, not the next one. To the Catholic communities of Ireland, especially the native Irish, the destruction of the Wentworth regime was a cause of apprehension, not of rejoicing. Bullying, grasping and thuggish though his administration had been, its tough independence (and willingness quite often to co-opt the native Irish in its schemes) was immeasurably better than what seemed most likely to replace it: the unrestricted domination of the New English and Scots Presbyterians. As recently as 1639 Wentworth's 'Black Acts' had been directed at the Protestant, rather than the Catholic, communities. Now that he was gone, the situation seemed especially ominous to the Catholic gentry of Ulster. They looked across the North Channel and saw the Covenanter conquest and settlement of the western Highlands and islands by the Earl of Argyll and could only imagine that it would be their turn next. For years they had been forbidden to increase their own land holdings while the Protestant New English and Scots had been encouraged to settle in ever greater numbers, and in responding to Wentworth's challenge to turn their own estates into models of 'improvement' they had incurred huge debts, building themselves grandiose English houses and attempting to introduce fine livestock and tillage. Now the improbable victory of the English parliament over the king, symbolized so dramatically by the execution of Strafford, had robbed them of any prospect of harvesting the fruits of all this hard work and money by securing their position in a rapidly changing Ireland. Instead, they were facing the nightmare of Presbyterian encirclement. And for the moment the Catholic Old English, in the middle of the conflict, had shown no wish to swerve from loyalty to the English state. So Ulster lords, like Phelim O'Neill, who claimed descent from the great leader of the Nine Years War, Hugh O'Neill, Earl of Tyrone, now turned to armed resistance as a last line of self-defence. When Phelim O'Neill captured Charlemont Castle early in the rebellion, he settled all kinds of scores by killing his chief creditor there, a Mr Fullerton.

Paradoxically, then, the leaders of the Irish rebellion thought that by planning to seize strongholds, including Dublin Castle, towards the end of October 1641 they were actually coming to the aid of the beleaguered king. At least at the beginning their action was presented not as a proto-nationalist, but as a fervently loyalist revolt. On 4 November O'Neill even went so far as to claim that he had had the commission of the king himself for his military action. It was an outrageous fabrication, probably targeted at the Old English (always the most genuinely loyal of the three communities), who, as yet, had stood aloof from the rebellion. O'Neill may have been hoping that by purporting to do the king's work he could draw the Earl of Ormonde, the most powerful of the Old English (a Protestant but very definitely not a Presbyterian), into the revolt. Instead, the ruse did massive damage to Charles's credibility in England. To many of the godly he now seemed beyond all doubt to be conniving at an Irish-Catholic plot.

Paranoia is the oxygen of revolution. But in November 1641, to men such as Harley and Wallington, Pym and St John, there seemed a great deal to be paranoid about. The king was still in Scotland and was reported to have attempted to overthrow the Covenant by a coup. News was beginning to pour across the Irish Sea, not just of castles and fortifications being over-run, but of much darker things—massacres visited by the Catholic rebels on isolated Protestant towns and villages of the New English. By the time it was

141

recycled for the Irish insurrection, anti-Catholic atrocity propaganda had become a formulaic part of the cultural war dividing Europe. The same pornography of violence, graphically illustrated with woodcuts and 'eye-witness' reports, which had been used to describe the behaviour of the Spanish in the Netherlands or of Wallenstein's troops in Germany, was rehearsed all over again: babies impaled on pikes; the wombs of pregnant women sliced open and the foetuses ripped out; skewered grandpas; decapitated preachers. Which is not to say that monstrous killings did not actually occur. At Portadown there was, unquestionably, terrible butchery: a hundred New English were herded on to the bridge, stripped and thrown into the river to drown. Those who looked as if they were swimming were clubbed or shot until they disappeared in the bloody water.

Little of this was countenanced by the military leadership of the rebellion, but they had only tenuous control over some sections of the Catholic rural population, which had suffered for generations at the hands of the planters and in some parts of Ireland now took the opportunity to make their point in blood. If they were not encouraged, neither were they stopped. The more isolated the plantations and villages—in Munster, for example—the more likely the target. Something like 4000 people lost their lives directly as a result of this violence and countless more as a result of being evicted, stripped naked and sent starving and unprotected into the cold, wet Irish winter. Among them were relatives of the Wallingtons, the family of Nehemiah's sister-in-law, the Rampaignes, rich farmers in Fermanagh. Attempting to flee to the coast, they were tracked down and Zachariah Rampaigne was killed in front of his children. The survivors had to protect themselves as best they could. Before long, of course, murderous retaliation would be inflicted on innocent Catholic populations, and the miserably unrelenting cycle of murder and counter-murder that stains Irish history would be well under way.

In England the Irish rising was immediately seen as an integral element in a pan-British conspiracy, ultimately aimed at itself. Wallington quoted in one of his notebooks the proverb 'He that England will win/Must first with Ireland begin'. Worse even than that, the rebellion brought back Elizabethan memories of Ireland being used as a back door to England by the armed league of Catholic powers. Whether England liked it or not, its fate now seemed to be tied up with the international wars of religion, a suspicion confirmed when Owen Roe O'Neill, nephew of the Earl of Tyrone, who had fled to Rome in 1607 and had served for thirty years in the armies of the king of Spain, crossed from Flanders in the spring of 1642 and took command of the rebel forces. It was not long before a papal nuncio, Cardinal Giovanni Rinuccini, arrived to press an all-out Counter-Reformation agenda on the rebels: the restoration of the Church as it had been before the Henrician Reformation.

This was a tragic turning-point in the life of the Old English Catholic community in Ireland. It was now in the same quandary over allegiance that had been so disastrous for its English counterpart during the Spanish-papal offensive in the 1580s. It seemed impossible to make men like Owen Roe O'Neill grasp that it had been historically feasible, especially under Strafford, to live a life of loyal Catholicism, practising their faith quietly and being tacitly tolerated as long as they kept clear of sedition. But the collapse of the protecting authority of the Crown had suddenly taken away this vital living space. They were now between the rock of the Roman Church and the hard place of the Presbyterians. So in December 1641 some of the leading Old English entered into an agreement with the Irish rebels. By the following spring they were being asked, more pressingly, to contribute men and money, and with some trepidation many of the Old English peers (though not the Protestant Ormonde) actively joined the revolt. One of them, John Preston, became the confederation's commander in Leinster. They may have consoled themselves with the thought that even in the spring of 1642 and the years ahead, the official line of the confederation, affirmed on its flags, was one of intense loyalism to Charles I. But that was not the way it was seen in England, either by the king or by his opponents. And once Robert Monro, a Scottish Presbyterian veteran of the Thirty Years War, took command of the Protestant forces, commissioned by the intensely Protestant Scots parliament, the polarization of Ireland into two armed religious camps was tragically complete. At Newry, where sixty men and women and two priests were murdered, Monro, who had been much affected by the atrocity literature, showed that he was perfectly capable of unloosing a massacre every bit as ugly as Portadown. 'Anti-Christ marcheth furiously,' wrote Wallington, and this was good news for it meant that the unsparing, long-heralded battle between the angels and demons could at last get under way.

Charles returned to London towards the end of November 1641 as news of the Irish slaughter, real and fictitious, was arriving, each day apparently bloodier than the last. A bill proposing to place control of a militia in the hands of parliament had already had a reading in the House of Commons, and Pym must have assumed that the Irish rebellion would work to complete, irreversibly, a momentous transfer of power from king to parliament. All sorts of demands—that Catholics be removed from the army, that parliament now have a decisive say in foreign policy—were being voiced. And, as a prelude to the capture of sovereignty, a Grand Remonstrance, drafted by the militants, was to capture history. The document represented a complete rewriting, for the present and for posterity, of the reign of Charles I, recording that from the beginning he had planned to violate the liberties of his subjects and impose on them a monstrous and detestable despotism. It recapitulated what had been done by the people's representatives to withstand that conspiracy and what still needed to be done.

The Grand Remonstrance became another immense public event in the life of an already feverishly politicized London. Wallington watched daily as troops of gentry and yeomen from Essex, Kent and Sussex clattered on horseback through the streets of the city towards Westminster, where they surrounded the parliament chambers. The showers of paper propaganda had turned into a virtual blizzard. But it was precisely this sense of being held hostage to the people—gentry and farmers in the provinces, artisans and apprentices in London—that turned a considerable number of both the Lords and Commons against the Remonstrance. Sir Edward Dering from Kent spoke for many when he expressed amazement at the 'descension from a parliament to a people . . . when I first heard of a Remonstrance, I presently imagined that like faithful councillors we should hold up a glass unto His Majesty . . . I did not dream that we should remonstrate downwards, tell stories to the people and talk of the King as a third person. I neither look for a cure for our complaints from the common people nor do desire to be cured by them.' Together with the sense that the gratuitously abusive tone of the Remonstrance had been deliberately calculated to put an accommodation with the king out of reach, it managed to pass the Commons by a majority of only eleven votes.

The discomfiture of Pym naturally presented an opportunity to a moderate group, with Edward Hyde as its presiding talent, to rally a reform-minded but non-Presbyterian party to the support of what he had been led to believe was a reasonably chastened king. Accordingly, Hyde drafted a response to the Remonstrance, which took the tone that royalist ideology would sustain throughout the civil war, namely that it was the king, and not a minority of Puritan zealots, who truly represented the well-being and interests of the people at large; that it was he, and not they, who was the true reformer. Those like Hyde who hoped to see the king wrap himself in the mantle of a non-Laudian, non-absolutist monarchy took heart from the warm reception that Charles, a figure who seemed more wronged than wrongful, had received on his journey back from Scotland to London. The narrow vote over the Remonstrance confirmed Hyde in his optimism that the tide of militancy could be pushed back.

But there was no political situation so fabulously promising for the revival of the king's fortunes that Charles could not still manage to undercut it by his ultimate belief in the arbitration of force. He had been persuaded by Hyde and Viscount Falkland, his new Secretary of State, and by the vote on the Remonstrance, that Pym and his fellows were indeed an isolated group within the Commons, who, once neutralized, could be brought back to the kind of parliament he cared to deal with and which would vote him money for an army to go to Ireland. But what he meant by neutralization was something more than just parliamentary defeat. So in December 1641 Charles, enthusiastically abetted by Lord George Digby, whose family castle at Sherborne was just a few miles from the Puritan citadel of Dorchester, systematically set about planning a *coup d'état*. The Earl of Essex's men—mostly trained bands from the City—who were guarding the approaches to parliament were replaced by Westminster troopers from the dependably royalist Earl of Dorset's regiment. For the first time the mutually derogatory epithets of 'Roundheads' (for the departing apprentices) and 'Cavaliers' (for the incoming guards) became part of the vocabulary of reciprocal hatred. Some sort of civil war had already started. The Warden of the Tower, right in the centre of the most riotously pro-parliamentary streets of the City, was likewise replaced with the notoriously brutal soldiers of Colonel

147

Lunsford's regiment.

And all this, of course, was exactly what Pym wanted. Since Charles's return from Scotland it had been Pym, not the king, who had been forced on the defensive. The failure of the Remonstrance had made this worse. But now, Charles's transparent and laborious plans for a strike against the integrity of parliament itself had miraculously played right into his hands. Had he himself written the script by which the king suddenly stood revealed not as a reasonable reformer but as a military conspirator Pym could hardly have improved on Charles's own performance. (The queen, as always, helped.) On 3 January 1642 five members of the Commons—Pym, Hampden, Holles, Haselrig and William Strode—together with Viscount Mandeville, were formally charged with impeachment by the Attorney General in the House of Lords. Their immediate arrest (carefully following the procedure used against Strafford and Laud) was demanded. Both houses of parliament made it clear that they would not surrender the accused, but articles charging the six with subverting the fundamental laws of the realm were now made public. If by now Pym, Holles and the rest were not sure of what was coming, the forced search of their houses gave them a pretty good idea. Charles must have felt confident—with control of the areas around both parliament and the Tower—that everything was in place for his strike.

Forewarned by spies at court, Pym and his friends were themselves playing with fire. They could have disappeared to safety on the night of 3–4 January, but they actually wanted the king to come and get them, exposing himself, unequivocally, as the violator of the independence of parliament. So on the morning of 4 January there they were in the Commons, informed by Lady Carlisle and other spies, of the king's progress from Whitehall. Once they were sure he was on his way, they made their departure. At the last minute William Strode, in a fit of misplaced bravura, nearly wrecked the strategy by announcing that he would rather like to stay and confront the king in person, and he had to be dragged off to the barge waiting to convey the members downstream to the City.

The famous scene played itself out: intruding tyrant versus absent champions of the people. No king had ever before presumed to intimidate the Commons with a display of armed force. The king arrived with a small personal guard, George Digby making sure that the door was left open with a clear view of the soldiers standing guard outside. Before long, the courtyard outside the parliament house was packed with anxious crowds. Doffing his hat in a gesture of respect, Charles asked politely for the use of the Speaker's chair, duly surrendered to him. He then asked for the accused to be delivered up. Silence. When Charles asked Speaker Lenthall to point out Pym and the others, Lenthall replied in the precise terms that Denzil Holles had forced on the terrified Finch in 1629: he had 'neither eyes to see nor tongue to speak in this place but as the House is pleased to direct me'. As it had always been, this was a drama of long political memories. Charles replied that he had eyes to see for himself and what he saw was that 'the birds are flown'. A huge caesura, full of silent rage, foolishness and foreboding, hung over the house. The embarrassed king, roiling in chagrin, departed whence he came, shouts of 'Privilege, privilege' following him through the door.

It was an unmitigated fiasco. The gamble had been worthwhile only if Charles could be absolutely sure of success. In abject failure he now stood nakedly exposed (just as Pym had wanted) as something worse than a despot—a blundering despot. With the abortive arrest of the MPs disappeared the last possibilities of constructing something like a moderate consensus for a reformed but sovereign monarchy. When the king demanded that the city yield up the accused, parliament responded by appointing a professional soldier and veteran of the European wars, Philip Skippon, to command the London militia and by declaring that anyone assisting the assault on parliament and its members was guilty of capital treason. London was, in any case, in uproar. On 11 January, Pym, Holles and the rest emerged to a delirious celebration, in which they appeared to the cheering crowds on a festive Thames barge. Court and government swiftly self-liquidated. Catcalls of 'privilege' hounded anyone recognized as having a court connection. Charles skulked around the periphery of London—at Hampton Court, Windsor, Greenwich—trying to find some way back to the moderate position he had already thrown away. But there was no way back. Contingency plans for outright conflict were now, in effect, operational. The queen was sent off to The Hague to pawn the crown jewels so as to fund an army. Prince Rupert of the Rhine, the king's twenty-two-year-old nephew, the laughing Cavalier himself, complete with a toy poodle called Boy, suddenly materialized at court. Preparations were made to try to secure key arsenals and ports. The king turned north, where he believed his best chance of rallying his forces lay. At Newmarket he was asked if he would agree to the militia being transferred to parliament's control for a limited time. 'By God, not for an hour,' was the answer. 'You have asked that of me in this which was never asked of a King and with which I will not trust my wife and children.'

What followed accelerated the likelihood, if not the certainty, of armed conflict. Since the king continued to refuse to sign the Militia Bill, its provisions were enacted unilaterally as an ordinance, transferring to parliament the right to commandeer men and munitions, and enabling it to appoint lord–lieutenants and deputy lieutenants in the counties to see to the execution of the orders. From his transplanted court at York the king countered by declaring anyone obeying those illegitimate officers to be guilty of treason. Invoking an ancient Lancastrian form of feudal mobilization, he then appointed his own 'Commissions of Array' in each shire to supply men to defend the Crown.

In its declaration to the king parliament had, for the first time, formally accused him of conspiring to wage 'civil war' against his own subjects. The words were out. They could not be unsaid. But even Puritan parliamentarians, like Bulstrode Whitelocke, were momentarily unnerved that actual bloodshed now seemed so near. The country, he told parliament, had 'insensibly slid into this beginning of a Civil War by one unexpected

Accident after another, as Waves of the Sea, which have brought us thus far: And we scarce know how, but from Paper Combats, by Declarations, Remonstrances, Protestations, Votes, Messages, Answers and Replies: We are now come to the question of raising of Forces.' There was one last chance at settlement, when parliament delivered its 'Nineteen Propositions' to the king at York. But they were more a clarification of its own ideas on the future of England's government than any kind of negotiating position, since they included things they knew the king could not possibly concede, like parliamentary control over the education and marriage of his children, the vigorous prosecution of all Catholics (which would include his wife) and the transfer of all ports, forts and castles to their officers. The fact was that parliament, along with Pym, now simply believed that Charles, together with the Irish, was committed to an English Counter-Reformation. So until he was made harmless they would put the monarchy out of commission—forcing it to exercise its powers through committees—creating, in effect, a parliamentary regency, as if he had become insane.

With that last hope gone, the months ahead were dominated by a scramble to secure martial assets—plate, money, guns, powder, horses and hay—so as to be best placed when hostilities actually began. At the same time attempts were made to sway the undecided. The showers of propaganda sheets now became downpours. The royal printing press had been prudently taken to York so that the work of influencing the north could proceed apace. A battle of the Mercuries took place with the parliamentary newspaper, the *Mercurius*

Civicus, answered and satirized by the royalist *Mercurius Aulicus.* And beneath the anathemas and the requisitioning something profoundly sad was happening: the Balkanization of England, not in the sense of its fracturing into coherent, warring regions (for there were virtually none), but in the collapse of communities and institutions—parishes and counties—which, despite differing sentiments and religious beliefs, had none the less managed to contain those conflicts in the interests of local peace and justice. Doubtless there must have been many places where the choice of allegiance was unthinking or even involuntary. Men and women followed habit, prejudice, their landlord, their preacher. And there were certainly those like Robert and Brilliana Harley on the one side and Viscount Scudamore on the other for whom the choice was pretty much a foregone conclusion. Just what they did about it, of course, was another matter. (Surprisingly, Scudamore showed himself to be a rather tepid royalist when the time came for action.) And there must have been many more, like poor Thomas Knyvett, a Norfolk landowner, whose purposefulness was not at all equal to his predicament. 'O sweete hart,' he wrote to his wife, 'I am nowe in a greate strayght what to doe.' Walking in Westminster he had run into Sir John Potts, who had presented him with his commission from the Earl of Warwick to raise a company for parliament. 'I was surpris'd what to doe, whether to take or refuse. 'Twas no place to dispute, so I tooke it and desierd som'time to Advise upon it. I had not receiv'd this many howers, but I met with a declaration point Blanck against it by the King.' Richard Atkyns, then twenty-seven years old and

153

living in strongly parliamentary Gloucester, believed that no one who had heard the trial of Strafford and 'weighed the concessions of the King' could be against him, but that 'fears, and jealousies, had so generally possessed the kingdom, that a man could hardly travel through any market town, but he should be asked whether he were for the King, or parliament'.

What is truly extraordinary about the spring and summer of 1642 is the wealth of evidence testifying to the agonies of allegiance, the painful rigour with which many thoughtful souls pondered the weightiest question of their lives and how earnestly and honestly they endeavoured to justify their decisions to their friends, their family and themselves. Different men and women reached their point of no return at different moments in the great crisis, which had been gathering head since the opening of the Long Parliament. Cornwall— which is often thought of, not altogether wrongly, as an especially cohesive community—was shattered right down the middle. For the two leading figures among the Cornish Members of Parliament, who had travelled to London optimistically expectant of peaceful reform, it had been their responses to Strafford's attainder that had separated them. Sir Bevil Grenville was the grandson of the pirate-patriot sea captain Richard Grenville, but after his education at Exeter College, Oxford, he became the very paragon of a learned, energetic country gentleman, devoted to his wife, children and land (in that order), an experimenter with new techniques for tin smelting, a breeder of Barbary stallions and a life-long enthusiast of classical history, philosophy and poetry. In 1626 he had been among the fiercest Cornish critics of the forced loan, had turned out his freeholders on behalf of Sir John Eliot and William Coryton and had been devastated by Eliot's death in the Tower. But in 1641 he was appalled at the attainder of Strafford, seeing it as the kind of naked manipulation of justice he had attacked when it was practised by the court. Grenville was one of eight MPs from Cornwall (including Coryton) who voted 'nay' and who tried to persuade Sir Alexander Carew to follow their example. 'Pray, Sir,' wrote Grenville to Carew, 'let it not be said that any member of our county should have a hand in this ominous business and therefore pray give your vote against the Bill.' Carew's reply was unclouded by equivocation (and would come to haunt him in the years that followed before his execution in 1644): 'If I were sure to be the next man on the scaffold with the same axe, I would give my consent to the passing of it.' Others in Cornwall who had long been friends, and had lived in mutual amity and respect, now divided: Sir Francis Godolphin of Godolphin (and his son, the poet Sidney) for the king; Sir Francis Godolphin of Trevneague for parliament.

Although none of Lord Falkland's Great Tew friends had any trouble with the act of attainder (one suspects none of them much liked the bleak, brusque Wentworth), they parted company, first over the attack on the bishops and then again over parliament's Militia Ordinance. Hyde and Falkland saw the Ordinance as a demonstrably unlawful usurpation of the sovereign's legitimate prerogative; indeed, a test case of whether the king was to be granted any sort of prerogative at all. But their legalistic friend and MP John Selden truly believed that it had been the king who had acted illegitimately, not being entitled to impress any of his subjects except when the realm was plainly threatened by *foreign* invasion. Selden thus remained loyal to parliament. Conversely, there were those like Lord Montagu, who were at pains to be understood as supporting the most parliamentary monarchy there could possibly be, short of conferring on the institution some sort of exclusive and transcendent sovereignty. To his son William, Montagu wrote that:

> It is most sure he is not of a true English spirit that will not shed life and all that he hath for the maintenance and preservation of parliaments consisting of the King, Lords and Commons. But to have the ordinance bind all the subjects to England without the consent of the King is of most dangerous consequence and a violation of all the privileges of parliament and the common liberty of the subject; therefore I would to God that the Lords and Commons would be pleased not to stand upon that. My heart, hand and life shall stand for parliaments but for no ordinance only by Lords and Commons.

For Sir Edmund Verney the choice was simpler, yet so very much harder. For he found himself governed by an unforgiving and unequivocal obligation of duty, even while his moral sense and his intellect told him the cause was worthless. Edward Hyde discovered his friend Verney's melancholy predicament at York, when he asked him to put on a face of public cheerfulness, the better to raise the spirits of the fearful royalist soldiers. Verney replied smilingly to Hyde that:

> I will willingly join with you the best I can but I shall act it very scurvily . . . you have satisfaction in your conscience that you are in the right; that the King ought not to grant what is required of him and so you do your duty and your business together. But for my part, I do not like the quarrel, and do heartily wish that the King would yield and consent to what they desire; so that my conscience is only concerned in honour and gratitude to follow my master. I have eaten his bread, and served him near thirty years, and will not do so base a thing as to forsake him; and choose rather to lose my life (which I am sure I shall do) to preserve and defend those things which are against my conscience to preserve and defend.

The Verneys, who had been the model of a companionable, loving gentry household, were now torn apart. Ralph, who had sat next to his father in the parliaments of 1640, had not just expressed his support for their cause but had taken the solemn oath of loyalty required of all members after the passing of the Militia Ordinance. Oaths were no light matter in the seventeenth century, especially to a Puritan. The act sharply separated him not just from his father but also from his younger brother, Edmund, who could not understand Ralph's failure to perceive his duty to his king as well as to his father. They were still, somehow, a family. In the early summer the steward at Claydon was getting letters from Sir Edmund at York asking him to prepare the defence of the house with carbines, powder and shot, 'for I feare a time maye come when Roags maye looke for booty in such houses; therefore bee not unprovided; but saye noething of it, for that maye invite more to mischeefe that thinek not of it yet . . . gett in all such monnys as are owing you with all speede, for wee shall certainly have a great warr. Have a care of harvest, and God send uss well to receave the blessing of and returne thancks for it. I can saye no more—Your loving master.' But the steward was also getting letters from Ralph in London asking him to search for his father's best pistols and carbines to be sent on to his father at York! For a time in the late spring of 1642, when tentative feelers were being put out between king and parliament, the Verneys and their friends clung to the hope that there might yet be peace. But on 1 June both houses of parliament passed the Nineteen Propositions for the future of England.

Not surprisingly, hopes of accommodation dwindled away to nothing. By late August it seemed certain that the Verneys, father and eldest son, would end up as enemies. Eleanor, Lady Sussex, an old friend of the family, parliamentarian by sympathy and conviction, but socially very much in both worlds, wrote to Ralph on 9 September that she had had a letter from his father. 'It was a very sade one and his worde was this of you: "Madam he hath ever lane near my hart and truly he is ther still", that he hade many afflictyon uppon him, and that you hade usede him unkandly.' Sir Edmund had, she said, become 'passynate, and much trublede I belive that you declarede yourselfe for the parlyment: a littil time will digest all I am confident'. And she asked Ralph in return to humour his father as much as he could: 'lett me intrete you as a frende that loves you most hartily, not to right passynatly to your father, but ovour com him with kandnes; good man I see he is infinitely malincoly, for many other thinges I belive besides the difference betwixt you.'

All over England, in the summer of 1642, disengagements and separations, often described as 'unnatural', like the prospect of civil war itself, were taking place in communities that for so long had shared customs, territory and beliefs. Very few counties or even towns were so politically homogeneous as to make the decision of allegiance a matter of course or obvious self-interest. Essex was overwhelmingly parliamentarian and much of Wales deeply royalist, but even in shires such as Warwickshire, where there were strong partisan presences—like the Grevilles—parts of those counties, in this instance in the north, were far more mixed in their loyalties. And there were a few regions—Cumberland and Westmorland—that tried to be studiously neutral and avoided organizing either parliamentary or royalist musters. The actual event of the musters—and the response they received in county and market towns—was a warning to those on the wrong side of the fence that they should either move to safer territory or prepare to defend their houses and farms as best they could.

Lady Brilliana Harley was one of those who decided against moving, being unafraid, as she later said, to die in defence of the family estates and godly religion. Her husband, Sir Robert, away in Westminster, very much a moving spirit in the committees of parliament, advised her to stay put: he could not quite believe that much harm could come to her in remote northwest Herefordshire, especially since there were friendly ties between the Harleys and fellow-gentry in the county, even when they parted company on religious beliefs. But in the summer and autumn of 1642 it quickly became plain to Brilliana that her household was an island of parliamentary puritanism in an ocean of royalism and that the old, dependable bonds of gentility might not survive the coming conflict. She was already the butt of popular abuse, some of it genuinely menacing. At Ludlow, she wrote to their son Edward, she had heard that a maypole had been set up 'and a thinge like a head upon it . . . and gathered a greate many about it, and shot at it in derision of roundheads'. And their old friend Sir William Croft had made it no secret that, while in private he still respected Lady Brilliana, this could have no effect whatsoever on his public conduct as a loyal servant of the king. Before long Brilliana and her household were enduring abuse while in the grounds of Brampton Bryan, from 'exceeding rude' country people on their way to market at Ludlow who shouted from the roadway that they wished 'all the Puritans and roundheads at Brampton hanged'. When, later that year, royalist soldiers took two of her servants away to prison, she asked Viscount Scudamore to intercede, appealing, anachronistically, to 'the many bonds by which most of the gentlemen in this country are tied to Sir Robert Harley, that of blood and some with alliance and all with his long professed and real friendship and for myself that of common courtesy, as to a stranger brought into their

160

country, I know not how all those I believed to be so good should break all these obligations'. But, little by little, Brampton Bryan was becoming a godly stockade, with frightened preachers and schoolmasters and Puritan friends coming to the house for shelter. How long it would remain safe was anyone's guess, but with royalism strong not only in Herefordshire but also in Shropshire to the north and in Wales to the south and west, Brilliana must have put in extra prayer-time for the help of the Almighty.

In the third week of August 1642 Charles I decided to raise his standard. He was, as yet, in no position to do more than wage the heraldic equivalent of war rather than the real thing. Far fewer counties had produced men, money and plate for him than for parliament. The navy had come out for parliament, and the king had suffered the indignity of being locked out of Hull by its governor, Sir John Hotham. An attempt by Lord Strange to seize an arms depot in the little Lancashire town of Manchester had ended with his troop of horse being chased out of the town by indignant, armed fustian weavers. But the king had been promised troops and horse in thousands from Wales and Shrewsbury, and he evidently felt confident that the quality of his officers and the rapid training that his professional soldiers, not least the young Prince Rupert, were giving the cavalry would prevail over the superior numbers of the parliamentary army, commanded by the dour veteran of the Dutch wars, the Earl of Essex—the first husband of the notorious Frances Howard. So the standard was to go up, the Rubicon to be crossed, and the man to whom this honour fell was the Knight Marshal, newly appointed standard-bearer, the fifty-two-year-old Sir Edmund Verney. It was a heavy duty, literally, for the thing needed twenty men to get it upright in the field just outside Nottingham castle. 'Much of the fashion of the City Streamers used at the Lord Mayor's Show,' one antiquarian remembered, several flags were mounted on a huge pole, the top one being the king's personal arms, with a hand pointing towards the crown and beneath it the imperious, optimistic motto 'Give Caesar His Due'. The flag was paraded around by three troops of horse and 600 infantrymen. Just as the trumpets were about to sound and the herald to read the royal proclamation, Charles suddenly asked for the paper, a quill and some ink and, still on horseback, started to make some last-minute revisions. When he was done and the herald nervously attempted to read the document, corrections and all, the flag went up, along with the army's hats, high in the air. The standard was carried back to the castle and hoisted to be seen for miles about. But that night a powerful storm got up and the flag was blown down. It was two days before the winds and rain abated enough for it to be raised once more. Those (and there were plenty) in the habit of searching for omens were not encouraged. For Sir Edmund Verney, though, the die was very definitely cast. His charge read 'that by the grace of God they that would wrest that standard from his hand must first wrest his soul from his body'.

By the time the royalist army assembled at Edgehill in Warwickshire, its prospects had been transformed. Charles's forces were now more than 20,000 strong, of whom about 14,000 mustered on the ridge in the early morning of 23 October. At the top of the hill, with his sons, Charles, the Prince of Wales, and James, the nine-year-old Duke of York (under the watchful eye of Hyde), as well as Prince Rupert carrying his toy poodle Boy, the king took his 'prospective glass' and looked down at the parliamentary troops drawn up in the vale of the Red Horse below. Not only did the king have the immense advantage of the sharply sloping terrain, with no trees and only a few hedges offering cover, he also knew that the Earl of Essex's army was exhausted even before a shot had been fired. Moving quickly from Shrewsbury, Charles had managed to slip between the parliamentary strongholds of Warwick and Coventry. Essex had had to play belated catch-up, attempting unsuccessfully to place his army across the route to London before it was too late. The first contact between the two armies had not been encouraging for Essex. A skirmish at Powick Bridge near Worcester the previous month, on 23 September, had ended in an embarrassing rout when Essex's Life Guard had evidently been incapable of understanding, much less performing, a 'wheel about' in the face of Prince Rupert's cavalry charge and had given themselves their own orders to flee.

Close to the king, surrounded by the royal Life Guard in their red coats and holding the standard (much reduced in size to make it portable) was Sir Edmund Verney. His family would have been horrified if they had known he was wearing no armour other than a helmet, being convinced that a full cuirass was more likely to kill a man by impeding his movement than to protect him. Some of his closest friends were there, too; Hyde with the

163

king, Falkland somewhere amid the cavalry. There were drums, the unfurling of regimental flags, coloured scarves tied like sashes over their armour to identify friends in the heat of battle. Already there had been serious trouble over the dispositions. The Earl of Forth and the commander of the infantry, the Earl of Lindsey, had got into an angry row over whether musketeers should be interspersed within the pikemen in the Swedish manner or whether, as Lindsey wished, in the older 'Dutch' style, in separate units—better fitted, he thought, for untried soldiers. Tactlessly, the king and Prince Rupert had voted Swedish, at which point the affronted Lindsey had thrown down his baton and marched off in a pout to head his own regiment. Cavaliers were like that. Still, there was much obvious affection for the king, who rode down the line dressed in a black velvet coat trimmed with ermine, the only flash of brightness the silvery starburst of his Garter badge. 'Your King is your cause, your quarrel and your captain,' he told the troops and promised them his grateful remembrance for their service. He spoke too quietly, as was his custom. But there were huzzahs anyway.

From his position in the valley, at the parliamentary centre, Denzil Holles, one of the five 'birds' of January, Dorchester's own MP in arms, would have had a good view of the formidable array of royal forces mustering on the ridge. From among the trained bands and apprentices in London he, like so many of his friends and colleagues, had raised his own troop of foot soldiers and had dressed them also in red coats, that being the cheapest of the available dyes. (One of the hoariest myths of the civil war is that there were no coloured uniforms. Lord Brooke's men were outfitted in bright purple!) John Hampden was supposed be *en route,* and Arthur Haselrig, he knew, had barely eluded capture by the king's army in the east Midlands. Of what lay in store for him should the parliamentary cause collapse on the battlefield, Holles could have no doubt. On their marches back and forth through the West Country these soldiers had already established a kind of brutal routine: taking what they could get when and as they needed it, abusing any church or priest or village they decided was 'papist', smashing and burning communion table rails, occasionally saying their prayers. Fortunately, it was harvest time and they were marching through the prolific west Midlands. 'Our food was fruit for those that could get it,' wrote one apprentice turned soldier, Nehemiah Wharton, in Worcestershire. 'Our drink was water; our beds the earth; our canopy the clouds, but we pulled up hedges, pales and gates and made good fires; his Excellency [Essex] promising us that, if the country relieved us not the day following, he would fire their towns.'

Their panicky encounters with Prince Rupert's cavalry along the way could not have done much for the morale of the foot soldiers, and there they were again on the brow of the hill. At least, now there were some guns. Scattered amid the lines of cumbersome 16-foot pikes were musketeers, busy now checking the tarred rope that would act as a fuse for their weapons, knocking firmly into place the forked and grooved supports on which the muskets and arquebuses had to rest before they had any chance at all of hitting their target. Some field guns were deployed in front of the centre, but firing upwards, against the bias of the hill, was not exactly going to be easy.

So indeed it proved. Around three o'clock Essex thought to compensate for his topographical disadvantage by cannonading the royalist infantry centre. Most of the replying cannonade came from guns positioned too far down the slope to get much ricochet effect, and it may have been the disappointing performance of the king's artillery, together with the sudden appearance of a parliamentary officer, Sir Faithful Fortescue, tearing off his orange scarf in a dramatic gesture of defection, that persuaded Rupert to begin his cavalry attack. For the parliamentary forces, sitting on their horses or standing with their long pikes in front of them, watching a trot become a canter and seeing the fire of their own muskets and carbines apparently having no effect on the advancing horsemen, the moment of truth had arrived and the reality of war slammed into them. Waves of horsemen came at the terrified parliamentary troops, cutting in at a sweeping angle, which ensured that they were completely unchecked by musket fire. Panic hit the parliamentary right. Their cavalry and some of the infantry broke and fled. Rupert's horsemen slashed a path right through and charged off in pursuit of the fleeing parliamentary troopers like so many huntsmen after the fox. Their chase was 3 miles all the way to the village of Kineton, where the parliamentary army had kept its baggage, now taken in a riotous triumph by Rupert's cavalry. A mile further on John Hampden, marching to the field with his own troops, collided with the runaways, heading for

166

cover like rabbits.

Rupert and his horsemen supposed the battle already won. Prepare the libations. At some point the prince decided he had better return to Edgehill, if only to help with the mopping up. What he found was carnage. The royalist army had been left completely unprotected when, against orders, the cavalry reserve stationed behind Rupert, its blood maddened by contempt for the runaway enemy, had joined the pursuit. Tally-ho!

It was a catastrophic mistake. By no means all the infantry in the parliamentary centre had disintegrated, although it was a close thing. Again it was the Scots or at least one old Covenanter, Sir William Balfour, who made the difference to the destiny of England. While Colonel Thomas Ballard plugged the infantry gap, Balfour rallied his cavalry reserve amid the flying mêlée. They charged the royalist foot soldiers, whom Sir Jacob Astley had led into the fight prefaced by a prayer: 'O Lord! Thou knowest how busy I must be this day. If I forget Thee, do not thou forget me.' A stand was made long enough and firmly enough for the shaken troops, including Holles' London apprentices, to begin to close and mount a gradual, slogging advance up the hill towards the unprotected royalist left flank. Further royalist charges impaled themselves on masses of pikemen. The two forces of pikemen and musketeers met, hand-to-hand, like two lumbering, predatory monsters caught in each other's bristling spikes. And they went at it, hour after hour. The little Duke of York, who had been moved further back for safety by his father, could still see the terrible slaughter below, and all his life he marvelled at the memory, neither side giving ground except to exhaustion. 'The foot being thus ingaged in such warm and close service,' he wrote later, 'it were reasonable to imagine that one side should run and be disorder'd; but it happen'd otherwise, for each as if by mutuall consent retired some few paces, and they stuck down their coulours, continuing to fire at one another even till night; a thing so very extraordinary that nothing less than so many witnesses as there were present, could make it credible.'

In the midst of all this push of pike, smoke and fire and banging of metal was Sir Edmund Verney. The flag gripped in his hand had, of course, made him the most obvious target of all. His eulogists would say that he cut down sixteen soldiers before seeing his own servant Jason die in front of him and then disappearing himself into a mass of oncoming troopers. The flag was carried off but then recaptured by a Life Guard, who disguised himself with the orange scarf of the parliamentarians and brought it back to the king.

Only the October nightfall and sheer dead-dog exhaustion ended the battle. The royalist army held the field. Essex, who thought he should keep together what remained of his force for a possible second engagement should the king decide to move on towards London, fell back on the security of Lord Brooke's Warwick Castle. But the royalist army, although attempting to celebrate a technical victory, was, in fact, torn to pieces. If it wasn't exactly a retreat neither was it a gesture of self-confidence. About 3000 lay dead in the Warwickshire valley, countless more were grievously wounded. The cold was bitter, so sharp that the few who were discovered alive the next morning owed their survival to the freezing temperatures, which had cold-staunched their wounds. The commanders of both armies, especially those who had not seen the bloodshed in Europe, were in shock. The tally-ho war was over.

Little help could be expected for the royalists from a countryside filled with the tenant farmers of Lord Brooke and Viscount Saye and Sele. Although Charles might have seized the moment and attempted a quick march to London, his depleted and mutilated army needed recuperation and reinforcement. So the king made for Banbury, whose garrison surrendered without a fight, then staunchly royalist Oxford, which was to be his capital for the duration of the war, and finally Reading.

In the House of Commons Ralph Verney had to sit through a reading of Lord General Essex's dispatch, which claimed optimistically that Edgehill (then known as the Kineton fight) had been a 'blessed Victory which God hath given us upon the Army of the Cavaliers, and of those Evil Persons, who upon Sunday the 23rd of this Instant, engaged his Majesty in a dangerous and bloody Fight against his faithful Subjects'. But Ralph was lost in a maelstrom of sorrow. His father, the enemy, had fallen holding the king's flag. No one seemed to know exactly what had happened to him or where his body could be found. Lady Sussex wrote to Ralph in condolence: 'I have the saddest heart and deepest wounded soul that ever creature had, he being, I confess to you, the greatest comfort of my life.' Ralph replied:

Madam, Last night I had a servant from my Lord of Essex's Army, that tells mee there is noe possibility of finding my Deare father's Body, for my Lord Generall, my Lord Brooke . . . and twenty others of my acquaintance assured him hee was never taken prisiner, neither were any of them ever possessed of his Body; but that hee was slaine by an ordinary trooper. Upon this my man went to all the ministers of severall parishes, that buried the dead that were slaine in the battle, and none of them can give him any information of the body. One of them told him my Lord Aubigney was like to have been buried in the fields, but that one came by chance that knew him and tooke him into a church, and there laid him in the ground without soe much as a sheete about him, and soe divers others of good quallity were buried: the ministers kept Tallies of all that were buried, and they amount to neare 4000. Madam, you see I am every way unhappy. I beseech you afford me your prayers.

Sir Edmund Verney did appear again—but only to the villagers (including a minister and a justice of the peace) who some months later swore they beheld a vision of a terrible engagement of phantom armies contending in the night sky, and there in the middle was the standard-bearer, holding fast to his king's flag. Others claimed that someone, somewhere had found Sir Edmund's severed hand, with the portrait ring of the king on his finger, still clutching a piece of the pole.

None of this was any consolation to Ralph Verney. His father's death shook his faith in the war.

In the following year, 1643, he was among many (including Denzil Holles) who tried to find some way out of it, if necessary by putting out feelers to the king. After the collapse of tentative negotiation with the court at Oxford, signatures were demanded for the Solemn League and Covenant with the Scots, an alliance committed to pursuing the war to total victory. Ralph Verney could not bring himself to sign. Instead he disappeared and took his family with him into exile in France.

That the war was to be a long, grim, grinding business had already been apparent when the king's attempt to smash parliament by taking London stalled at Turnham Green, on the western outskirts of the capital, in November 1642. A week before the royalist army, now somewhat depleted by leaving garrisons at Reading and Oxford, had been confronted with trained bands at Brentford, including Denzil Holles' redcoats. Another of Rupert's cavalry charges had cut through their lines, however, and pushed the troopers stumbling back into the Thames, where many of them floundered and drowned, weighed down by their armour. But the fear that gripped London also produced an immense outpouring of volunteers, determined to stand in the way of the Cavaliers' retribution. On Sunday, 12 November, 24,000 of them, plus hordes of women and civilians supplying them with food and encouragement, faced 12,000 soldiers of the royalist army. Many of the defenders were armed with nothing better than cudgels or pitchforks, but there were a lot of them. And after a day-long, nervous stand-off at Turnham Green Charles decided against risking his army and took it back to Oxford.

Edgehill had taught Charles that the conflict would not be settled by a single, epic battle. Turnham Green taught him that, however disorganized and amateurish, parliament was capable of mobilizing resources that could equal or outgun his own. It was crucial, then, to husband and strengthen his own assets in regions of the country where he could depend on a solid base of gentry support and where the population might be more receptive to the heavy taxation needed to fund the war effort. This boiled down, essentially, to the west and northeast and Wales. Once his military power base was solid, he could move from the periphery of the country towards the strategic centre, gradually drawing a noose around the neck of London. Parliament, on the other hand, knew that as its core supply areas in eastern and southeastern England were held secure, the capital would be fed and armed. Preventing the royalist army from making inroads into East Anglia and the east Midlands, lying as they did between the king's northern and western power bases, became crucial for parliament. In 1643 the establishment of an Eastern Association, linking the county defence committees under the unified command of Lord Mandeville, now the Earl of Manchester and one of the few peers to remain with parliament, was meant to make the rapid deployment of Cromwell's foot soldiers, guns and horse, when and where they were needed, more efficient.

The war that year broke down into regional theatres of conflict, especially in Yorkshire and the West Country. They were no less nasty or bloody, and no less ruinous to the towns and country that felt their shock, for being such local events. And they were both very unpredictable. The size of the forces waxed and waned with the enthusiasm and loyalty of the gentry who brought them into the war, and they were constantly plagued by defections of common foot soldiers and troopers who deserted in large numbers after battles, whether victorious or defeated. ('Home, home' was the repeated cry of London apprentices in Devon and Cornwall, who knew they were very far away from Cheapside and Southwark.) But then, after all, their gentlemen officers seemed to change sides with dismaying regularity, at least during 1643, and mostly in one direction—towards the king, whose fortunes were certainly in the ascendant that year. In Yorkshire Sir John Hotham, who had turned the king away from Hull, and Sir Hugh Cholmley, a ship-money resister, both switched sides. In Cornwall Sir Alexander Carew, who had been so implacably determined to see Strafford beheaded, plotted to hand over Plymouth to the royalists, was exposed by one of his servants, arrested, taken to London and summarily tried and executed. With things definitely not going according to plan in the western campaign, Sir Richard Grenville, the brother of Sir Bevil, suddenly discovered that, after all, religion had been 'a cloke for rebellion' and changed his allegiance, becoming one of the most ruthlessly cold-blooded of all the royalist generals.

The fact that, especially in the early years of the war, many of the generals on either side were so alike in their social and cultural personality, indeed had often known each other well, either in parliament or in the country, and spoke the same kind of language of patriotic disinterest, must also have weakened, or at least constantly tested, their allegiance. The two generals who faced each other in the murderous little war in the West Country, Sir William Waller and Sir Ralph Hopton, respectively from Gloucestershire and Somerset, and both professional soldiers, were virtually interchangeable types, even in religion, where Hopton the royalist was as much of a sober Puritan as Waller and had voted not only for Strafford's attainder but even for that bugbear of the royalist cause, the Grand Remonstrance. It had only been when parliament arrogated to itself power over the militia that Hopton had changed allegiance. He was, then, as close as possible to the mind-set of his adversaries. During a brief lull in their campaign, Hopton wrote to Waller asking for a meeting. Waller had to turn him down but in terms that suggest just how deeply the distress of their broken friendship went.

> To my noble frend, Sr Ralphe Hopton at Wells
>   Sr
> The experience I have had of your worth, and the happiness I have enjoyed in your freindshipp, are wounding considerations to me when I looke upon this present distance between us. Certainly my affections to you are so unchangeable, that hostility itself cannot violate my freindshipp to your person, but I must be true to the cause wherein I serve. The ould limitation usque ad aras holds still, and where my conscience is interested all other obligations are swallowed upp. I should most gladly waite upon you, according to your desire, but that I looke upon you as you are ingaged in that party, beyond the possibility of a retreat

and consequently uncapable of being wrought upon by any persuasions. And I know the conference could never be so close between us, but that it would take winde and receive a construction to my dishonour. That great God, who is the searcher of my heart, knowes with what a sad sence I go on upon this service, and with what a perfect hatred I detest this warr without an ennemy. But I looke upon it as Opus Domini, and that is enough to silence all passion in mee. The God of Peace in his good time send us the blessing of peace and in the meane time fitt us to receive itt. Wee are both upon the stage, and must act those parts that are assigned us in this Tragedy. Lett us do itt in a way of honour, and without personall animosities. Whatsoever the issue be, I shall never relinquish the dear title of

Your most affectionated friend
and faithfull servant
Wm Waller

Three weeks later at Lansdown, near Bath, Hopton's army charged Waller's hilltop position and captured it, along with guns and prisoners but at savage cost to himself. Of the 2000 who had ridden up the hill, only 600 were left alive in the pyrrhic victory. Among the 200 infantry who had died in the same attack was Sir Bevil Grenville, another friend of Waller's, pole-axed at the summit. Hopton himself had been badly slashed in the arm. Inspecting prisoners the next day an ammunition wagon exploded, burning and temporarily blinding him, so that he needed to be carried in a litter, knowing that at any time Waller's troops, defeated but rested at Bath, might swoop down on his battered and bedraggled army. On Roundway Down outside Devizes a week later, Hopton's army, despite its general being more or less unable to see or ride, again triumphed, this time overwhelmingly. Two weeks later, on 26 July, the walls of Bristol, thought to be impregnable, were stormed by Hopton's Cornish army and the city, under the command of Saye and Sele's son Nathaniel, surrendered to Prince Rupert.

The fall of Bristol sent shock waves through all the godly hold-outs in the southwest. To the godliest of them all, Dorchester, William Strode brought disturbing news of Cavalier besiegers who had thought nothing of climbing up 20-foot walls. In his view Dorchester's defences would keep the town safe for about half an hour. Those who had vowed to live and die with their Covenant now had a sudden change of heart. John White fled to London; William Whiteway tried to take ship out of Weymouth and was intercepted by a royalist patrol. On 2 August, having been assured that a quick surrender would guarantee them against plunder, the citizens of Dorchester opened the town to Cavalier troops. They were plundered anyway.

With the royalists now in command of most of the strongholds and towns of the west, Lady Brilliana Harley, locked up in Brampton Bryan, braced herself for the worst. She was in dire peril. Sir Robert (who belatedly had reconsidered his advice that she should remain in Herefordshire) was still in London without any way to reach home. Her sons Ned and Robert were in Waller's army and, she hoped, safe. Most of the godly clergy and families had long since fled, many to Gloucester, which was holding out against a royalist siege. Her friends' abandoned houses had been gutted and vandalized, their livestock taken and slaughtered, the tenant farmers and labourers terrorized, and the lands themselves forfeit to the king. Defending Brampton behind its fourteenth-century gatehouse were fifty musketeers, attempting to protect another fifty civilians, including her family physician, a few of her godly lady friends and her three youngest children, Thomas, Dorothy and Margaret. By late July, 700 foot soldiers and horse troopers were camped around Brampton, building breastworks close to her garden from which they could fire cannonballs and musket shot at the house. There was nothing much that Brilliana could do except pray, wait and inspect her own defensive works. The siege, when it began in earnest, went on for six and a half weeks. There were daily bombardments, the defenders reduced to using hand-mills to grind their grain into flour for bread. The roof of the hall was smashed in, but despite the relentless regularity of the fire surprisingly few were killed, except Brilliana's cook, another servant and one of her woman friends. Priam Davies, a parliamentarian captain present throughout the siege, claimed, not implausibly, that Brilliana was most upset by the perpetual and noisy enemy cursing coming from the 'breast works in our gardens and walks, where their rotten and poisoned language annoyed us more than their poisoned bullets'.

Throughout the siege Brilliana remained in regular contact with the besiegers, who themselves hoped for a negotiated end rather than having to storm the house, and kept them talking as a ploy, while hoping for some relief from parliamentary troops. Eventually, in September, the royalists were called away to reinforce the siege of Gloucester and left her still the mistress of Brampton Bryan. She set about levelling the earthworks and replanting her garden and orchards. She also badly needed to restock the estate with cattle and took them from neighbours who had become enemies. Brilliana the pious had become Brilliana the plunderer, but God, she knew, understood the compulsion of her plight.

God, in fact, had other plans for Brilliana Harley. In October, apparently quite suddenly she fell into a 'defluxion' of the lungs, convulsed with terrible bloody coughing, and on Sunday 31 October 1643, to general shock and grief, she died. When Sir Robert got the news, like the Calvinist he was, he bent before the inscrutable design of the Almighty: 'having received the sad news that the Lord has taken from me my dear wife, to whose wise hand of providence I desire with a heart of resignation humbly to submit'. Stirred by Brilliana's example, the defenders of Brampton Bryan continued to hold out against further attacks until April 1644, when they finally gave up the house to troops acting in the name of the governor of Hereford, Barnabas Scudamore, the viscount's brother.

The autumn of 1643 was perhaps the time of greatest gloom for the parliamentary cause. The 'birds' of 1642 had been plucked by defections and death. In June 1643 Hampden had been mortally wounded at the battle of Chalgrove Field. Denzil Holles had been so shaken by the adversities of the year that he was among the most conspicuous of those who were trying to reach a negotiated peace with the king. Haselrig's troop of cuirassiers, known from their armour and red coats as the 'lobsterbacks', were among those destroyed in Hopton's great victory at Roundway Down in July, although Haselrig himself lived to fight many more political battles. John Pym was dying, horribly, of intestinal cancer, but not before he had put together the alliance that, more than any other single event, would rescue the parliamentary position and determine the eventual outcome of the war: the Solemn League and Covenant with the Scots.

In 1637 Scotland had begun the resistance to the absolutism of Charles I, and seven years later the Covenant would all but finish him off. Only the obstinately anglocentric need for home-grown heroes can explain the general impression that Oliver Cromwell was somehow single-handedly responsible for defeating Charles I in the first civil war, when his role was late and limited (although often decisive and invariably successful). Without the intervention of the great Covenanter general, Alexander Leslie (at the Scottish parliament's request elevated by Charles to be Earl of Leven in 1641), Cromwell might never have had a chance to celebrate those victories. Ironically, the League between the Covenanters and the English parliament, which delivered a huge army to the critical campaign in Yorkshire, was the first concerted attempt to make a British union since the abortive efforts of James VI and I. To seal the alliance, Pym and the godly party in the Lords and Commons had, in effect, to promise that there

179

would be a Presbyterian concordance among the Churches of England, Scotland and Wales. Since there was a Scots army under Monro vigorously (not to say brutally) campaigning there, it seemed only a matter of time before Ireland, too, was brought into the fold. So when the Lords and Commons gathered on 25 September 1643 to take the oath of loyalty to the Solemn League and Covenant in St Margaret's Chapel, Westminster, an astoundingly inverted version of the Stuart dream of union—a godly Great Britain—seemed wondrously within reach.

On 19 January Leven crossed the Tweed with 18,000 foot soldiers, 3000 horse, 500 dragoons and 16 cannon. For the second time in five years Northumberland was under Scottish occupation. To defend the Tyne, Newcastle had 500 foot and 300 horse. A royalist disaster was obviously looming. Troops were hastily rushed from wherever Charles could get them, especially from the south and west, but Waller's victory in the next round of his war games with Hopton, at Cheriton in March 1644, took one of those resources away.

York, which for so long had seemed impregnable as the king's capital of the north, found itself the target of a huge eleven-week siege, the city surrounded on all sides by parliamentary and Scottish troops. Its outlying villages were laid to waste, and everything in the farms was taken and used by the besiegers. An observer of the destruction inside the city, Simeon Ashe, wrote: 'Had thine eyes yesternight with me seen York burning thy heart would have been heavye. The Lord affect us with the sad fruits of wasting warres and speedily and mercifully end our combustions which are carried on with high sinnes and heavy desolations. Truly my heart sometimes is ready to breake with what I see here.'

Gradually, the fate of York and with it the north of England came to be seen, by both sides, as the fulcrum on which the fate of the entire war would turn. The king kept just enough of his army in the southwest to keep the Earl of Essex and Waller detained, while, with an immense effort, the Duke of Newcastle and Prince Rupert assembled an army large enough to break the siege and compete on equal terms with the combined forces of the Covenant and parliament. Early on a sultry 2 July, 40,000 men faced each other on Marston Moor, a few miles from the city. It was neither a good place nor a good time for a battle. There had been a violent rainstorm, making the Yorkshire heath boggy, and there was a wide ditch separating the two armies, which stood a half mile from each other, sweating into their armour. For once Rupert was not especially anxious to begin the proceedings—not even, for that matter, to give battle. The afternoon wore on, a long cat-and-mouse game, with Rupert waiting for a premature cavalry attack to stumble over the ditch and be ready to be picked off. But before he knew it, Cromwell's horse, on the parliamentary left, was charging over the ditch and on to his soldiers, slashing its way through to the rear. In the furiousness of the charge Cromwell took a wound to the neck and head and had to leave the field, which, since the royalist left had badly beaten Sir Thomas Fairfax's troops, should have given them their opportunity, with the pikemen and musketeers as usual pushing and firing at the centre. But, at the defining moment of his career, Cromwell came back into the fray, along with the Covenanter general David Leslie. Cromwell had become justly famous for the battlefield discipline of his horse, and instead of letting them waste precious time and energy rampaging through the enemy's baggage train, he wheeled his troopers round to the now unprotected rear of the royalist right flank. It was this fast-moving parliamentary cavalry that had the advantage of the lie of the land and rode down on the virtually surrounded royalist centre, folding in on itself.

After three hours, there were 6000 dead on Marston Moor. The cream of the king's infantry had been wiped out. The Duke of Newcastle, who had emptied his own coffers to supply Charles with an army, had witnessed its complete destruction and had nothing left to finance another. He would not, he said, remain to hear the laughter of the court, preferring instead to go into exile with just £90 to his name. For Oliver Cromwell, though, the victory was an unmistakable sign that the Lord of Hosts was fighting alongside his godly soldiers. Writing to his brother-in-law, Colonel Valentine Walton, he declared that 'God made them as stubble to our swords', before going on to darken the rejoicing by telling Walton: 'Sir, God hath taken away your eldest son by a cannon-shot. It brake his leg. We were necessitated to have it cut off, whereof he died. Sir, you know my trials this way [Cromwell had lost his own son, Oliver junior, to sickness while he was serving in the army]; but the Lord supported me with this: that the Lord took him into the happiness we all pant after and live for. There is your precious child full of glory, not to know sin nor sorrow any more.'

By the end of the month York had capitulated. The only bright spot for the king was Cornwall, where the Earl of Essex (who had insisted on taking command over Waller) had managed to get an army of 10,000 hopelessly trapped within a 5-mile strip of land between Lostwithiel and Fowey. Charles, who was personally commanding the campaign (and enjoying it), asked the earl if he would now consider joining him in a united campaign to clear the Scots from the north, but Essex declined, preferring to depart from his army by boat once he had seen the cavalry break through and escape. Philip Skippon (another who was offered a place in the royalist army by Charles and who rejected it) was left to deal with the débâcle at Fowey, negotiating for his foot soldiers an honourable retreat that turned into a logistical and human nightmare. One of the royalist soldiers who was watching the retreat saw a 'rout of soldiers prest all of a heap like sheep . . . so dirty and dejected as was rare to see'. Stripped of food, clothes, boots and shelter, attacked by the country people (especially the women), Skippon's men slept in soaking fields and drank from puddles and ditches. One of them remembered being 'inhumanly dealt with, abused, reviled, scorned, torn, kicked, pillaged and many stript of all they had, quite contrary to the articles of war'. Disease, starvation and untended wounds made short shrift of the army, so that just 1000 of the 6000 who had left Fowey dragged themselves into Poole.

By the end of the year parliament was in control of thirty-seven of the fifty-seven counties of England and Wales and the majority of the most populous and strategically important towns, with the exception of Bristol, Exeter and Chester. But the king was not yet defeated. At the second battle of Newbury in October he had managed to avoid a potentially lethal pincer movement by the armies of Waller and Essex and slugged out the day to an exhausted tie. The wear and tear of Newbury was enough to prevent Charles from breaking through, but not enough to finish him off. And Charles was aware, as much as parliament, of the increasingly acrimonious relations between Waller and Essex on the one hand and Manchester and Cromwell on the other, all of whom were barely on speaking terms, so much did they suspect and despise each other. Attempting to flatten the king was like trying to swat a particularly annoying and nimble housefly. And, although by all measure of the military arithmetic, Charles was losing ground, there was an ominous sense among the military commanders on the parliamentary side that he was prevailing—at least politically—just by avoiding obliteration. As the Earl of Manchester put it: 'If we beat the king ninety and nine times yet he is a king still and so will his posterity be after him. But if the king beat us once we shall all be hanged and our posterity be made slaves.' To which Oliver Cromwell, who was rapidly coming to despise what he thought was Manchester's inertia and pusillanimity, retorted, pithily: 'If this be so, why did we take up arms at first?'

Manchester and Cromwell's arguments over how best to use the now formidable army of the Eastern Association were much more than a tactical squabble. Cromwell suspected that what he said—in public—was Manchester's reluctance to prosecute the war with all possible energy and severity resulted from a misguided anxiety not to destroy the king too completely lest a great void in the polity be opened up. For his part, Manchester accused Cromwell of filling his regiments with social inferiors of dangerously unorthodox religious opinions, who would be unlikely to subscribe to the Presbyterian rule they were all supposed to be fighting for, north and south of the Scottish border. Oliver Cromwell was, as time would show, no social leveller, nor did he see the army as a school of political radicalism. But he was a recognizably modern soldier in his belief that men fought better when officers and men had a common moral purpose, a bonding ideology. The old knightly ideal by which gentlemen would lead and their loyal men would follow was, he thought, no longer adequate for the times nor for their cause. It was necessarily the Cavalier ethos, not their own. This is what Cromwell meant after Edgehill when he had told Hampden, 'Your troopers . . . are most of them old decayed serving men and tapsters, and such kind of fellows, and . . . their troopers are gentlemen's sons . . . You must get men of a spirit . . . that is like to go as far as a gentleman will go, or else I am sure you will be beaten still.' And when he told the Suffolk committee that 'I had rather have a plain russet-coated captain that knows what he fights for, and loves what he knows, than that which you call a gentleman and is nothing else,' he was not so much asking for a democratized army as for a morally and ideologically motivated godly army. In the bitter debate with Manchester, which lasted into the winter of 1645 and was aired in the House of Commons, Cromwell made it clear that a godly

185

army need not (as the Covenanters assumed) be a rigidly Presbyterian one. More than once he came to the defence of a junior officer accused of being a Baptist or some other kind of unofficial Protestant, on the grounds that those who were prepared to die for the righteous cause should not be slighted to appease the Scots. Whatever Britain Cromwell thought he was fighting for, it was not a Presbyterian united kingdom.

Presbyterians, like Manchester, Essex and Harley, and 'Independents', as those who took the more inclusive and tolerant line on worship called themselves, could at least agree that the war needed to be brought to the king with maximum force in 1645. To that end, parliament attempted to separate politics from the military command by enacting a Self-Denying Ordinance, which required all members of the Lords and Commons to resign their military posts, or vice versa. This effectively removed most of the principal protagonists—Essex, Manchester and Waller—while creating a unified New Model Army under the command of Sir Thomas Fairfax, the only senior general for whom no one (yet) had a bad word and who made a point of being politically neutral. Apolitical though he was, Fairfax did share with Cromwell a sense of how this core parliamentary army ought to be run. It was to be zealous and godly (a lot more psalm-singing), and it was to be exemplary in its discipline. The standard unwinding techniques for soldiers—drink, cursing and whoring—were to be replaced by quiet sessions with *The Souldiers Catechisme*. Plunder would be savagely punished. (That, at any rate, was the idea: all very nice and Christian in principle but suicidal to enforce in the aftermath of a particularly hideous and prolonged siege.) In return for their sobriety and enthusiastic self-sacrifice, the soldiers were to be made to feel that their generals—all their officers, in fact—genuinely cared for their welfare, that they would be provided with boots, food and shelter, and that when they were lying screaming as their arm was being sawn off they would know there had been a point to it all. Cromwell and Fairfax were in absolutely no doubt of the point to it all.

Translating that certainty into total victory was another matter. Although by the spring of 1645 it looked unlikely (if not impossible) that Charles could win in England, he was now fighting for, and in, Britain. A setback in one of his kingdoms might always be compensated by success in another, and to the wearied and vexed parliamentary generals it seemed that he could go on playing this military shell game indefinitely, until his enemies were all at each other's throats. For there were now internal civil wars in all four of the British nations. They were not taking place in discrete theatres of conflict but were all tangled up in each other's fate. Because Charles could thank his remote Plantagenet ancestors for the most indestructible of his fortresses in Wales, what happened there, especially in the Marches, at castles like Chepstow and Monmouth, would ultimately affect the course of the war in England. Welsh soldiers were already making up a significant part of the royalist armies fighting in the west. Scottish Covenanter troops were stuck in Ireland protecting Presbyterian Ulster against the Gaelic Confederacy, which, given the central importance of the papacy and Owen Roe O'Neill, they believed was the same

187

thing as protecting Scotland and England from impending invasion by the Antichrist. That eventuality seemed much closer in June 1646 when Monro lost a crucial battle at Benburb in County Tyrone against Owen Roe O'Neill.

And in the autumn of 1644, the Covenanter-Catholic, Scots-Irish war came back to Scotland itself, when Alasdair MacColla landed in the western Highlands with a force of 2000 Irish, supplied by his Clan Donald kinsman, the Earl of Antrim, and drawn almost exclusively from Catholic Ulster. It linked up with the even smaller army of James Graham, Marquis of Montrose, whose ambition was to open a second front for Charles in northern and western Scotland. With the bulk of the Covenanter army still in England (from which the English parliamentary command could certainly not afford to release it), Montrose was gambling that he could open a back door to power, rally the Highlands and islands, cut through the weakened Lowlands and go all the way to Edinburgh, where he would overthrow the Covenant and establish a Scottish royalist regime. With that army, he would then invade England and turn the tide there as well.

That was the plan, at any rate—a pan-British, anti-Covenanter solution for the whole country— and it was blessed initially with a spectacular series of military successes against the weakened Covenanter-Lowland armies. But the reason Montrose and MacColla were winning in the autumn and winter of 1644–5 had almost nothing to do with the Marquis' British strategy or his personal alienation from the Covenanters and everything to do with two ancient Scottish feuds.

The first was the relentless war between the Calvinist Lowlands and the largely Catholic northwestern Highlands. But even within the Highlands, the obscene slaughters of the Scottish wars were powered by the visceral, unforgiving hatred between Clan Donald (both its Irish and Scots branches) and the Campbells of Argyll. The further away from the killing hills the campaign went, the harder it was for Montrose to keep his army together, although the lure of sacking cities like Perth and Aberdeen helped. The butchery at Aberdeen was especially sadistic, lasting over three days and involving the cold-blooded murder of anyone thought to exercise any sort of public office or authority—advocates, merchants, the masters of the hospitals and almshouses, and scores of other civilians—and leaving a deep legacy of enmity between Irish and Scots. There was, said a contemporary Aberdonian: 'killing, robbing and plunder of this town at their pleasure. And nothing hard bot pitiful howling, crying, weeping, mourning through all the streets. Som women they preseet to defloir and uther sum they took perforce to serve them in the camp.'

Even the tactical style of the Irish-Highland army defied expectations of modern warfare. Like its English counterpart, the Covenanter infantry had at its heart six-deep platoons of musketeers who, to be effective, were supposed to execute a 'countermarch'. This involved the first line filing to the back of the six once its weapons had been fired, with the next line replacing them. By the time the original row returned to the front they were supposed to have completed a flawless and extremely rapid reloading. But without intensive

189

drill practice the movement was, in fact, seldom either flawless or swift, and it was precisely at that moment that the Highland and Irish soldiers dropped their own muskets and charged with sword and shield, cutting a bloody route through the floundering musketeers and pikemen. The 'Highland' charge (already much used in the Irish war by the Gaelic-Catholic soldiers) was primitive but astonishingly effective. And there were other ways in which the armies of Montrose and MacColla inconveniently refused to abide by the rules, continuing their campaign into the deep Highland winter, especially in the Campbell lands, where villages were devastated, and (as would remain the practice all through 1645 and into 1646) indiscriminately killing any men or boys who might one day serve as soldiers. After a while, strategy simply dissolved into clan cleansing. For MacColla killing as many Campbells as possible became the main point of the campaign, while for Archibald Campbell, Earl of Argyll, counter-killing as many of the Clan Donald and their allies, the MacLean, was equally satisfying. And so the carnage went on and on and on, indifferent to seasons or landscape: blood in the snow, blood in the heather, blood in the pinewoods. In one particularly gruesome atrocity, some hundreds of Campbell men, women and children were herded into a barn, which was then burned to the ground.

Montrose did, in the end, succeed in reaching deep into the Covenanter Lowlands, establishing himself not at Edinburgh, then in the grip of a terrible wave of the plague, but at Glasgow. At Philiphaugh in 1645 his army suffered its first serious defeat, but by early 1646 he was still in a position to do great damage in Scotland on behalf of the royalist cause. So it must have been a shock when, at the beginning of May 1646, Charles himself went to the Covenanter army then besieging the town of Newark and put himself in the hands of the Scots.

But then Montrose's campaign (and the battle of Benburb in Ireland) had been the *only* thing that had gone right for the king in 1645 and early 1646. By the time the New Model Army was deployed in April 1645, parliament, together with its Scots allies, could put 50,000 men in the field and had perhaps the same number in garrisons—much the biggest military force ever to be seen in Britain. The king could field half that number at most. Penned up in Oxford, he had few choices. The first was to cut his losses and respond positively to peace terms set at Uxbridge earlier in the year. But the Solemn League and Covenant had required the king to accept a bishopless Presbyterian regime along with the new Directory of Worship, already distributed in place of the Book of Common Prayer, and this Charles found just as repugnant as he always had. Fighting on, unless he just sat in Oxford waiting for the inevitable siege, meant choosing between moving west or north.

A second option for Charles, recommended by Prince Rupert, was to play to his strengths by moving west and maintaining his military power base along a line of strongholds from Exeter through Bristol and Cardiff to Carlisle, to join with the still undefeated army of General Goring, drawing the parliamentary army into deeply hostile territory and keeping the crucial seaways open to Ireland from whence cometh, it was hoped, some help. Alternatively, a third choice would be to move north towards Montrose, hoping his victories would prove contagious and uniting their armies. After a good deal of dithering, mesmerized by Montrose's success and by an understandable feeling that everything decisive that happened in his reign happened in Scotland, Charles chose the northern option. At the end of May 1645 his army took and sacked Leicester and was moving northeast. Its break-out had the effect, as intended, of drawing Fairfax away from the siege of Oxford and hastening Cromwell eastwards to protect East Anglia. But it also had the undesired effect of bringing those two armies together to face the king in what was obviously going to be a decisive battle, near the Northamptonshire village of Naseby.

Even without the New Model Army forces, Charles was outnumbered by Fairfax. But again over-ruling Rupert's caution, he decided to give battle anyway. By the time they deployed on two facing hilltops with a marshy little vale between them, the two forces were massively disproportionate. Cromwell and Fairfax had about 14,000 men, the king only half that number. And numbers counted. Remembering his mistake in waiting at Marston Moor, Rupert took the initiative, charged right away down his hill and, carried by the momentum up the facing slope, sliced through the cavalry on the left flank, commanded by Cromwell's future son-in-law, Henry Ireton, who was wounded in the onslaught. But only about half of Ireton's cavalry strength broke from this initial hit. Yet again, Rupert's horse was soon off plundering the baggage train, leaving the royalist infantry in the centre to push pikes with Fairfax's foot soldiers and the Scots. At just the moment when it looked as though Fairfax's numbers would inevitably take their toll, Cromwell charged, his tight lines of horses crashing into the royalist cavalry that remained on the left flank. At the critical moment Charles, dressed in a gilt suit of armour, tried to charge Cromwell's victorious troopers with his Life Guard. Horrified aides took the reins of his Flemish horse and led it away, a move that was misread in the field as a command for tactical withdrawal. The crumbling became a collapse. In two hours it was all over. Seeing his men exposed to a slaughter, Astley surrendered 4000 foot and 500 officers, as well as the complete royalist artillery train and thousands of muskets and arquebuses. Virtually nothing was left of the royalist army except its dead on the field of Naseby. In the captured baggage train were the king's correspondence, personal and military, as well as £100,000 worth of jewels, coaches and plate. A troop of Welsh women, called 'Irish whores' by the victorious troopers, were, needless to say, mercilessly butchered or mutilated.

Within a month or two there was almost nothing left of the royalist war machine in England. Another decisive victory by Fairfax over Lord Goring at Langport in Somerset destroyed its surviving western command. One by one the major centres—Bristol, Cardiff, Carlisle—fell. Garrisons that held out were besieged with the utmost ferocity. When, after a massive siege in October, Cromwell's army finally took the heavily fortified Basing House built by the Catholic Marquis of Winchester (Mary Tudor's Lord Treasurer) and still owned by his heir, they were convinced they were rooting out a nest of filthy idolatry and put to the sword everyone they could find in the burning ruins, civilians as well as soldiers, women as well if they offered any resistance. The great architect and orchestrator of the court masques, Inigo Jones, fled with only a rough blanket to protect him from naked indignity. Paintings and books were taken to London to be burned in a great public bonfire, and whatever was left of the furniture or jewels found there was the soldiers' to sell.

On 26 April 1646 Charles left Oxford. He had cut his hair; wore a false beard and was dressed without any of the trappings of a gentleman, much less those of a king. Only his chaplain and a single manservant went with him. For a while he hid in disguise in Norfolk, hoping he might yet escape by sea and perhaps join the queen in France. But this was the heart of Cromwell country, and the ports were being watched. His better chance lay with the Scots, even the Covenanter Scots, for he knew that, Presbyterian though they were, their vision of the future assumed the continuing presence of a king. Exactly what sort of king, however, was evidently open to dispute.

And dispute the nations of Britain did, in words and fire for another three years, which were almost as ruinous and certainly as divisive as the previous three. For if peace had broken out in 1646, it was only in the sense that sieges and battles had, for the time being, ended.

Just what the new England, what the new Britain, was supposed to be, what the prize was for which so many had laid down their life, was unresolved. So many of the principles for which parliament had gone to war in the first place in

1642 had been made redundant by the transforming brutality of the conflict. The one thing that had not changed was the conviction, shared by a majority of parliament, that they needed some sort of king, chastened, emasculated, restrained and reformed, but a king none the less, as an indispensable element in the constitution. So the traditional political fiction that the king had been 'led astray' into the war by wicked and malignant 'men of blood' was maintained, the better to cleanse the Crown of permanent, institutional guilt. By the same token, those held responsible for the crime of civil war and who were exempt from any kind of pardon and indemnity— and who therefore might well be brought to trial— were no fewer than seventy-three, starting with Prince Rupert. Equally, anyone who had fought for the royalist side or aided or abetted them in any identifiable way was to be excluded forever from holding any kind of local office or trust. This, in effect, was to perpetuate the painful division of the governing and law community that had opened up in 1642. And since the king had shown such contempt for what, in retrospect, seemed like the modest proposals for his restraint set out by parliament five years before, he now had to be fettered with bands of steel. Control of the militia and armed forces was to be transferred to parliament for twenty years, and it went without saying that neither high officers of state nor his council could be appointed without parliament's consent, nor foreign policy action taken without its approval. While Presbyterianism was the order of the day, the eventual fate of England's Church was left, for good political reasons, to future settlement.

What kind of Britain did this augur? The Marquis of Argyll, for one, believed that at last a 'true union' of Scotland and England—unforced, sympathetic in godly amity, the opposite of James VI and I's marriage of high Churches, and certainly the opposite of Charles's Arminian coercion—was now at hand. But then, of course, with the Clan Donald still torching his villages and murdering his clansmen, and with the Catholic-Irish Confederacy unsubdued and capable of supplying new armies to make his people wretched, Argyll had very practical reasons to sound so fraternal. The war that at the beginning had been fought to keep the several nations of the British archipelago apart was now pulling them together, although on terms that were often mutually at odds. Driven by the imperatives of the Catholic Counter-Reformation, the Irish revolt had now accepted a view of itself that had once been only the fantasy of its enemies: that the restoration of the old Church was the prelude to the destruction of heresy in England and Scotland. Conversely, the Presbyterians in Ulster now thought there would never be any peace or safety for themselves in Ireland without the active military involvement of the rest of Protestant Britain. We are still living with the consequences of that assumption.

Oddly enough, in 1646–7 it was England that rather wanted to be left alone and paid the Scots army £400,000 to go away, leaving the king behind. (The Scots, Charles remarked with grim irony, had bartered him away rather cheaply.) To be left alone, though, was not the same as to be left in peace. Militarily pacified, politically England was a vacuum filled by an uproar. The old polite community of law and government that had ruled since the Reformation had been shattered, some thought (wrongly, as it would turn out) beyond repair. In counties ravaged by war, justices of the peace were partially replaced by county committees empowered to mobilize money and arms, while JPs survived to look after traditional administration and crime. The county committees were hated by civilians for billeting soldiers and levying taxes, and they were hated by the army for failing to pay them adequately and reducing them to either beggary or theft. By 1646–7, however, as parliamentarian control was established throughout England, JPs everywhere started making a comeback. The wielder of power in England now was not, as everyone had imagined when the war began, parliament, but the army: a massive military machine the likes of which had never before been seen in Britain. And when the fighting was more or less done, the men of this hungry, angry and poorly paid army were perfectly prepared to mutiny, seize their officers, march to new quarters without permission or refuse to decamp. In the last years of the war, the New Model Army at least had also been socially transformed, with the officer corps drawn from sections of society that were much broader and lower down in the pecking order than anything thought possible before 1645. This did not necessarily mean that its opinions were more radical—the startlingly proto-democratic Levellers, such as John Lilburne, were still an influential minority. But it did mean that something new had been unloosed on the English polity: a reading, debating soldiery with a burning desire to settle accounts with its parliamentary paymasters. And while they were at it, an extremely important element in the army, beginning with Cromwell and Ireton, was becoming increasingly hostile to the 'Scottish' Presbyterianism that had been imposed on England by the Solemn League and Covenant. Let the Scots have a Kirk, said the Independents, and let godly English congregations elect ministers according to their own understanding of faith and desired forms of worship.

In the summer of 1647 this perilously volatile mixture of religious hostility and economic anger brought England very close to another civil war, this time between parliament and the army. But it was a contest in which only one side had the guns. Parliament's idea of neutralizing its problems with the army had been to demobilize it, even before it had come to terms with the king. For its part, the army was hardly likely to agree to its disbandment before its grievances had been properly addressed. Indignant that their orders were not being obeyed, parliamentary leaders, especially Denzil Holles, began to wax constitutional. They claimed (with some reason) that the protection of parliament's authority was the reason for which the war had been fought in the first place and that threats against the integrity and independence of the 'representatives of the people' were a kind of tyranny no less mischievous than that of the king. But in 1647 the army not only had the guns; they also had ideologues—although they did not always share the same ideology—such as Ireton or Colonel Rainborough, who ventured to argue that parliament was in fact a 'decayed' body and that the army was a great deal more representative of the people than was the genteel body at

Westminster.

On 3 June the quarrel over sovereignty turned literal when a detachment of Fairfax's soldiers, led by Cornet George Joyce, seized the king himself from Holmby House in Northamptonshire. Two days earlier they had hijacked the bullion intended for their disbandment. In the same week Fairfax agreed to the establishment of an unprecedented institution, a General Council of the New Model Army to consist of both officers and elected men from each regiment. With money, force and the king in hand, the army could now literally call the shots. It began to demand the impeachment of Holles and ten other members of the Commons, including Sir Robert's son, Edward Harley, who resisted the redress of their grievances, in particular their arrears of pay, indemnity for conduct during the war and adequate pensions, all genuinely matters of life and death for the battle-hardened soldiers. The army also wanted the kind of religious regime dear to Cromwell, one that respected the independence of congregational preference rather than one that surrendered to Presbyterian enforcement.

There were no heroes (and perhaps no villains) in this sorry showdown. The summer of 1647 witnessed the peculiar spectacle of a professedly apolitical commander, Fairfax, leading (out of conscience for the welfare of his men) a highly politicized army prepared to impose religious liberty at the point of the sword. If that were not paradoxical enough, the men they hated, the parliamentary Presbyterians, were defending the right of the elected representatives of the nation to impose a Calvinist Church on England by virtue of their votes! Holles and his friends, including Edward Harley, the champions of parliamentary sovereignty against the army (as they had been against the king five years before), were prepared, if necessary, once more to use the pressure of the crowd (another tactic revived from 1642) to get *their* own way. Mobs were excited, 'monster petitions' drawn up. The London apprentices and soldiers who had already disbanded from armies other than the New Model mobilized for their protection. When, at the end of July, a vast and heavily armed demonstration forced both houses of parliament to support the Holles Presbyterian line, bloodshed seemed inevitable. MPs and peers on the losing side, including Manchester, escaped from London to Fairfax's camp and the Lord General began a march on London, making it clear that if the city did not open its gates he would blow them open. On 2 August the New Model Army was peacefully admitted. London—and by extension England—was now under the gun.

In its turn, the army now set out terms for settlement with the king in its Heads of the Proposals. Needless to say, Charles was delighted to be able to play one lot off against the other, especially as the army's conditions turned out to be a good deal more lenient than those currently on the table from parliament. Only four, not seventy-three, royalists were to be exempt from a general pardon. Parliament, called biennially, would exercise control over the armed forces for just ten, not twenty, years, and royalists could be eligible to return to local office after five years. Charles was now in the agreeable and unlooked-for position of watching a Dutch auction for his signature. He waited for the bids to go ever lower.

$$* \qquad * \qquad *$$

Amid the debris of the English state were survivors who were desperately trying to put the pieces of their lives back together and attempt to make some sense of what had happened to them, their beliefs and their country. For some, this was close to impossible. In 1647 Nehemiah Wallington's sister-in-law, Dorothy Rampaigne, the widow of Zachariah, came back to England to see what she could recover of her deceased husband's estate. But the Wallingtons were horrified to learn that since Zachariah's death Dorothy had taken an Irish Catholic as her lover and protector. This turned upside down everything the Wallingtons had ever believed. 'Oh, my sister,' moaned Nehemiah, 'my heart aches and trembles to consider of yoiur sad and miserable condition . . . in regard to your poor soul.' Dorothy had not only lain 'with that Irish rebel' and hidden her pregnancy but had carried on with her 'sins and wicked ways' with such shamelessness as to guarantee a terrible judgement from heaven. Nehemiah's wife, Grace, implored her sister to send her only remaining child by Zachariah, a boy called Charles, to London to be protected from the infections of the Antichrist and to be brought up in a proper godly household. For whatever reasons, Dorothy did, indeed, send Charles to the Wallingtons, where he was trained as an apprentice turner by Nehemiah, becoming a master himself in 1655.

Ralph Verney's life also changed in 1647–8 as dramatically and as painfully as the condition of

England. Although he had never been a royalist, his flight and continued absence in Blois had made him officially a 'delinquent', subject to the sequestration of his estates. In 1647, after much deliberation, he sent his capable wife Mary back to England to see if something could be done to recover them. He had hoped to use his connection with Lady Sussex, who had waxed so considerate at the time of his father's death, to advance his cause but she was now on her next aged husband, who turned out to be none other than the Puritan Earl of Warwick. Faced with the embarrassing reminder of her past in the shape of Mary Verney, Lady Warwick became suddenly hard of hearing to her propositions. Mary none the less persevered with the county committee and eventually 'Old Men's Wife', as Ralph and Mary called her in their private code, did her bit. In January 1648 the sequestration was lifted. But Mary paid a terrible price for her tireless efforts. Claydon itself, when she finally got to it, was miraculously still standing, though it had been used as a barracks for soldiers, and the rats and moths had munched their way through much of the furniture and hangings, especially, to Ralph's distress, the 'Turkie Worke' rugs. But their house's dilapidation was nothing compared to the personal tragedy that followed. Pregnant throughout her lobbying campaigns, Mary was finally delivered of a boy, whom she christened Ralph, only for him to die while still an infant. The same week she heard from her husband that their little daughter Peg had died as well. Ralph, though full of grief, wrote to his distraught wife bravely, in the stoical Christian manner: 'Tis true they are taken from us, (and thats theire happinesse); but wee shall goe to them, (and that should bee our comfort). And is it not much the better both for us and them, that wee should rather assend to heaven to partake of theire perpetuall blisse, than they descend to Earth to share with us our misfortunes?' But he was, in fact, unhinged by sorrow and told his nephew Dr Denton that he would leave France and travel somewhere—Italy or the 'barbary desert' where he could seek out his death. Once gone, he thought his widow and their remaining children would be free to start a new life unencumbered by the taint of his political past. The rescue of his estate, though, thanks to Mary, lifted his spirits out of the slough of despond, and after all their troubles the couple were reunited in Paris in the spring of 1648. They had two more years together in France before Mary's death from a lung disease. It was still not safe for Ralph to return, and he was obliged to ship her body back to Buckinghamshire in its coffin where it was buried before a little company of friends in Middle Claydon church.

An endgame began. In November 1647 Charles had escaped the custody of the New Model Army, but only as far as the Isle of Wight, where he was swiftly shut up in Carisbrooke Castle. It was, none the less, a kind of political liberty, since he was still allowed to entertain offers for his endorsement from the lowest bidder. They now included the Scots—not, of course, the purest of the Covenanters (who were appalled by the overture) but a critical element of the less zealous nobles, fearful that the formidable English army, which had neutered parliament, would target them next. A Scotland subjected to the New Model Army would be a Scotland in which a bedlam of sects would be unloosed. It was not to be thought of. The Scots also knew that in his troubles Charles was more popular than he had ever been at the height of his powers. So they came to the Isle of Wight and made him the best offer yet: a Presbyterian settlement for just three years in the first instance and a voluntary acknowledgement of the Covenant. Under the terms of this 'Engagement' (seen also as a way to end the Scottish civil war), the Scots army, together with a newly raised royalist army from northern England, would, if necessary, impose the settlement by force.

Charles, the Duke of Hamilton and royalist stalwarts like Sir Marmaduke Langdale, who had somehow survived Marston Moor and Naseby, could only imagine that they might well reverse the outcome of the first civil war, because since December 1647 whole regions of southern England and Wales had risen in revolt. Unfortunately, for those who wanted to turn a rebellion into a cohesive army, the cause for which they were in insurrection was not Charles (though he was extremely popular) but Father Christmas. Maypoles and the celebration of St George's Day and, of course, Charles's accession day, along with other heathen and seditious revels, had already been outlawed by the Presbyterian parliament. But Christmas—the longest festive celebration and the one arguably that everyone needed at the darkest time of year—was the major target for those bent on cleaning up the calendar and making the Lord's Sabbath on Sunday the only day of rest, and 5 November, the festival of redemption from papist despotism, the only permissible celebration. But to force shopkeepers to keep their businesses open on

Christmas Day was hard work for the constabulary, who were already busy ripping down the holly and ivy in towns like Bury St Edmunds and Ipswich, where the citizens festooned the streets in deliberate defiance. The greatest Christmas riots occurred in Kent and rapidly swelled into an all-out armed rebellion. The insurrection was bloodily put down, but 3000 of the rebels escaped over the Thames to Essex, where they held out against Fairfax for months on end behind the great Roman walls of Colchester.

The only real chance of a serious royalist revival, though, depended on the rest of Britain. And in the summer of 1648, the rest of Britain failed Charles. A rebellion in south and central Wales was smashed, leaving Cromwell to besiege Chepstow and Pembroke and mop up the resistance. While relatively charitable terms had previously been offered to those surrendering to besiegers, this second round of war had made iron enter Cromwell's soul, and he often let his soldiers do their worst. Having cleaned up Wales like some latter-day Edward I, he turned to the Scots and between 17 and 19 August 1648 annihilated them first at Preston and then at Winwick.

Although parliament in the spring of 1648 had passed a resolution continuing to declare that the government of England should still consist of king, lords and commons, Cromwell, and more particularly his increasingly militant son-in-law Henry Ireton, no longer really thought so. After the first civil war they had been prepared to buy into the fiction that Charles had been misled by 'men of blood'. And many of those surviving culprits were summarily tried and executed. But now there was nowhere else for blame to go. The chief sanguinary was Charles Stuart himself. In the previous year, the Leveller *Agreement of the People* had already spelled out the unmentionable: a kingless, bishopless Britain. As a demand from the army's rank and file it was not to be tolerated by such as Ireton, but now in the bitter aftermath of the second civil war they sought to make it their own. They had not come to this conclusion in any delirium of constitutional experiment, but rather with the intense pessimism with which parliament itself had concluded that Strafford had to go for 'reasons of the security of state'. If anything, Strafford had been much more blameless than Charles I. Ireton reasoned now that Charles's escape and the second civil war, not to mention the still unsubdued Irish Confederacy, ruled out ever considering another negotiated treaty with the king. He would never abide in good faith by its terms, nor fail to be a magnet for the disaffected, especially in such difficult times of soaring prices and plague. And perhaps more decisive than all of this, at least for Oliver Cromwell, was his infuriated conviction that Charles had defied the judgement of Providence, so clearly declared at Marston Moor and Naseby. Perhaps then (Cromwell still could not quite bring himself to this) the monarchy had to go. Whether Charles had to die was quite another matter. What, after all, was the point, when a whole club of healthy little Stuarts were standing in line in France and Holland as potential successors?

It was when the parliamentary Presbyterians realized that the trial of the king was now a distinct possibility that they hastened to pre-empt it. In September 1648 a deputation went to Newport on the Isle of Wight to talk to the king one last time. But Charles was himself now lost to a peculiar euphoria, both wily and holy. One day he would imagine that he could continue to exploit the deep differences between parliament and army, that one or the other would *need* him to prevail. And on the next day he would meditate on his coming martyrdom. His grandmother had felt and behaved in precisely the same way at Fotheringhay. But if Mary had been certain of her martyrdom, she died not quite knowing where the allegiance of her son James stood. Charles, on the other hand, had no such anxiety about the Prince of Wales. All those Van Dyck family portraits, it turned out, were in their way no more than the truth. The Stuarts were, whatever their many other character failings, a loving and loyal family. So Charles was increasingly prepared, even eager, to deliver himself to his fate, convinced that his death would wipe clean his transgressions and follies, excite popular revulsion and guarantee the throne for his son. 'The English nation are a sober people,' he wrote to the Prince of Wales, 'however at present under some infatuation.' He was sure that sooner or later they would recover from this unfortunate delirium. So why should he have any interest in baling out the Presbyterians by agreeing to terms that he had already turned down? He might even have privately enjoyed their transparent desperation.

On 16 November 1648 Fairfax, who had failed to persuade the king to sign a version of the army's 'Heads of the Proposals', was now more or less compelled to agree to a ferocious 'Remonstrance', largely written by Henry Ireton. It demanded the trial of the king and the abolition of the monarchy.

But none of this, by now, could have been much of a shock to Charles. At his most apparently impotent, there was a weird sense in which Charles was at last in control, if not of his immediate destiny, then of his posterity. His worst moment became his best moment, his execution his vindication. He must have taken satisfaction from the knowledge that everything that would be done to him could only be done by making a nonsense of the principles for which parliament had claimed to go to war: the protection of the liberties of the subject. It was but a small step now for Charles Stuart to claim that, all along, *he* and not they had been the shield of his subjects, the defender of the people.

And so it fell out. When Colonel Thomas Pride stood at the door of the Commons on 6 December with his sword-carrying heavies, stopping members who had voted for the Newport Treaty from entering and arresting others, he was violating precisely the parliamentary independence that the war had been fought to preserve. The truncated 'Rump' Parliament that resulted was more a mockery of the institution than anything the Stuarts had ever convened or dissolved. Of the original stalwart tribunes of the Long Parliament, only Oliver St John and Henry Vane the younger embraced the military *coup d'état* with any enthusiasm. The 'high court', packed and processed into compliance by manager Ireton, was more farcically arbitrary than any of the prerogative courts that the Long Parliament had abolished as the tools of despotism. It seems that Cromwell was, for a long time, painfully aware of these transparent manipulations of legality and deeply troubled by the prospect of a trial. As late as December 1648 he still referred to those who had 'carried on a design' to depose Charles as traitors. But at some point over the next few weeks he had decided that Providence was, after all, unmistakably demanding the punishment of the 'man of blood', the 'author' of the civil woes. A special high court of 135 commissioners was hand-picked, with a great deal of trouble taken to include a cross-section of the English notability—landowners, army officers and MPs. One commissioner who absented himself from the proceedings was Fairfax. When his name was called at the very beginning of the roll, it was answered by Lady Fairfax, sitting veiled in the public gallery: 'No, nor will he be here; he has more wit than to be here.' Oliver St John likewise decided against making an appearance. Certain precautions had to be taken. The presiding judge, John Bradshaw, wore a hat with a special metal lining 'to ward off blows', and the prisoner was kept well away from the public galleries.

Anyone with even a passing acquaintance with the history of the previous century might have known that it was a bad idea to put members of the house of Stuart on trial. Exacting and nimble displays of legal punctiliousness, followed by a dignified preparation for martyrdom, were their forte. Charles had been brought from Windsor to Westminster, where he dined and lodged as 'Charles Stuart', without any of the service and courtesies due to a sovereign. It was as though legally he were dead already. But there were formalities to go through. On 20 January, beneath Richard II's great hammerbeam roof in

Westminster Hall, the short figure in the black hat and grey beard, his face drawn and haggard, was told by the lawyer John Cook that he was being arraigned for his chief and prime responsibility for 'all the treasons, murders, ravages, burnings, spoils, desolations, damages and mischiefs to this nation'. Asked to plead, he refused, demanding instead to know by 'what power I am called hither . . . I would know by what Authority, I mean, lawful; [for] there are many unlawful Authorities in the world, Theeves and Robbers by the high ways . . . Remember I am your King, your lawful King, and what sins you bring on your heads, and the Judgement of God upon this Land, think well upon it . . . before you go further from one sin to a greater.'

Denying the court its show trial, complete with witnesses, Charles, without his habitual stammer, reiterated his refusal to acknowledge the competence of its jurisdiction. When he reappeared on 22 January he was hoping to read the text of a written explanation of his reasons for refusing to plead, insisting that as king he could not be held accountable to any earthly judges and that nothing lawful could possibly be derived from a body that had removed one part of its indivisible law-making sovereignty. The only possible claim to such jurisdiction was through the revolutionary utterance, already made by the Rump Parliament when it asserted on 4 January that 'the people are, under God, the source of all just power'. Charles, not hesitating to expose the coercion behind the fig leaf, protested that it was common knowledge that this parliament's claim to represent the people was belied by the detention and exclusion of many of its representatives. Here was Charles Stuart in effect making the claim that he, and not the army or a fraudulent parliament, was the true guardian of the welfare and freedom of the people. That, of course, was what his most articulate and disinterested champions, like Edward Hyde, had wanted him to say all along. Needless to say, the impresarios of the trial were not going to allow Charles to say these things out loud. He was silenced before getting very far with his statement and after much protest taken away from the court. The following day the same exchange ended when Bradshaw admonished Charles that he was 'notwithstanding you will not understand it . . . before a Court of Justice'.

'I see I am before a power,' was Charles's accurately laconic response. For the remainder of the proceedings the court merely sat as a committee eventually passing judgement on 27 January and sentencing him to be 'put to death, by the severing his Head from his Body'. The following day Charles was brought back to hear his fate. When he asked to be heard again, he was about to be denied when one of the commissioners, John Downes, protested that Charles ought to be allowed to speak, drawing from Cromwell an intimidating rebuke—'What ails thee?' When he heard himself condemned as a 'tyrant, traitor and murderer, a public and implacable enemy to the Commonwealth of England', Charles allowed himself a last, droll chuckle. Once again he asked to speak and once again was denied on the not unreasonable grounds that he 'had not owned us as a court'. He was taken away protesting, 'I am not suffered to speak. Expect what Justice other people will have.' A bare fifty-nine members of the court signed the death warrant, Cromwell and Ireton prominent among them.

Elizabeth I had wanted Mary Stuart's execution to be carried out in the utmost secrecy, away from the public gaze. Cromwell and Ireton were convinced that as many people as possible should see Charles beheaded, both to dissuade any attempts at rescue and to do God's work without the slightest tremor of shame or hesitation. So a scaffold was erected in Whitehall and a huge throng gathered on the cold morning of 30 January. Charles was walked up the back stairs of Inigo Jones's Banqueting House through the great hall where he and Henrietta Maria had danced in royal masques celebrating their loving communion with Britannia and with each other. The Palladian windows of the palace had long been boarded up, so that Rubens' great paintings in the ceiling overhead could hardly have been visible to the little king as he stepped through the room and out through an opened window on to the platform, where death awaited. But up there none the less were the great painted jubilations of Stuart power and wisdom: Peace clasping Prosperity; the protection of Mercury and Minerva; the enraptured union of the crowns embodied in embracing putti. This insistent, unreal vision of a happy, united Britain, this compulsion to bring together those ill-matched partners, Scotland and England, was what had sustained the Stuarts and what (not for the last time) had ruined them.

Perfectly composed and dressed in two shirts, lest shivering be mistaken for fear, Charles noticed that the block was extremely low to the wooden platform and asked if it might not be raised a little. Apparently it could not, no reason being given. And at last he was allowed to give his speech, written out on a paper that he opened on the scaffold. 'I never did begin a War with the two Houses of Parliament, and I call God to witness, to whom I must shortly make an account, That I never did intend for to incroach upon their Privileges, they began upon me.' Then followed an instant history lecture, his much delayed, personal response to the Grand Remonstrance of 1642. But it was not Edward Hyde's thought-out political theory of a constitutional monarchy so much as an expression of personal sorrow and anger. Charles remained indignant that the power of the militia had been taken from him and deeply remorseful for his collusion in the unjust death of Strafford for which God was now properly punishing him. He ended by declaring that 'For the People . . . truly I desire their Liberty and Freedom as much as any body whomsoever; but I must tell you, That their Liberty and Freedom consist in having of Government, those Laws, by which their Life and their Goods may be most their own. It is not for having share in Government (Sir) that is nothing pertaining to them. A Subject and a Soveraign are clean different things.'

No one had ever accused Charles I of pandering to the public. From beginning to end, through all the tactical twists and turns of his short-sighted but not ignoble career, he had remained utterly constant in his belief in the divinity of his appointment. The celestial hosannas of Rubens' pictures were for the likes of him and him alone. 'I go from a corruptible to an incorruptible Crown;

where no disturbance can be, no disturbance in the world,' he said, in that deep, quiet voice. Stray hairs tucked back into his white cap, he lay down before the low block, and the executioner, Richard Brandon, cut through his neck with a single blow.

Cromwell had given notice that he would 'cut his head off with the Crown on it'. But the famous 'groan by the thousands then present' that greeted the king's head as it dropped into the bloody basket and was then held aloft by Brandon could not have been very reassuring. For the person of the monarchy had already proved to be separable from the institution. In his last days, while yielding nothing of the highness of his sovereignty, Charles had managed, despite all the attempts to gag him, to assert a teaching that he would have done better to have learned seven years before: that armed power could not remake the broken legitimacy of the English, much less the Scottish, state. The point was well taken. But if anything had been learned from the tragic experience of the reign of Charles I, it was that henceforth the mere assertion of a divinely appointed right to rule would not suffice for political peace. It would only be when a monarch of both England and Scotland would manage to square the circle, and see that the authority of the Crown might actually be strengthened not compromised by parliamentary partnership, that the violent pendulum swings of the English and Scots polities would find their equipoise. That is what the notoriously anachronistic, Whiggish and self-congratulatory Victorians believed, at any rate. And, as a matter of fact, they were right.

214

CHAPTER THREE

LOOKING FOR LEVIATHAN

For the forthright and the adamant, it was time to begin again; to bleach the country of the stains of the past. 'Whatever our Fore-fathers were,' declared Henry Marten in parliament, 'or whatever they did or suffered or were enforced to yeeld unto, we are the men of the present age and ought to be absolutely free from all kinds of exorbitancie, molestation or Arbitrary Power.' All over the country in the early months of 1649, acts of obliteration, big and little, got under way. Young Isaac Archer, living near Colchester, had been spending time innocently gluing pieces of decorative silk to prints, when his father, William, 'with a knife, I know not why, cutt out the picture'. The picture was of Charles I. In the weeks after the king's execution, the remnant of the purged parliament lopped off its own head by abolishing the House of Lords as 'useless and dangerous'. The monarchy itself followed the peerage into the trash, denounced as 'unnecessary, burdensome, and dangerous to the liberty, safety and publick interest of the people'. The Great Seal, which gave acts of parliament the force of law and which bore the likeness of the monarch, was defaced and replaced by the stamp of the House of Commons, bearing the optimistic inscription 'In the First Year of Freedom by God's blessing restored 1648'. Writs, which had formerly required acts to be carried out in the name of the king, were now issued in 'the name of the Keepers of the Liberty of England'.

So there was a 'Commonwealth'. But what was that—an absence or a presence? Official bravura papered over popular uncertainty and confusion as to where, exactly, sovereignty now lay. There was no shortage of suggestions, of course. 'At that time,' wrote Lucy Hutchinson, the wife of a staunchly Puritan soldier, 'every man allmost was fancying forms of government.' The problem was who was to judge between them. To look for arbitration was to stare at a void.

As it happens, voids were a topic of compulsive fascination among philosophers, both natural and political. Learned disputes raged over whether vacuums could occur at all in nature; and if they did, whether they indicated utter vacancy, or the presence of a mysteriously 'subtle matter', albeit invisible and indeterminate. In 1644 the Italian physicist Evangelista Torricelli had performed the famous experiment which set off the debate. Torricelli took a glass tube, sealed at one end, filled it with mercury and then put it upside down into a basin, also filled with mercury. He had made, in effect, a primitive barometer. Atmospheric pressure pushed the mercury up the tube, but not all the way. Between the top of the mercury level and the sealed end of the tube was a space. But what was inside that space: a something or a nothing? This was what divided 'vacuists' from 'plenists', those for whom a vacuum was a possibility in nature and those for whom the *horror vacui* was a paramount truth.

The philosopher Thomas Hobbes was a plenist, someone for whom a vacuum was as abhorrent in the government of the state as in the operations of nature. When Charles I was executed in January 1649, Hobbes was living in Paris, debating the mystery of the Torricellian gap with French philosophers like Marin Mersenne, and writing, among other works, his answer to the dilemma posed by the vacuum of sovereignty. Published two years later, in 1651, his *Leviathan* would be profoundly shocking to the royalists who had confidently assumed Hobbes to be one of their own, for it seemed to counsel submission, indeed *unconditional* submission, to the self-appointed powers which had rushed into the space left by the dead king. Worse, in that same year, Hobbes acted on his convictions by returning to England, now governed by parliament and Council of State, both filled with unrepentant regicides. For someone thought to have owed everything he had—station, employment, security—to royalist families like the Cavendishes, this was unforgivable apostasy.

Hobbes, the son of a Wiltshire parson and the nephew of a prosperous glover who had given him the means to be educated at Oxford, had subsequently been tutor to the future second Earl of Devonshire, William Cavendish. No sooner had he come into his own than he proceeded to squander it, to the detriment of his old tutor who, according to his friend John Aubrey (the nonpareil of seventeenth-century gossips), wore out his shoes and caught colds from wet feet going 'up and downe to borrow money'. But after the second earl died in 1628, Hobbes continued to collect monies for the Devonshires, extracting the forced loan of 1628 and billeting soldiers in the homes of loan refusers. In 1640 he had stood, unsuccessfully, for parliament from Derby, as a loyal champion of royal prerogative and the personal rule. Perhaps, though, his defeat in the polls made Hobbes (who prided himself on the clarity of his prescience) see the writing on the wall. For he took himself off to exile in Paris well before the war began. His patrons the Cavendishes duly lost battles and fortunes and then trooped to Paris themselves to join the court in exile. Still in favour, Hobbes became mathematics tutor to the Prince of Wales and to his prematurely dissipated companion, the second Duke of Buckingham. Geometry, which for Hobbes was one of the few uncontestable realities in the universe, bored both his charges. According to Aubrey, Buckingham relieved the tedium of his instruction by languidly masturbating, while Charles thought his tutor 'the oddest fellow he ever met with'.

The publication of *Leviathan* would certainly not have made the prince any less bemused. Apart from supplying arguments for accepting the outcome of the civil war, it also seemed to attack institutional Christianity with such withering scepticism that in court circles Hobbes was deemed little better than an atheist. 'It was below the education of Mr. Hobbes,' complained Edward Hyde, who had enjoyed his company in the circle of Viscount Falkland at Great Tew, '& a very ungenerous and vile thing to publish his *Leviathan* with so much malice and acrimony against the Church of England when it was scarce struggling in its own ruins.'

Hobbes was a materialist, a rationalist, and not really a Christian in the sense of subscribing to gospels full of miracles and sacred apparitions. But he certainly believed in some sort of deity to whom alone otherwise absolute sovereigns had to render account. If for nothing else, Hobbes's God was needed to keep Leviathan honest. And he was certainly unequivocal in his condemnation of the rebellion against the king. His later history of the civil war, *Behemoth* (1679), begins with an imaginary view from the Devil's mountain, of 'all kind of Injustice, and of all kinds of Folly that the world could afford'. But in 1650 he believed that moral anathema was no help at all in answering the paramount questions for everyone caught in the sovereignty vacuum. It was all very well to follow the lament 'the king is dead' with the shout 'long live the king' if you happened to be in Paris, since that was indeed where the new king could be found. But suppose you were stuck in Wiltshire? Then the questions that preyed on you were not about propriety but self-preservation. To pretend otherwise was self-deluding humbug. Simple but inescapable anxieties forced themselves on any rational person. What will become of me and mine? Who should be obeyed? On whom can we depend for our elementary needs of safety? Who will stop differences of opinion and differences of religion—for, argued Hobbes, there will always be such differences, incapable of adjudication—from becoming causes for endless, murderous war? Who will stop soldiers from burning dwellings, stealing animals and assaulting the defenceless? Who will enforce contracts—the very touchstone of justice? Who would allow us to sleep quietly in our beds? And how may such a protector be known: by faith or by reason?

They are the terrors of orphaned children who

219

had seen their father-ruler killed in front of them; who, in counties ravaged by war, had seen familiar adjudicators—bishops and priests—effaced from the landscape of authority. Those anxieties would not be put to rest with the return of the bishops and the judges when Charles II was restored to his throne in 1660 and received his old maths tutor once more at court. For the Restoration closed, but it did not heal, the puncture wounds with which the civil war had pierced the body politic. Beneath the skin there was still traumatized tissue, which could be made raw and bloody again by collisions with misfortune. Plague, fire, defeat and paranoia would shake the confidence of the English in the protective authority of the throne and would make allegiance once more arguable, contingent. Forty years after the Great Seal of the beheaded king was defaced, his son James would drop it into the Thames in an act of perverse self-destruction. The political barometer would feel the pressure of altered atmosphere. The mercury of liberty would rise. A vacancy at the top would be declared.

The cure for fearfulness, Hobbes thought, was the frank acknowledgement that it was the natural and universal condition of man. Hobbes knew all about fear. According to John Aubrey, the philosopher claimed that he had been born prematurely in 1588 as the result of his mother taking fright at the prospect of the Spanish Armada. Terror of the unknown, 'feare of power invisible . . . imagined from tales publiquely allowed', Hobbes daringly claimed, was the source of most if not all religious experience. Pious fictions—like miracles, revelations or the existence of the soul itself—which could neither be proved nor disproved, might be a consolation for the anxious, but they were of no use in helping men escape the pitiless war of all against all, which was their lot in a state of nature. The only true asylum from anarchy lay in the surrender of liberty to an omnipotent sovereign—the Leviathan —in whom all individuals would be subsumed. What, after all, was the point of clinging to the freedom of mutual self-destruction? Neither sanctity, nor tradition, nor moral pedigree could confer on a government the authority to claim obedience. If Leviathan offered safety and justice, if Leviathan could keep disputes over beliefs from becoming acts of violence, then Leviathan was legitimate.

If this was not an atheistic answer, it was a shockingly amoral and impious one. And it was an affront to royalists because, in the aftermath of the death of Charles I, all they had was piety. Hobbes mocked 'immaterial' things. But for the devoutly loyal, the immaterial presence of the king was their solace and their hope, and they clung with desperate consolation to any and every purported relic that came their way: to little pieces of brown cloth said to be stained with the blood of the royal martyr; to the ribbon-bound locks of hair sworn to have come from the decapitated head. Above all they hung on the every last word of Charles, collected in the *Eikon Basilike*, the book of his meditations. Despite the attempts of the Commonwealth to suppress it, 'The King's Book' was an immediate publishing sensation. No fewer than thirty-five editions (plus an extra twenty-five for unvanquished Ireland) appeared in 1649 alone, the first just a week after the beheading. In March 1649 an especially popular expanded edition, complete with the king's prayers and his speech on the scaffold, was made available. Charles's posthumous campaign of persuasion was perhaps the most successful he ever waged. Dead, he seemed more ubiquitous and materially present in England, Scotland and Ireland than he had ever been when he was alive. And this was exactly what Charles had intended. For although the editorial genius behind his book was the clergyman Dr John Gauden, Charles had taken enormous pains to present himself (like his grandmother Mary) as a martyr for the Church (in this case the Church of England).

The *Eikon Basilike* was designed as the king's spiritual legacy, the gospel according to St Charles, in sure and pious hope of the resurrection of the monarchy. Complicated (but to contemporaries intelligible) Christian symbolism dominated the frontispiece designed by William Marshall, engraved by Wenceslaus Hollar and obviously in tune with the king's presentation of his posterity. Its themes were consolatory: comfort for the bereft, steadfastness in turmoil, light in the darkness. Palm trees—the trees thought never to die and thus the ancient emblems of the resurrection—continue to grow, even under the weight of royal virtue, while the rock of faith (also an emblem of the true Church) remains immovable in the storm-tossed sea. The grace bestowed on the king-martyr was represented as an illumination, the reception of light. Out of the murky skies a shaft of sublime light strikes the head of the kneeling king and imbues him with vision. Blessed with celestial sight he is able, as his parting words promise, to leave his corruptible, earthly crown at his feet and behold his reward, the heavenly crown of glory, radiant with stars.

By the end of the first year of the Commonwealth, 'The King's Book' was everywhere, showing up like an irrepressible phantom, even in miniature editions designed for concealment. Its undeniable popularity disconcerted the stewards of the new state whose own sense of legitimacy depended on their conviction that it was they who represented the 'honest' and 'godly' kind of people. Apparently there were more of their countrymen enslaved to the old despotism than they had anticipated. Royalist newspapers like John Crouch's scabrous weekly *The Man in the Moon* 'shone its light' on the devilish Commonwealth, while the Man's dog, Towzer, shamelessly lifted his leg on proclamations of the Rump Parliament. Something had to be done to counter these scandalous influences. So John Milton, already established as a dedicated propagandist for parliament, was mobilized to enlighten the deluded. Milton was fast losing his own sight. His greatest works—*Paradise Lost* and *Samson Agonistes*—would be the masterpieces of his long years of blindness and defeat. He had published a volume of poetry in 1645 and thought of prose writing as merely 'the work of my left hand'. But he also thought of himself in the classical tradition of virtuous republicans such as Cicero who had laid aside 'idle' pursuits to place their eloquence at the service of the state. With his own vision dimming, Milton would none the less be the physician of the 'blind afflictions' of the common people, the kind of myopia that made them hanker, sentimentally, for the late,

223

unregretted tyrant.

So in February 1649, in the midst of the royalist hagiography, Milton published the essay that brought him to the attention of the beleaguered leaders of the Commonwealth, not least Oliver Cromwell, for whom Milton made no secret of his ardent admiration. *The Tenure of Kings and Magistrates* went unerringly to the vacuum-anxiety, attacking the parliamentarians who had become queasy or even indignant at the king's trial and punishment, beginning to 'swerve and almost shiver ... as if they were newly enter'd into a great sin ... when the Commonwealth nigh perishes for want of deeds in substance, don with just and faithfull expedition'. Why, if they now flinched from its proper and legal outcome, had they embarked on the resistance against the king in the first place? Could they not see that by resorting to arms, the king had unilaterally torn up the contract with his subjects: the bedrock on which his authority rested. When he had raised his standard at Nottingham he had dethroned himself. God and parliament had merely affirmed that fall from grace by his defeat. For Milton there *was* no vacuum of authority to lose sleep over. It had always been lodged in the sovereign people whose conditionally appointed executive the king had been. Once stripped of that shared and limited power, Charles Stuart had to be judged for his crimes like any other felon. To accept his assertion that only God could judge him was a dangerous absurdity, since it put in question his earthly accountability for *any* laws or treaties he signed or promises he forswore (including his coronation oaths).

Historically, this was entirely back to front. The

224

war had begun in 1642 not to remove Charles but to constrain him. The 'people' had not existed as a party to the conflict except through their representatives in parliament. But everything had changed in the brutal second civil war, the war of 1648, which had indeed turned into a life-or-death struggle, at least to Cromwell, who treated Milton's publication like the job application it more or less was. The poet duly became secretary of foreign tongues to the Council, responsible for translating Latin and European documents into English and vice versa. So it was as a dependable attack propagandist that, in October 1649, Milton took his polemical sledgehammer to the *Eikon Basilike*. His *Eikonoklastes*, 'The Image Breaker' (1649), took the carefully manufactured image of sanctity apart, extracting from the book the passages he thought most fraudulently self-serving. But chopping up 'The King's Book' proved untidier work than chopping up the king, and not much more popular. Milton later confessed that this was a job he had been told to do, which may account for the hectoring manner of its tone and style, alternating between needling, posthumous interrogations (as if Milton regretted not having sat himself on the court which had judged Charles) and bursts of epic denunciation. To Charles's famous comments in the House of Commons that 'the birds have flown', Milton added images which turned the king into a carrion carnivore feeding off the carcasses of the free: 'If some Vultur in the Mountains could have open'd his beak intelligibly and spoke, what fitter words could he have utter'd at the loss of his prey?'

Milton's invective may have been more persuasive than his political theory. For his daringly advanced argument, that the authority of governments was based on popular consent and that they were at all times beholden to, and limited by, the will of the sovereign people, left wide open the problem of how the people were supposed to exercise their rediscovered majesty and in whom they could safely put their trust? Parliament, of course, ought to have been the answer. But to many among the traditional governing class—even those who had fought under its flag—the purged, single-chamber assembly of 1649, that came to be known derisively as 'the Rump', bore no resemblance at all to the representative institution that had taken to the field in defence of the nation's liberties in 1642. Those who had been 'excluded' in 1648 for their known opposition to the trial of the king never regarded the Rump and its executive Council of State as anything more than an illegitimate usurping power.

Attacks on the presumption of the Rump Parliament and its councillors to fill the void left by the defunct monarchy came from those who thought it was not nearly bold enough, as well as from those who questioned its audacity. For the hottest Protestants, free to speak their minds in the void left by bishopless England, the only proper successor to King Charles was King Jesus. Prophecies abounded that a new millennium was at hand, and that the destruction of Antichrist and the coming of the Last Days were imminent. Combing through the books of Daniel and Revelation, the most fervent declared that the Four Monarchies—of Egypt, Persia, Greece and Rome—would now be succeeded by a Fifth: the reign of the godly, the visible saints. To those gripped by this ecstatic fervour, the execution of the king had not just been a political act but a sign from God that he had indeed chosen England as his appointed instrument for a universal redemption. And the freshly sanctified country would look like no other realm, for its mighty would be laid low and its humble raised up. Under the rule of the saints 'no creature comfort, no outward blessing' would be denied.

For the Fifth Monarchists and a multitude of other equally fervent sects, the emptiness left by the dethroned king was not a void at all but the antechamber to glory. Their preachers and prophets said so in the streets and to rapt congregations of apprentices and artisans. But the message resonated with special force in the army where sabres had been honed by the fire of sermons. The army remained, as it had been since 1647, the dominant institution in the country, for although royalism had been defeated in England, it was very much alive elsewhere in the islands. On learning the news of Charles's execution, the Presbyterian regime in Scotland had immediately declared his son King Charles II of England and Scotland. In Ireland, not only had the Catholic confederacy not been defeated, it was now reinforced by the explicitly royalist army of the Duke of Ormonde. And since over the past decade the outcome of power struggles in England had been determined by events in Scotland and Ireland, it was impossible for the military to let its guard down and be lulled into a fool's peace.

So England remained an armed camp, a place of troopers and horses and armourers and arsenals; an occupied country in all but name, where law might as easily be delivered on the point of a sword as in the magistrates' court. It was an army, moreover, which had changed almost out of all recognition in the course of a decade. The officer corps, especially at the junior level, was younger, less traditionally educated, drawn from lower down the social scale and passionately religious. Since something like 70 per cent of artisans—shoemakers, weavers, coopers, tanners and so on—could read, the rank and file had a political awareness of its destiny and that of the country, and of their own part in shaping it, that was absolutely new in England. In the autumn of 1647, each regiment had elected two Agitators to represent it at the army Council and they had the audacity to debate with Cromwell and Ireton at Putney on the future of the country's political and social institutions. Their grievances with parliament over arrears of pay and pensions had likely been in part inspired by Leveller writers and orators like John Lilburne, Richard Overton and William Walwyn into a crusade to transform England into something which, if not quite a representative democracy, was none the less shockingly radical by seventeenth-century standards. Under the Leveller proposals, the franchise would go to all male householders over the age of twenty-one. Parliaments would be annual and members debarred from sitting consecutive terms. Tithes supporting the clergy and excise taxes on food would be abolished, and the law would be simplified and made accessible to the whole people.

As far as Lilburne and his fellow-Levellers were concerned, they were not asking for the moon, just the 'free-born' natural rights which Anglo-Saxons

228

had apparently enjoyed before being crushed beneath the Norman yoke, rights which had only been partly restored by Magna Carta. Twenty to thirty per cent of adult males in England in fact *already* had the vote, and once the categories that the Levellers continued to exclude (servants, apprentices and paupers) were subtracted they could reasonably argue that they were merely extending to the rest of the country what was already *de facto* household suffrage in towns like Cambridge and Exeter. For the most part, Walwyn, Overton and Lilburne were at pains to distance themselves from any imputation of social egalitarianism. The label of 'Leveller' had originally been a hostile accusation. When they called their newspaper *The Moderate* there was no irony intended. They believed in rank, they insisted. They believed in orderly government.

All the same, they could hardly avoid the impression that they were radicals since it was unquestionably true. If they did not want to see a great social levelling, they did want some sort of attention to the just complaints of the poor. The Levellers were trying to make more fortunate citizens see that these starvelings were not the armies of travelling beggars that haunted the imaginations of constables and magistrates, and which could be whipped out of sight and out of mind. The new poor were often settled folk— agricultural labourers and artisans, or even tenant farmers—who had been distressed or made destitute by the disruptions of the war, their fields burned and their carts and animals requisitioned (in other words stolen) for the troops. The abolition of the tithe was meant to help the tenant farmers, but the Levellers also wanted the Commonwealth government to initiate some sort of sustained programme of relief for the needy rather than abandon them to the Elizabethan poor laws. Even more daringly, they argued that those immediately above pauperdom should be considered active members of political society. At the Putney Debates the naval officer and MP Colonel Thomas Rainborough declared that 'The poorest he that is in England hath a life to live as the greatest he,' and insisted that no man should have to live under laws to which he had not personally given his own express consent.

This was an argument of genuinely revolutionary boldness and it appalled the officers whom Lilburne assailed as the 'grandees' of the army—Ireton, Fairfax and Cromwell. They came to believe that the Levellers and their allies in the army were hell-bent on subverting both the godly discipline of the troops and, for that matter, the entire social and political order. Against Rainborough's literal interpretation of the sovereignty of the people, Ireton argued the sovereignty of property: 'no person hath a right to an interest or share in the disposing of the affairs of the kingdom . . . that hath not a permanent fixed interest . . . and those persons together are properly the represented of this kingdom.' In other words, a man's estate counted when it came to the vote. A parliament stuffed with lawyers, moreover, was unlikely to feel warmly about the Levellers' proposals to democratize the law. Oliver Cromwell's own attitude to the importance of social rank was best summed up in his later dictum: 'A nobleman, a gentleman, a yeoman. That is a good interest of the nation and a great one.'

Bitter enemies though they became, Oliver Cromwell and John Lilburne none the less shared a history. Lilburne, who like Cromwell came from a family of county gentry, was always one of those restless souls, easier to recognize in the nineteenth than the seventeenth century, who seem destined to be outsiders. In his twenties he had been arrested for circulating pamphlets attacking Laud and the bishops, and his savage sentence in 1637 had been one of the *causes célèbres* which helped make the Star Chamber notorious. Lilburne had been flogged through the streets of London from the Fleet to Palace Yard, then set in the pillory (from which he continued to harangue the crowds) and finally incarcerated in the Tower of London for more than two years in conditions of brutal deprivation and restraint. It had been Cromwell, in fact, who had brought Lilburne's plight to the attention of the Long Parliament and got his release. Commissioned as a captain in the regiment of Lord Brooke, Lilburne was captured by Prince Rupert's soldiers in the rout at Brentford and was subjected to an exemplary trial for high treason at Oxford. Had not parliament made it clear it would exact retribution on its own royalist prisoners, he would have been executed then and there. For the bravery of his demeanour during the trial the Earl of Essex offered Lilburne £300, a sum his chronically indebted family could hardly afford to turn down. But, of course, Lilburne did just that, announcing he would 'rather fight for eightpence a day until the liberties and peace of England was settled'. As an officer in the Eastern Association he would certainly have encountered Cromwell, and

231

he made no secret of sharing Oliver's dim view of the Earl of Manchester's capacity for command. Shot through the arm at Wakefield, repeatedly robbed and plundered and seldom paid, Lilburne was in a sorry enough plight in 1645 for Cromwell to write to the Commons recommending he receive the special pension he had been voted on account of his treatment by the Star Chamber, but which had failed to materialize.

This, however, was as far as their comradeship went. Cromwell raised no objection to Lilburne's imprisonment twice in 1646, first in Newgate, then in the Tower where he was committed by the House of Lords for accusing the peers of, among other things, 'Tyranny, Usurpation, Perjury, Injustice and Breach of Trust in them reposed'. It didn't help that when Lilburne appeared before the Lords, he refused to take off his hat, which was taken (as intended) as a refusal to acknowledge their right to try a 'freeborn Englishman'. In Newgate he barricaded himself in his cell and stuck his fingers in his ears to avoid hearing the charges against him. It was two more years before Lilburne was finally released. But nothing, not even being deprived of writing materials, seemed to be able to gag him as pamphlet after pamphlet somehow issued from the Tower and into the streets, apprentice shops, garrisons and Baptist churches. During 1647 the Levellers began to mobilize mass petitions, often delivered by noisy crowds wearing the Leveller token of a sea-green ribbon in their hats. Cromwell was in no doubt at all that Leveller agitations, with their demands for direct political representation, were undermining military discipline. After the high command had forbidden a 'general rendezvous' of the army, two regiments none the less showed up at Corkbush Fields near Ware in Hertfordshire to hear the Leveller Agitators, carrying their literature. The papers and green ribbons were ripped from their hats, the meeting broken up at sword point, and one mutineer shot.

The Levellers were not yet finished as a threat to the 'grandees'. Through the second civil war *The Moderate* continued to voice the programme set out the year before in their 'Agreement of the People', as well as to point fingers at backsliders and adventurers in parliament. (Astonishingly, some of the Leveller chiefs even began to make contact with the king in hopes of persuading him to become a patron of their household democracy.) After Charles's defeat Ireton grafted some of their principal demands—the abolition of the House of Lords and the monarchy, and annual parliaments —on to his own official proposals for republican government. But by the beginning of 1649 Overton, Lilburne and Walwyn were convinced that the Commonwealth had been delivered into the hands of an oligarchy every bit as rapacious, self-serving and heedless of the needs of the masses as the one it had replaced. Lilburne's snarling rebuke to the House of Lords in 1646 held just as well for the Rump Commons three years later: 'All you intended when you set us a-fighting was merely to unhorse and dismount our old riders and tyrants, that so you might get up and ride in their stead.'

Lilburne detested everything about the new regime. He had been against the execution of the king and had refused to support his trial on the grounds that it violated all the principles of equity encoded in the common law. Even Charles Stuart he believed was entitled to the same benefits of Magna Carta as Freeborn John, including the right to trial by jury. When three of the captured royalist commanders—the Scots Duke of Hamilton, Lord Holland and Lord Arthur Capel —were awaiting trial in the Tower (they would be beheaded shortly after the king in front of the parliament house), Lilburne sent them law books for their own defence. The response of the Leveller leaders to a formal ban on political discussions in the army was a two-part pamphlet called *England's New Chains*, which at the very least put in question any kind of obedience to a regime they condemned as illegitimate. On 28 March 1649 Lilburne, Overton and Walwyn, together with a fourth colleague Thomas Prince, were arrested and dragged before the Council of State. There (according to Lilburne), both they and the councillors were treated to a fist-pounding eruption of rage by Oliver Cromwell:

> I tell you . . . you have no other way to deal with these men but to break them or they will break you; yea, and bring all the guilt of the blood and treasure shed and spent in this kingdom upon your heads and shoulders, and frustrate and make void all that work that, with so many years' industry, toil and pains, you have done, and so render you to all rational men in the world as the most contemptible generation of silly, low-spirited men in the earth . . . I tell you again, you are necessitated to break them.

Not surprisingly, then, the Levellers who refused

to acknowledge the authority of the Council were packed off to the Tower. But then something quite astonishing—and to the hardened grandees of the army incomprehensible—happened. A petitioning campaign for their release immediately broke out in London, mobilized by Leveller women. In 1646 Lilburne had already gone against the grain of virtually every household manual (a Puritan speciality) by insisting, and in print, that women 'were by nature all equall and alike in power, dignity, authority and majesty [to men]'. Leveller women had always been directly involved in the movement's campaigns. Elizabeth Lilburne had been politicized through her early efforts to spring her reckless spouse from one prison or another, moving from the expected tear-stained pleas to unexpected assertions of the rights of man and woman. Mary Overton seems to have been, from the beginning, a radical at heart. For printing and distributing her husband's tracts, she had been brutally punished, dragged through the London streets by a cart, as she was holding her six-month-old infant, while being pelted and abused like a common whore. But the most articulate and impassioned of the sisters was the charismatic preacher-turned-Leveller Katherine Chidley, who tried to make the Commonwealth understand the particular sufferings of their sex and to institute poor relief for their assistance:

Considering that we have an equal share and interest with men in the Commonwealth and it cannot be laid waste (as it now is) and not we be the greatest and most helpless sufferers therein; and considering that poverty, misery and

235

famine, like a mighty torrent is breaking in upon us . . . and we are not able to see our children hang upon us, and cry out for bread, and not have wherewithal to feed them, we had rather die than see that day.

The outrageous temerity of women giving voice to these grievances was profoundly shocking to mainstream Puritan culture, devoted as it was to an especially draconian hierarchy of the sexes in which the woman's role was that of obedient, quietly devoted helpmate. When Elizabeth Lilburne and Katherine Chidley, at the head of a mass demonstration of women, presumed to petition parliament for the release of the Leveller leaders, they met with a predictably dusty response: 'The matter you petition about is of a higher concernment than you understand, the House have an answer to your Husbands and therefore you are desired to go home and looke after your own businesse, and meddle with your huswifery.'

But the Leveller women did not go home. Instead they made sure that the *Manifestation,* published from the Tower under the names of all the imprisoned Levellers, was widely distributed in London. Its quasi-theological touches—comparisons between the sufferings endured by the Levellers and those inflicted on Christ and his disciples—suggest the authorship of William Walwyn, the grandson of a bishop. But the *Manifestation* was less of a treatise and more an explanation to the obtuse of why, after so much persecution, deprivation and frustration, they had no choice but to persevere, whatever further ordeals might come their way. In its

236

determination and bleak pathos, the *Manifestation* is a vocational manifesto of an unmistakably modern profession: the revolutionary calling.

> 'Tis a very great unhappinesse we well know, to be always strugling and striving in the world, and does wholly keep us from the enjoyment of those contentments our severall Conditions reach unto: So that if we should consult only with our selves, and regard only our own ease, Wee should never enterpose as we have done, in behalfe of the Common-wealth: But when so much has been done for recovery of our Liberties, and seeing God hath so blest that which . . . has been desired, but could never be atained, of making this a truly happy and wholly Free Nation; We think our selves bound by the greatest obligations that may be, to prevent the neglect of this opportunity, and to hinder as much as lyes in us, that the bloud which has been shed be not spilt like water upon the ground, nor that after the abundant Calamities, which have overspread all quarters of the Land, the change be onely Notionall, Nominall, Circumstantiall, whilst the reall Burdens, Grievances, and Bondages, be continued, even when the Monarchy is changed into a Republike.

All the same, the four denied that they were 'impatient and over-violent in our motions for the Publick Good', hoping to achieve their ends through another 'Agreement of the Free People', which they proceeded to publish from their 'causelesse captivity' on 1 May 1649. The document was serious and not impractical: a legislature of 400 chosen 'according to naturall right' by all males over twenty-one years old, other than paupers, royalists and servants. Neither military forces nor taxes could be raised without its consent, but the limits of that parliament's power were spelled out as forcefully as its jurisdiction. It was not to infringe freedom of conscience; it was not to coerce anyone into the military, nor to create any kind of legal procedures not provided for in the common law. It was neither to limit trade, nor to impose capital punishments or mutilations for anything other than murder and certainly not for 'trivial offences'. No one, except Catholics who insisted on papal supremacy, was to be disqualified from office on account of their religion. Judged by what was thought politically acceptable, in the Commonwealth, this *'(third and final) Agreement of the [Free] People'* was a non-starter. But this did not mean that the kind of assumptions and arguments made by the Levellers should be thought of as utopian (hence their desperation to mark out clear differences from Gerrard Winstanley's 'Diggers', who preached community of land and goods). Leveller principles would have a future, in fact, and not just in America.

But the soldiers who continued to read Lilburne, Overton and Walwyn (and who knows, perhaps Katherine Chidley too) could not wait around for the future. In April a mutiny over pay in London turned into a mass demonstration at the funeral of one of the executed mutineers. In mid-May, another mutiny broke out among some troops passing through the garrison stationed in the staunchly Puritan town of Banbury in Oxfordshire. Two more regiments mutinied near Salisbury and attempted (but failed) to join the Oxfordshire rebels. On 13 May, Cromwell and Fairfax marched a pursuit force 50 miles in a single day, catching the mutineers in the middle of the night at Burford on the edge of the Cotswolds. Seven or eight hundred fled, but 400 were captured of whom four were sentenced to be shot and three were. The next day, Cromwell went off to receive an honorary degree in law from Oxford University. Ringing Leveller statements continued to be published from Bristol before the heavy hand of the army came crashing down again. There was nothing to connect Lilburne directly with the mutiny, but he did his best to remedy that by publishing *An Impeachment of High Treason against Oliver Cromwell and Henry Ireton* in August. In October, though, it was Lilburne who was tried for treason at the Guildhall in the City of London, where he played brilliantly to the gallery by insisting that the jury alone was empowered to issue a verdict and the judges merely 'cyphers' of the people's will. It duly acquitted him and Lilburne was freed without conditions, the other three in the Tower following, provided they subscribed to the oath of engagement which the Commonwealth now required of all its citizens. Walwyn, Overton and Prince agreed, but everyone from Cromwell down knew better than to ask John Lilburne.

By the autumn of 1649 it was clear that, whatever else was going to fill the space left by the monarchy, it was not going to be the visionary Commonwealth of the Levellers. Bought off, intimidated or imprisoned, their officers dispersed;

the rank and file of regiments thought unreliable were shipped off to Ireland where they could vent their fervour and frustration on the benighted rebels. Their leaders eventually went their separate ways. The philosophical Walwyn became an amateur authority on matters medical, John Wildman made a packet from speculating in confiscated royalist property, Overton went to France, while Lilburne took up sundry social causes and grievances before being banished for life in 1651. In exile in the Netherlands, he attempted to make sense of what had happened by reading deeply in the classical literature of Roman republicanism: Livy and Sallust. But the texts only seemed to confirm for him the gloomy likelihood of oligarchy or tyranny. Returning to England in 1653 he published again, was imprisoned again and eventually ended up a Quaker.

Leveller fire transmuted into Quaker light is less startling than it might seem, for any number of former political zealots faced with the ferocity of the republic's repression turned to religion in their search for truth and deliverance. And this spiritual migration was not just a matter of consolation for thwarted populists. If Levelling had failed, it had to be because God had willed it so, wanting the brethren to turn aside from the 'carnal' world and look elsewhere for salvation. Elsewhere meant, first and foremost, within themselves, in the recesses of their being, which had been overlaid by carnal things: appetites, words, ambitions. Buried beneath all that worldly muck were the spotless hearts and souls of the children they remained in their innermost spirit and which, once released from the bondage of the carnal world, could be opened to receive the light of God's grace.

The first apostles of this personal redemption were utterly convinced, even when locked up in the stinking darkness of a dungeon, that they were walking in the time of light. God had willed the terrible wars, not for carnal alterations—a parliament, a republic—but so that the institutions of false authority should fall away. Away had gone bishops. Away had gone presbyteries. What was left was freedom—the precious freedom for them to find their way. In Rome 1650 may have been the Jubilee year, and Pope Innocent X was erecting his own column of light, the obelisk, in the Piazza Navona. But it was an age of miracles for the seekers after grace. For while the Commonwealth and the generals were adamant about the monopoly of armed force and the control of expressly political opinions, they were (especially Cromwell) equally insistent on freedom of conscience for any sect or confession (other than Catholics, naturally) who caused no threat to the public peace. Just what constituted such a threat, of course, was often left to the judgement of local magistrates whose threshold of outrage was often much lower than Cromwell's, as the Quakers in particular were to discover. But this brief period of benign neglect produced the most fertile proliferation of spiritual enthusiasms since (or for that matter before) the Reformation. Some were organized, like the Baptists, into Churches, but others were frequently no more than cult followings gathered around the personality of charismatic preachers like Abiezer Coppe or the Ranter Laurence Clarkson.

From group to group they differed wildly on,

for example, the status of Scripture (some of the Ranters and Quakers thought it no more than an historical document) or the importance of baptism and church marriage (which the Quakers rejected along with any other outward sign of communion). But what they all had in common was an intense aversion to any kind of formal ecclesiastical authority or institutional discipline. Calvinism's dogma of predestination, with its irreversible separation of the elect and the damned, they rejected out of hand as utterly inconsistent with God's love, which could be received by any who opened themselves truly to his grace. The most extreme of their number, such as Laurence Clarkson, taught that, since God was perfect, the idea of sin, and the shame which went with it, must have been a human invention, and to the scandal of other Christians went about conspicuously testing their theory by living openly with a series of concubines. The disregard for formal authority, pushed to its logical extreme and professed by Quakers as well as Ranters, was that God lived in each and every one, and was simply waiting to take possession of the transformed believer.

Separated from the fraudulent and redundant authority of the clergy, salvation could now be a free, voluntary act by anyone old enough to know what she or he was doing (hence the Baptists' refusal to countenance infant baptism). The mere idea of a parish was an arbitrary geographical absurdity, a jurisdictional convenience masquerading as a Church. Why should all the people who happened to live within the same bounded area be supposed, by that fact alone, to be brethren or sisters in Christ? Church buildings themselves the

Quakers ridiculed as 'steeple houses', mere piles of stones built for carnal admiration and which had to be broken up, in spirit if not in fact, before the enslaved flocks could be converted into Children of Light.

The sects satisfied two quite different visions of the imperfect alteration of the state from kingdom to Commonwealth and pointed a way ahead in two quite separate directions. For Fifth Monarchists like John Rogers, Vavasor Powell and Major-General Thomas Harrison, their noses buried in scriptural prophecy, the new, last age had dawned with the beheading of the king. So they were under an obligation not to turn their back on the state but to convert it to the rule of the Saints, and so be in a position to prepare the Commonwealth for the consummation of prophecy. Their soldiers, magistrates and preachers had to infiltrate, not abandon, the public world, the better to bend it to God's command.

For the Quakers and those who thought like them, this obstinate attachment to carnal affairs was only compounding the problem. Polities were, by their very nature, incapable of spiritual transformation, and hence should simply be shunned, the better to concentrate on what counted—the alteration of individual personalities to fit them for the admission of light. Self-assertion, the quality that made men leaders, had to give way to self-nullification.

Their lives, then, became journeys towards sweet nothingness, which began, necessarily, with an uprooting from familiar habits. When he was barely nineteen, George Fox, a Puritan weaver's son, began his wanderings away from his home in

Drayton-in-the-Clay in Leicestershire (much to his father's displeasure). It was 1643 and Fox walked through a landscape torn apart by the war, plodding patiently in his grey leather coat along roads travelled by troopers and munitions wagons. In the garrison town of Newport Pagnell on the Bedfordshire/Buckinghamshire border, he watched Sir Samuel Luke's soldiers rip out statues from the churches and smash them in the streets. And he listened to the ex-tailor and army captain Paul Hobson sermonize the troops, denouncing the vanity of 'steeple houses' and insisting that a church was but a gathered body of believers. Two years later, while Fox was roaming the orchards in Leicestershire, he began to experience the 'openings' which exposed him to illumination. By 1649 he was now ready to begin his wanderings in earnest. It helped that he had a modest inheritance from which he could supply his even more modest wants on the road. In Derbyshire villages populated by hungry lead miners, for whom neither king nor parliament had done much, he preached against tithes and approached potential converts, unbidden, to attempt a 'convincement'. More perilously, he began to disrupt Presbyterian lectures, shouting of the woe to come and the awaiting light.

Soon, Fox was planning his interventions to provoke the maximum attention and became, to the Presbyterians especially, first a nuisance and then an intolerable menace. For his fearless temerity Fox spent months at a time in prison, in the filthiest of conditions. But (just as with Lilburne) his confinement only enhanced his reputation and did nothing at all to quiet him. In fact he began to get attentive visitors. In Derby, where he was sentenced to a six-month spell in 1650, a jailer asked if he might share his cell for a night to listen to Fox's instruction. Irrepressible, Fox moved north to Lancashire and Yorkshire, gathering converts not just from the poor but also from the propertied classes—the wonderfully named high sheriff of Nottingham, John Reckless, and Margaret Fell, the pious wife of a Lancashire JP, both of whom opened their houses to Fox to use as an asylum and recruiting headquarters. At Wakefield he brought in the ex-weaver and New Model Army quartermaster James Nayler, who was already a gifted preacher and would be for Fox both a blessing and a curse.

The quaking began. Although he used them freely enough to attack 'sprinkling' and 'steeple houses', Fox taught his flock to despise and mistrust words; reason was the enemy of the light. When suffused by it, the 'Children of the Light', as they called themselves, felt a great trembling of the earth as if it was opening like their own souls, and they themselves began to shake and sway and sometimes sing for joy. The community they felt in this state of grace was important, for it insulated them, up to a point, from the very real perils and penalties they faced from the carnal world. For without question the Commonwealth, and the Protectorate after it, felt threatened by the Quakers, notwithstanding their continual protestations of indifference to politics and loyalty to the powers that be. They were somehow deeply offensive. They refused to doff their hats or to be quiet in church. Indeed, they came to church specifically to make an ungodly noise. Fox was punched in York

Minster, and in Tickhill, Yorkshire, he was smacked in the face with a Bible, dragged from the church and tossed over a hedge. He was sat in stocks, pilloried, repeatedly arrested and jailed, despite a modicum of protection from John Bradshaw, president of the court that had tried Charles, a Councillor of State and a friend of Margaret's husband Thomas Fell.

Yet he remained indomitable. In the spring of 1652 Fox climbed to the top of Pendle Hill, on the border between west Yorkshire and Lancashire, and beheld, if not the Promised Land, then the green Ribble valley stretching west to the Irish Sea, a whole country waiting to be gathered. 'I was moved', he wrote, 'to sound the day of the Lord.' He bathed in the Light.

As far as Thomas Hobbes was concerned light was just a 'fancy of the mind caused by motion in the brain'. Like everything else in the human world, it was not mystery but matter and capable of explanation by sound reasoning. At the same time that Fox was in the throes of his illuminations, *Leviathan* appeared, its premise being that matters of religion ought to be shunted off into the realm of metaphysical speculation where they belonged. Politics and government could only be decided by hard-headed, unflinching logic. Moral distaste was neither here nor there. Reason demanded submission to whatever sovereign had the capacity of providing peace and law.

When he got back to England in the spring of 1651, Hobbes discovered that, for all the shouting and prating, there were others who thought very much like himself when it came to the criteria of allegiance. One of them was Marchamont Nedham, the most prolific and ingenious of the parliamentary journalists, whose *Mercurius Britannicus* jousted with its royalist rival *Mercurius Aulicus*. For a brief spell in the late 1640s, Nedham had switched sides. But once the war was over, he reverted to the Commonwealth and was its leading propagandist. Not only did Nedham now subscribe readily to the official 'Engagement' that the Commonwealth required of all its citizens, he was prepared to develop a public position which might be used to reconcile the countless thousands of royalists in England to accepting the *de facto* power of the Rump Parliament and its government. Nedham started from the same premise as Hobbes: that the paramount reason to institute any government and to accept subjection to it was its power to offer protection to subjects, otherwise prey to anarchy. Nedham's argument, reinforced by Hobbes, replaced the question 'Is it proper?' with the question 'Does it work?' And with that apparently simple change in perspective, for better or worse, modern political science was born.

*　　　*　　　*

So was Oliver Cromwell Leviathan, the 'artificial man' in whom all men were combined in one indisputable, unarguable sovereign? Later, when he was Lord Protector, his steward John Maidstone described his appearance as though it was indeed a one-man national monument: 'his head so shaped, as you might see it a storehouse and shop . . . a vast treasury of natural parts'. But however slavish the sycophancy, it's to Cromwell's credit that he never quite seemed to fall for it. Nor is there any serious evidence that, from the beginning of the Commonwealth, Cromwell aimed at any sort of personal supremacy, regal or otherwise. Though those who came to hate him, like Edmund Ludlow, believed that his repeated declarations of aversion to high office were hypocritical, masking a monomaniacal ambition, there is good reason to believe them sincere. Cromwell certainly showed some of the symptoms of absolutism—colossal self-righteousness, haughty intolerance, a frighteningly low threshold of rage, a coarse instinct for bullying his way past any opposition. But he also lacked the one essential characteristic for true dictatorship: a hunger to accumulate power for its own sake. For Cromwell, the exercise of power was a necessary chore, not a pleasure. And it was not undertaken for personal gratification. Whatever his many failings, vanity was not one of them. He saw the warts clearly and without extenuation, and they were not merely on his face. Throughout his life as a public figure, Cromwell believed himself to be no more than the weak and imperfect instrument through which an almighty Providence worked its will on the history of Britain. Often he sounded like the stammering Moses, drafted by an insistent Almighty into business he would rather leave to someone else.

But there was, as he wrote to Oliver St John in 1648, no shirking the call: 'The Lord spake thus unto me with a strong hand and instructed me.' Cromwell, then, believed he worked for God. Real dictators believe they are God. It was those who fancied themselves little gods, from Charles I to the republican oligarchs of the Rump like Henry Marten and Sir Arthur Haselrig, who most aroused

Cromwell's contempt. He mistrusted power-seekers and personal empire-builders and constantly questioned their motives, including his own. 'Simplicity' was a word he used repeatedly of himself and his conduct, and it was the highest of moral compliments. Better, always, to be thought naïve than wickedly sophisticated. If he was no manipulator, then nor was Cromwell (unlike Ireton) much of an ideologist of the new Britain. Arguably, the survival of the republic was jeopardized by his complete indifference to creating anything like a true commonwealth culture to replace that of the defunct royal regime. In the last analysis Cromwell was not that far from Fox (whom he found both fascinating and repellent) in believing in the ultimate triviality of 'carnal' forms of government. They were all, he said, following St Paul, 'dross and dung in comparison of Christ'. This spiritual loftiness was personally admirable, but it was also politically fatal to the perpetuation of the Republic. To prolong itself, the Protectorate needed Cromwell to be more of a Leviathan, more of a ruthless sovereign, than he could ever manage to stomach. This is both his exoneration and his failure.

Though he is an obligatory fixture in the pantheon of heroes, along with Caesar, Napoleon and all the usual darlings of destiny, the wonder of Oliver Cromwell is that for so much of his life he showed absolutely no inkling of what awaited him, nor any precocious impatience to be recognized as exceptional. For the greater part of his fifty-nine years he toiled away in dim mid-Anglian obscurity, amid the cabbage fields, very much the provincial country gentleman-farmer. For most of his career

249

the man who was to become the arbiter of power in Britain was breathtakingly innocent of it. Likewise, the greatest general of his age was completely unschooled and unpractised in the arts of war. Cromwell was not, then, someone who instinctively knew that he was fated to ascend. On the contrary, he thought of himself as a casualty of a triple fall—social, political and spiritual. His rise was the ungainly clambering of a man making his way up the forbidding stone face of Purgatory.

Socially, Cromwell spent most of his early life on the narrow edge of respectability rather than embedded comfortably within it, for he was the son of a second son. He was tantalizingly close to real fortune. His grandfather, Sir Henry, had been sheriff of both Huntingdonshire and Cambridgeshire, a member of the Elizabethan parliament and opulent enough in his entertainments at least to be called 'the Golden Knight' by the Queen. His oldest son (also called Oliver) also managed to cut a stylish figure both at court and in East Anglia: a herald at the funeral of James I; married into Dutch and Genoese banking money. All of which made the much more modest circumstances of Oliver's father, Robert, glaringly uncomfortable. Uncle Oliver's money was needed to keep the modest estate afloat and to send young Oliver (the only surviving boy in a family of seven children) to the Inns of Court in London. There, however, he made what seemed to be his saving fortune by marrying Elizabeth Bourchier, a wealthy London fur-trader's daughter. He seemed very much on his way up. With a legal education and some funds in hand he was elected to the parliament of 1628 which saw the dramatic struggle over the Petition of Right.

But there was no sign, in that momentous year, that Oliver Cromwell was anything but a silent back-bencher while the debates over prerogative and the common law were thundering around him. All that is known of his presence amid the political furore was that the royal physician, Sir Theodore Mayerne, treated Cromwell for severe depression —*valde melancholicus*—a condition that would often revisit him. (In fact, his wild mood swings— from bursts of disconcerting laughter while praising the Lord for a particularly comprehensive annihilation of the enemy, to his descents into scowling gloom—suggest the classic symptoms of clinical depression.)

Whatever the cause, around 1629–30 Cromwell's fortunes seem to have collapsed. By 1631 his circumstances had become so parlous that he was forced to sell almost all of his land and transplant himself to St Ives in Huntingdonshire. There he farmed about 17 acres, not as the squire of the manor but as a yeoman tenant, leasing holdings from Cambridge colleges and working the land alongside his hired hands. Cromwell's social descent and his experience of rural toil in these years gave him a closeness to the speech and habits of ordinary people which became a priceless asset when he translated it into the charisma of military command. He never lost the soft East Anglian burr in his voice, and when he spoke about the 'plain russet-coated captains', the 'honest' men he wanted at the core of his army, Cromwell knew exactly what and whom he was talking about. Before his fall from genteel ease, he had also been on the losing end of a bitter local political dispute in Huntingdon when the royal government had changed the borough charter. Cromwell was among the local gentry discomfited by the changes and, for the first but not the last time, let the vainglorious winners feel the rough edge of his tongue. One of his adversaries complained about the 'disgraceful and unseemly speeches' he made against the mayor and recorder of Huntingdon, which were aggressive enough to get him reported to the Privy Council.

De profundis, politically marginalized, socially demoted, submerged below sea-level in the sodden Fens, Cromwell was suddenly reborn. It was this conversion experience, so he believed (rather than a timely inheritance from a bachelor uncle), which started him on the road to redemption. A justly famous letter to his cousin, the wife of Oliver St John, written later in 1638, but recalling his redemption, is a classic of Pauline-Calvinist reawakening: 'Oh, I lived in and loved darkness, and hated the light. I was a chief, the chief of sinners. This is true; I hated godliness, yet God had mercy on me. O the riches of His mercy!'

His political election—to the Short and then the Long Parliament in 1640 as member for Cambridge—was less important than his spiritual election to stand forth and do God's bidding. Or rather, political life for Oliver Cromwell *was* a spiritual office. Whatever accountability he might nominally have to his electors or to the king was as nothing compared to his accountability before God. Although he had become a man of some substance again, living in Ely, Cromwell still thought of himself as a marginal man in the world of the grandees. His distance from and deep scepticism of oligarchs and aristocrats, even those who professed proper parliamentary opinions,

252

gave him the unwavering resolution they often lacked. While he was deeply committed (and would always be) to the prevailing social order, he did not believe it would be subverted by a forthright challenge to the king's presumptions. On the contrary, only by resisting those presumptions, the corrupt arrogance of a court, could this ancient and essentially benevolent English hierarchy be securely preserved. Unlike many, in and out of the parliaments of 1640–2, Cromwell was not afraid of a fight, always provided that it was for a godly cause. He was convinced, much earlier than most, that a great struggle between the forces of righteousness and unrighteousness was inevitable and that to pretend otherwise was false comfort. By knowing that it would be so Cromwell made it so, becoming the most vocal member of the Commons to demand that the authority to appoint Lords-Lieutenant and to muster militia be transferred from the king to parliament. As far as Cromwell was concerned, the war did not begin with the raising of the royal standard in Nottingham but much earlier, in the Irish rebellion behind which he saw the bloody hand of Stuart machination. Putting the country 'into a posture of defence', he urged, with a clarity which Hobbes would have grudgingly admired, was no more than an act of timely self-preservation.

So where others dithered and hesitated, Oliver Cromwell acted. Having raised a troop of sixty horse in Cambridgeshire, he used it to seize Cambridge Castle for the parliament and to stop the removal of college and university plate to the king's war chest. Dead straight-ahead decisiveness was to be the hallmark of Cromwell's spectacular career during the war itself (in such contrast to his later indecisiveness in the world of pure politics). He had no time for those whom he suspected—first Denzil Holles, then the Earl of Manchester—who fought, always with an eye to negotiation rather than to total victory, or for those like Essex who he thought shrank from engagement. Equivocation was unworthy of the helmeted Jehovah who he knew fought on his side. Inside the hymn-singing, pocket Bible-carrying New Model Army, Cromwell turned Gideon: the leader of a godly troop. He played it for all it was worth, helping John Dillingham, editor of *The Parliament Scout,* to drum up the Cromwellian reputation as a general in his newsbook, because he undoubtedly believed that he had been designated by the Lord of Hosts to lead his captains and corporals. And Cromwell also understood that the rank-and-file soldiers would respond better to an officer who never betrayed any doubts about the rightness of the cause or the certainty of eventual victory. This spiritual armour-plating did not make Cromwell any less of an intelligent tactician, for all his lack of military experience or training. What he brought to Marston Moor and Naseby (and learned from the failure at Edgehill) was a cavalry strong enough to take the impact of an enemy charge and flexible enough to regroup for a counter-offensive to which an undeployed reserve could be added for additional force. He was also blessed with the one quality without which all paper planning would be useless: an infallible sense of timing. Cromwell could 'read' a battle, right through the din and the choking smoke and the chaos, and have an uncanny sense of how to react to its ebb and flow. This did not mean, however, that he sat at a distance surveying the carnage with his perspective glass. On the contrary, he was usually to be found in the thick of it, leading charges, urging on pikemen and dragoons, risking (and sometimes taking) a wound but always surviving. His personal bravery and steely composure in the heat of battle won the trust of men who were being asked to put themselves in harm's way. How could they not believe in a general who never lost? (Even the indecisive second battle of Newbury was at worst an unsatisfying draw.) With every fresh victory, Cromwell's soldiers had proof that they were themselves protected by the general's close relations with Providence. Faith that his soldiers were truly doing God's work was not the same, though, as assuming that the army rather than parliament should dictate the political fate of the nation.

The two Cromwells—the socially conservative believer in the ancient constitution and the zealous evangelical reformer—were still at odds within his own personality. Despite the presence of true Puritans like Sir Robert Harley in the parliament, Cromwell, like Ireton, was unsure of its commitment to godly reformation. But the thought of imposing a settlement at sword point on parliament still made him uneasy, right through the crisis of the summer and autumn of 1647. A regime of generals, however pious, was not what he had fought for. A year later, though, many of these reservations had fallen away in the ferocity of the second civil war. Presbyterianism no longer seemed the vanguard, but the rearguard, of the pure. Its parliamentary champions such as Holles seemed frightened by true liberty of conscience and even prepared, like the Scots, to make a cheap bargain with the king to secure the interests of their own narrow Church. They had 'withdrawn their shoulder from the Lord's work through fleshly reasonings', he wrote. So even though he let Ireton do the hatchet work and disingenuously remained at a distance from Colonel Pride's Purge, Cromwell was no longer a devout believer in the sacrosanct untouchability of the Long Parliament. He was already the sceptic of the mask of legalism. 'If nothing should be done but what is according to the law,' he would say before yet another of the purges he sponsored (that of the second Protectorate parliament), 'the throat of the nation may be cut while we send for some to make a law.' This is the rationalization of all *coups d'état*.

When Cromwell joined the republic's Council of State in 1649, however, he never imagined he was presiding over the conversion of a parliamentary state into a military-theocratic dictatorship. It was merely the old parliament, riddled with equivocation and bad faith, that had needed to be got rid of. And when on 15 March he accepted the command of the expedition to suppress the Irish revolt Cromwell did so, in his own mind, as the servant rather than the master of the 'Keepers of the Nation's Liberties', as the Rump styled itself. Even as 'Lord-Lieutenant' Cromwell was still, in theory at least, subordinate to the commander-in-chief of the Commonwealth armies, Fairfax. All the issues of titles and authority, which seemed to exercise many people, were for Cromwell beside the point. 'I would not have the army now so much look at considerations that are personal,' he told the Council of State, 'whether or no we shall go if such a Commander or such a Commander go and make that any part of our measure or foundation: but let us go if God go.' He was clear in his own mind that, unless Ireland was subjugated, it would always remain the springboard of an invasion of England: perhaps even half of a pincer movement, with the other thrust coming from Scotland where Charles II had been declared king. So while the innocent might think 1649 a time to sit back and settle the Commonwealth, for Cromwell it was still very much a pressing wartime emergency.

But emergency or not, what Oliver Cromwell then perpetrated in Ireland in the autumn of 1649 has been remembered as one of the most infamous atrocities in the entirety of British history, an enormity so monstrous that it has shadowed the possibility of Anglo-Irish co-existence ever since. Unquestionably, events of appalling cruelty took place at Drogheda and Wexford. But exactly what happened, and to whom, has for centuries been clouded with misunderstanding. Only recently have Irish historians like Tom Reilly, a native son of Drogheda, had the courage and scholarly integrity to get the story right. Getting it right, moreover, is not in any sense exoneration or extenuation. It is explanation.

The first thing to get right is just who the victims at Drogheda were. The vast majority were neither Catholic nor Gaelic Irish, nor were any of them unarmed civilians, the women and children of Father Murphy's largely mythical history published in 1883. For in the first instance Cromwell was being sent by the Council of State and the Rump Parliament to confront not the Catholic

Confederates who had risen in 1641, but a royalist, largely Protestant army led by the Duke of Ormonde, which for many years, until the execution of the king, had been fighting against, not alongside, the rebels led by Owen Roe O'Neill. Drogheda, from the beginning a staunchly loyalist Old English town, had in fact defied the siege of Phelim O'Neill's insurgent army in 1641. At the time, then, when Cromwell and thirty-five of his fleet of 130 ships, carrying 12,000 troops, set sail from Milford Haven, there were no fewer than four distinct armies in Ireland: the Gaelic-Irish forces of the Confederacy, dominated by Owen Roe O'Neill and Cardinal Rinuccini; the royalist army of Ormonde; the Scots-Presbyterian army in Ulster of General Monro, which had been pro-parliament but since the proclamation of Charles II in Scotland was now potentially another enemy of the English; and finally the English parliamentary forces commanded by Lieutenant-Colonel Michael Jones. It's quite true that a negotiated truce between the royalist army and the Irish-Catholic Confederation had simplified this military quadrille for Cromwell, but as much as he heartily detested Roman Catholicism and believed that the Irish rebellion was a Trojan Horse, not just for the Stuarts but for Rome and even Spain (he was to his marrow an Elizabethan in this respect), he also identified the immediate and most formidable enemy in Ireland not as Irish Catholic but as royalist. If he was about to be merciless in his onslaught it was because he had been equally implacable in his prosecution of the evidently unfinished second civil war.

Cromwell made no secret of his contempt for

the native Irish population. In common with many of his Puritan contemporaries, he believed the pornographic exaggerations of the atrocity propaganda by which most Englishmen got news of the rebellion of 1641: all those impaled Presbyterian babies and mutilated patriarchs in Ulster and Leinster. 'You, unprovoked,' he wrote to the Irish bishops in 1650, 'put the English to the most unheard-of and most barbarous massacre (without respect of sex and age) that ever the sun beheld.' There's also no doubt that his credulous belief in the bestiality of the Irish hardened him against any suffering that might be inflicted on the native population as a result of the campaign. But this did not turn him to genocide. Soldiers, not civilians, were the targets of his fury. In fact, and in keeping with his practice in past campaigns in England, Cromwell went out of his way, publicly, to threaten retribution against any of his troops found assaulting the unarmed and unresisting population. Before the siege of Drogheda ever got under way, two of his men were hanged expressly for violating that prohibition. Nor did Cromwell have any particular relish for the inevitable bloodshed. It was precisely because he might have anticipated General Sherman's dictum that 'war is hell' that he resolved to wage it with maximum ferocity, the better to shorten its duration.

Whenever there was a chance of intimidating a defending stronghold into capitulation without loss of life, Cromwell did whatever he could to make that happen. At Drogheda, commanding the main road between Dublin and Ulster, he believed there was just such a chance, since the commander, the royalist veteran (and one of its few Catholics) Sir

Arthur Aston, was hopelessly outnumbered, not least in the heavy artillery department where Cromwell could bring massive siege mortars to bear on any attack. In an attempt to obtain Aston's peaceful surrender on the morning of 10 September Cromwell delivered a chilling ultimatum to him:

> Sir, having brought the army belonging to the parliament of England before this place, to reduce it to obedience, to the end the effusion of blood may be prevented, I thought fit to summon you to deliver the same into my hands to their use. If this be refused you will have no cause to blame me. I expect your answer and rest, your servant, O. Cromwell.

Aston, of course, summarily rejected the ultimatum. The experience of the long-drawn-out siege of 1641–2 and the apparently imposing walls of Drogheda made him believe that the town could hold out against the first shock of Cromwell's assault, at least long enough for him to be relieved by troops supplied by Ormonde. As it turned out, he was tragically deluded twice over. Drogheda's walls did not hold, and on the day of the attack Ormonde's troops were nowhere in sight, though he had sent a small number of reinforcements to the garrison the day before. It took Cromwell's guns no more than a few hours to blast breaches in the outer walls, but longer for his infantry to penetrate those breaches, furiously defended by royalist soldiers among whom was young Edmund Verney, Ralph's brother. The gaps choked with wounded and dying, Cromwell himself led a third and decisive charge into the breach. The defenders fell back into a flimsily defended stockade area on Mill Mount, while some of them retreated to the tower and steeple of the Protestant Church of St Peter.

What then happened was not unprecedented in the appalling history of seventeenth-century warfare, and especially not in the Irish wars. The Scottish-Presbyterian General Monro massacred 3000 at Island Magee. After the battle of Knockanauss in 1647 Colonel Michael Jones had 600 prisoners killed in cold blood and deserters from his own side (including his own nephew) hanged. But it was, all the same, an obscenity. Cromwell's own account of what he did is startlingly unapologetic and without any kind of procrastination or euphemism: 'our men getting up to them (Aston and his men on Mill Mount), were ordered by me to put them all to the sword. And indeed, being in the heat of action, I forbade them to spare any that were in arms in the town, and, I think, that night they put to the sword about 2000 men.' At least 3000 royalist soldiers were massacred in Drogheda, the vast majority not as they were frantically fighting the parliamentary troops, but when they had all but given up and were either surrendered or disarmed. The refusal of quarter to unresisting, defeated men was a calculated slaughter. At St Peter's Church, Cromwell had his soldiers burn the pews beneath the steeple to smoke out the defenders who had taken refuge in the tower, with the result that many fell to their deaths in flames along with the bells and masonry which came crashing down. The murders were so inhuman that it seems certain that not all of Cromwell's officers could bring themselves to obey his orders and that some actually went out of their way to save their enemies.

This atrocity inflicted on soldiers, few of whom were either Irish or Catholic, is surely sufficiently unforgivable to indict Cromwell, without any additional need to subscribe to the fiction that he deliberately or even passively extended the massacre to civilians. As Reilly correctly points out, the stories of women and children raped and mutilated, derive in their entirety from non eye-witnesses, virtually all of them either passionate royalists (like the antiquarian Anthony Wood), who published the stories during the Restoration witch-hunts against republicans, or compilers of accounts at least one or two centuries after the fact. Wood's brother Thomas, who had fought for the royalists in England, then switched sides to parliament, then reversed his allegiance again in the Restoration, was notorious for his buffooning and indulgence in tall tales, and, obviously anxious to exonerate himself, was the source of many of the juiciest stories. His version of Drogheda, repeated by Wood, supplied the story of Aston being beaten to death with his own wooden leg (though he was certainly robbed by his killers of gold worn on a belt around his body), and that of the mysterious martyred 'virgin' (how would they know in the heat of battle?) arrayed in her finest jewels and finery, who was stabbed in the 'belly or fundament' by marauding troopers. None of this apocrypha is needed to make the case for the prosecution. The most damning witness against Cromwell is Cromwell, who makes no bones about his deliberate intention to perpetrate a slaughter so

262

ghastly that it would dissuade other strongholds from making Drogheda's mistake and refusing peaceful capitulation.

The strategy of terror worked. In many other places along his march—New Ross, for example—the fate of Drogheda did indeed guarantee a bloodless surrender. Even at Wexford, where the defending troops and civilian inhabitants, unlike those at Drogheda, were Catholic and holding the town for the Irish Confederacy, and where there was another terrible slaughter, the military governor had not in fact refused to capitulate before the violence began on 11 October. Although he had, as usual, made it unequivocally clear what would happen were his ultimatum refused, Cromwell promised the governor, Colonel Sinnott, that should there be a surrender he would let the soldiers and non-commissioned officers depart peacefully, once they had undertaken not to take up arms again, and make the officers prisoners. 'And as for the inhabitants, I shall engage myself that no violence shall be offered to their goods, and that I shall protect the town from plunder.' Sinnott never got this note. While negotiations were still under way firing broke out, and in no time at all the parliamentary troops were inside the city killing as many of the other side as they possibly could. Once again it's no mitigation of the horror to realize that civilians were not among the masses of dead at Wexford. The most tragic and numerous civilian deaths occurred when there was a panicky rush for the boats moored at the quayside. Overloaded, they inevitably capsized, drowning people. At least 2000 perished—300 by drowning—at Wexford that day, including priests (some of whom, understandably, may have been armed) as well as soldiers.

Cromwell is unlikely to have shed tears for the fate of the Fathers. He made no secret of the fact that he did not regard the priesthood as innocent bystanders to the conflict, but as conspiring agents of the forces of Antichrist. When the Catholic prelates of Ireland accused him, at the end of 1649, of deliberately aiming to 'extirpate' their religion from the country, Cromwell responded, in January 1650, with a lengthy, thunderous denunciation which exposed in the most extraordinary way the intensity of his passions and prejudices and his selective, Protestant version of Anglo-Irish history:

> You say your union is against a common enemy . . . I will give you some wormwood to bite on, by which it will appear God is not with you. Who is it that created this common enemy? I suppose you mean Englishmen. The English! Remember ye Hypocrites, Ireland was once united to England; Englishmen had good Inheritances, which many of them purchased with their money; they or their Ancestors from many of you and your Ancestors . . . They lived Peaceably honestly amongst you. . . . You broke this union!

It was the clergy, he asserted, who were responsible for deluding the poor common people in the snares of their theological fraud, while reaping the benefits of wealth and rank. Cromwell bluntly owned up to his refusal neither to tolerate the saying of the Mass 'nor suffer you that are Papists: where I can find you seducing the People, or by any overt act violating the Lawes established'. Catholics in Ireland, in other words, were to be treated just as harshly as, but no worse than, Catholics in England. As far as private practice was concerned, they were to be left alone: 'As for the People, what thoughts they have in matters of Religion in their owne breasts I cannot reach; but thinke it my duty, if they walk honestly and peaceably, not to cause them in the least to suffer for the same, but shall endeavour to walke patiently and in love towards them: to see if at any time it shall please God to give them another or a better minde.' As for the charges of 'extirpation' through 'Massacring, destroying or banishing the Catholique Inhabitants . . . good now, give us an instance of one man since my coming into Ireland, not in armse, massacred, destroyed or banished; concerning the two first of which, justice hath not been done or endeavoured to be done.' As the evidence shows, he had a point. But Cromwell's passions, rather than his reason, rose like a tidal wave at the end of his tirade. Scornfully rejecting the notion that the English army had come expressly to rob the Irish of lands, he readily conceded that the soldiers had been, as usual, promised recompense from the confiscated lands of proven rebels, but:

I can give you a better reason for the Armies comming over then this; *England* hath had experience of the blessing of God in prosecuting just and righteous causes, what ever the cost and hazard be. And if ever men were engaged in a righteous cause in the World, this wil be scarce a second to it . . . We come to breake the power of a company of lawlesse

265

Rebels, who having cast off the authority of *England*, live as enemies to humane society, whose Principles (the world hath experience of) are to destroy and subjugate all men not complying with them. We come (by the assistance of God) to hold forth and maintaine the lustre and glory of English liberty in a Nation where we have an undoubted right to doe it.

This is, to the core, absolutely authentic Cromwell and today it makes unbearable reading. It is not the same as the unwitting confession of a genocidal lunatic, but it is the unwitting confession of a pig-headed, narrow-minded, Protestant bigot and English imperialist. And that is quite bad enough.

Even for his most devoted warrior, however, God could occasionally drop his guard. Except at Clonmel in County Tipperary, where Cromwell botched an attack, there was not a lot the remaining royalist and Irish armies could do to stop the relentless campaign of subjugation. Most of the strongholds in Munster in the south fell to his army. But his own troops were not immune to Major Hunger and Colonel Sickness, which launched a pitiless offensive in the awful winter of 1649–50. Cromwell himself became seriously ill as the attrition rate in his army rose to devastating levels. Even though he issued draconian prohibitions forbidding his soldiers from wantonly stealing and looting from the native population, the orders were unenforceable. In all likelihood, several hundred thousand more died from those kinds of depredations, as well as from the epidemics of plague and dysenteric fevers which swept through war-ravaged Ireland, than from the direct assault of English soldiers. It was, all the same, a horror, and it went on and on and on.

Cromwell was recalled by the Council of State in April 1650 and appointed Ireton as his deputy, but the country was still by no means pacified. Ireton would die on campaign the following year, and Ludlow, with good reason for trepidation, became temporary commander-in-chief, until July 1652, when he was replaced by Charles Fleetwood. Forcibly reunited with England, Ireland went through another huge transfer of land: the gentry and nobility associated with the revolt were stripped of their estates in the east, centre and south, and transplanted to much smaller and much less fertile lands in stony Connacht in the west. Some of the officers and men taken prisoner on the campaign—at Wexford, for example—were treated as chattel prizes and sold as indentured quasi-slaves for transport to Barbados.

Cromwell returned to England the Puritan Caesar. More than Marston Moor, Naseby or Preston, it was the Irish campaign in all its gruesome ugliness which had made him an English hero. He had revenged 1641. He had laid the lash on the barbarians. He was covered in laurels and greeted by shouts of acclamation. Thousands cheered him on Hounslow Heath. The young Andrew Marvell addressed a Horatian ode to the victor, confident that he remained unspoiled by triumph:

> How good he is, how *just*,
> And fit for highest Trust:
> Nor yet grown stiffer with Command,

But still in the *Republik's* hand:
How fit he is to sway
That can so well obey.

Whether or not Cromwell's head was beginning to be turned by all this noisy adulation, he continued to insist that he was still the servant of God and the Commonwealth. And, debilitated as he was by whatever sickness he had contracted in Ireland, Cromwell also knew there was at least one more decisive campaign to fight in the interminable British wars before the task of 'healing and settling', as he often referred to it, could be undertaken. Marvell agreed:

But thou the Wars and Fortunes son
March indefatigably on.

This next war would be in the north. For in the summer of 1650, the twenty-year-old Charles II had arrived to assume his throne in Scotland. It had not been his first choice for a theatre of counterattack. In every way, not least the presence of Ormonde's army, Ireland would have been (as Cromwell had guessed) a much more desirable operational base, but the events of late 1649 had put paid to that hope. So, more in desperation than jubilation, Charles had met with Scots negotiators in Holland and had agreed to their dismayingly severe condition that he sign the National Covenant which had first seen the light of day as a battle-cry against his father. Much had happened since 1637, of course, and *in extremis* even Charles I had been prepared to accept it as the price for Scottish support. All the same, Charles II was, as the Scots themselves knew, an even more unlikely Presbyterian, being not much given to professions of Calvinist repentance. He was, even at twenty, working hard on accumulating sins to repent of, beginning with the first of a long string of mistresses, Lucy Walter, who bore him the bastard Duke of Monmouth. As a young man Charles was already what he would be all his life: effortlessly charming, affable, intelligent, languid and hungrily addicted to sex, in every respect the polar opposite of his chaste, austere, publicly conscientious but neurotically reserved father. When Charles II was introduced to Lady Anne Murray, who had helped his younger brother James escape from England disguised as a girl, he promised that, if ever it was in his power to reward her as she should deserve, he would do so. 'And with that,' she wrote, 'the King laid his hand upon mine as they lay upon my breast.' This was the sort of gesture that came naturally—for better or worse—to Charles. It was almost impossible not to like him and almost as impossible to take him seriously. But once in Scotland, he chafed against the vigilance imposed on him by the Covenanter leaders like the Marquis of Argyll, hoping somehow to be liberated by a genuinely royalist Scottish army led by Montrose—until that is, the hitherto indestructible and elusive Montrose was betrayed by the Scottish parliament, seized, taken to Edinburgh and hanged and quartered, his several parts distributed throughout Scotland.

The Covenanter suspicion of royalist contamination of their army led them to purge it of any officers and troops whom they believed to be potentially disloyal. The result was a large but unwieldy and amateurish force, led by General David Leslie. It was this army that Cromwell smashed at the battle of Dunbar in September 1650. He had come to the command only after Fairfax (whose wife was a Presbyterian Scot and who had fought alongside the Covenanters) had refused to lead the northern expedition. The numerical odds were against Cromwell, but he offset them with one of his headlong cavalry-led onslaughts right at the thick of the Scottish force an hour before dawn when they were not yet properly mustered. Thousands were killed in the brief mêlée, thousands more taken prisoner.

The Scots retreated, as so often before, out of Midlothian and Fife across the Forth to Stirling, and Charles was duly inaugurated at Scone on 1 January 1651. But despite appalling weather and over-extended supply-lines, Cromwell took the war to them, crossing the Firth of Forth. In the summer of 1651, Charles and Leslie took what they thought was the audacious step of leaving Cromwell's army floundering in the rain and mud while they marched west and south into England itself. The hope was (as it would be for Charles's great-nephew Bonnie Prince Charlie in 1745) that, once inside England, a nation of burning Stuart royalists would flock to his standard. And, as in 1745, it never happened. It was not that the entire country was so devoted to the new Commonwealth that rallying to Charles was under any circumstances unthinkable. It was rather that the armies of the republic were so obviously still formidable that it made absolutely no sense to anyone but the most blindly devoted royalist to hazard their safety by supporting so reckless a gamble. So the march down western England to Worcester—where, as Cromwell noted, the civil wars had begun—was a lonely and exclusively Scottish business. Cromwell had let them go deep into the heart of England from which there could be no way back. What had begun as a daring venture had become a steel trap closing fast on Charles II. Another substantial army moved north and west to join Cromwell. Together, outside Worcester, some 28,000 Commonwealth troops faced a royalist-Scottish army of hardly more than half that number. The result was a bloody catastrophe, which ended at twilight with men still hacking at each other in the streets of the city.

Oliver Cromwell returned to an even noisier triumph in London than had greeted his Irish victory. Charles embarked on the extraordinary six-week flight from captivity, which was the coolest and bravest thing he would ever do. Although once he got back to Paris and the exiled court he invented a great number of details—to avoid incriminating his helpers, it was said, but also because he evidently enjoyed telling the stories— the truth of his adventure was astonishing enough. Disguised as a country yeoman, with his mane of black curls cropped short, his face darkened with nut juice to look more weather-beaten and wearing a rough leather doublet, Charles outsmarted and outran his pursuers. Relying on a network of royalists in the West Country, many of them Catholics and thus expert at improvised concealment, Charles hid first in the Staffordshire woods around Boscobel House, the home of the Penderel brothers. Then, having failed to cross the Severn in an attempt to get to Wales, Charles was first hidden in a hayloft and then walked in the rain back to Boscobel, where he slept exhausted in one of the great oaks in the park while troopers searched the estate for him. For royalist legend-makers it was a perfectly emblematic moment: the young hope of the future safely cradled in the fatherly embrace of the ancient English tree. There followed a ride across country disguised as 'William Jackson', the manservant of Jane Lane; failure to find a safe passage either from Bristol or from Bridport in Dorset, where the quays and taverns were crawling with Commonwealth soldiers about to be shipped to the Channel Islands; and then abortive wanderings along the south coast before finally finding a reliable ship, the *Surprise,* at Shoreham in Sussex. Given the £1000 price on his head, and his willingness to test the limits of his disguise by engaging in reckless banter about the rogue Charles Stuart (the sort of game that amused the king), it was astonishing that he was not, in fact, betrayed or discovered. To royalists who had reconciled themselves to submitting for the time being to Leviathan, his near miraculous survival gave them a consoling legend to develop in competition with Cromwell's depressing record of invincibility.

Charles II's escape, dependent as it was on so many helping hands, says something important about this very English revolution: that it was (for its own good) deficient in those elements which make for the survival of republics—police and paranoia. Whether you were a gung-ho republican like Edmund Ludlow, a visionary like John Lilburne or a wistful royalist like John Evelyn, it was glaringly obvious that the Commonwealth had signally failed to develop an independent republican culture to replace the banished monarchy. No revolution, especially not those in eighteenth-century France or twentieth-century Russia or China, could hope to survive for even as long as they did without a conscious cultural programme for the redirection of allegiance. Those programmes were aggressively, even brutally, executed to orchestrate loyalty in the interests of the new state. (Hobbes would have understood this very well.) In their requirements of public demonstrations of allegiance—sung, sworn, chanted, enthusiasm reinforced by fear—they would make political neutrality either an impossibility or a crime. There could be no going back.

Nothing of the sort happened in the Britain of the 1650s. And in this sense the shocking drama of the beheading of Charles I is a misleading guide to the true nature of the Commonwealth and Cromwell's Protectorate. For the men who ran the country were not Jacobins, much less Bolsheviks, in stove-pipe hats and fallen collars. They were clear-eyed pragmatists who were prepared to mouth the necessary shibboleths about 'Liberty', always provided these were vague enough to avoid a commitment to anything like a systematic programme of radical change in, for example, the procedures of the law (as the Levellers had wanted). There had been a lopping all right, a lopping such as has never happened before or since. The king, court, house of peers and bishops had all gone. But this still left a lot of England undisturbed—the England that most of the bigwigs who now ran it, like Henry Marten and Arthur

Haselrig, had grown up with, and were partial to and, for all the sound and fury of 1649, had never dreamed of doing away with in the name of some imagined new Jerusalem. Their Zion was still comfortably seated, thank you very much, in the magistrate's chair, in the county hunts and in city counting houses, and in the 1650s it was doing very nicely. So it was possible for unrepentant royalists like John Evelyn (again in startling contrast to the fate of émigrés in the French Revolution) to travel back and forth between London and the Stuart court in Paris, armed with a passport issued to him personally by John Bradshaw, the judge who had presided over the court which had tried the king and who had sentenced him to death! In that same year, 1649, Evelyn bought himself another country estate, and in February 1652 he came back for good, in effect taking the Leviathan option offered by another of the returnees, his friend Hobbes, 'no more intending to go out of England, but endeavor a settled life, either in this place [Deptford], or some other, there being now so little appearance of any change for the better, all being intirely in the rebells hands'.

But no prospect, either, for Evelyn of some nightmarish descent into revolutionary terror. In fact he saw, at first hand, an impressive demonstration of the republic's commitment to upholding the traditional regime of law and order after he had been relieved by a pair of robbers at knife point, while riding through Bromley forest, of two rings (one emerald, one onyx) and a pair of buckles 'set with rubies and diamonds'. The mere fact that Evelyn wore all this glittering hardware at all while out for a ride scarcely suggests he thought of the Commonwealth to which he had returned as an inferno of social chaos and disorder. And he was right. After two hours tied up against an oak 'tormented with the flies, the ants, the sunn', he managed to get loose, find his horse and ride to 'Colonel Blount's, a greate justiciarie of the times, who sent out a hugh & crie immediately'. In London Evelyn had notices of the mugging printed and distributed, and within a mere two days knew exactly what had become of his valuables, which were duly restored to him. A month later he was summoned to appear at the trial of one of the thieves, but not being 'willing to hang the fellow . . . I did not appeare'. For the swift return of his jewellery and the exemplary apprehension of the malefactors Evelyn was 'eternaly obliged to give thanks to God my Savior'. But he might also have given some credit to the smooth operation of the law in regicide England. For the next eight years of the interregnum he spent his days much as he would had there been a king on the throne, the significant exception being the difficulty of finding acceptable sermons to hear and the prohibition on celebrating Christmas, which upset him greatly (especially when one clandestine service was raided). But he went about his business, attending to his own estates and advising acquaintances and learned colleagues and gentry on the landscaping and arboriculture of their properties.

In the summer of 1654 Evelyn was able to stay for an extended time in Oxford, now transformed from the Laudian capital of the king and governed by heads of colleges like his host Dr Wilkins of Wadham, approved of by the Protector. Obedient or not, Oxford was none the less a congenial place of science and learning where Evelyn made the acquaintance of many of the prodigies who would be his colleagues in the Royal Society, including 'that prodigious young Scholar Mr. Christopher Wren, who presented me with a piece of White Marble he had stained with a lively red [presumably in imitation of porphyry], very deepe, as beautifull as if it had ben naturall'. In fact Evelyn's entire journey through England—through the West Country and back to East Anglia and Cromwell's Cambridge—is a record of a country conspicuously going about its business, war damage being repaired, farms flourishing (even in a decade of some economic dislocation), gentlemen planning 'beautifications' to their houses and gardens. It was certainly not a country in shock.

And it was still being run largely by men of a practical, rather than a messianic, temper. To read the journal of a man like Bulstrode Whitelocke, the Middle Temple lawyer turned Buckinghamshire gentleman and MP, Commissioner of the Great Seal and a friend of Cromwell's, is to be struck once more by the relentless normality of his life, by the imperturbable continuity before and after the killing of the monarch. What electrified Whitelocke in 1649 was not Charles I's death. A staunch parliamentarian and moderate Puritan inclining towards the Independent view of liberty of conscience, he had none the less been against the trial and had declined to serve as one of the commissioners of the court (a gesture which in Jacobin Paris would have booked him a certain date with the guillotine). But Whitelocke had more important things to think about—above all the death of his second wife, Frances, a trauma which almost unhinged him. With all his misgivings about what the Commonwealth was supposed to be, and his sense that any English state ought to have 'something of a monarchy' about it (he suggested the youngest Stuart, Prince Henry of Gloucester, as a potential replacement, being of an age to be re-educated in political virtue and moderation), Whitelocke sailed on serenely in public life.

Men like Whitelocke, as well as the other dominant figures of the Council of State and the Rump Parliament, invested far more time and energy in preventing any sort of radical change than in promoting it. Their tenure in power suggests perhaps what a pragmatic government might have looked like had Charles I actually succeeded in winning over men like John Pym, rather than just appointing a few token opposition figures to his Privy Council in 1641. Instead of the firebrands he feared, Charles might have had what men like Henry Marten, Henry Vane and Arthur Haselrig had become—businessmen of state, mercantilists, money-managers. And, in their swaggering, beady-eyed way, fierce patriots. For if there *was* some sort of republican ideology that had replaced the inadequate and suspect policy of the Stuarts and around which the English (rather than the British) could indeed rally, it was that of the aggressive prosecution of the national interest. It's all too easy to think of the Commonwealth after the battle of Worcester as living in a kind of pious peace. In fact, it lived in profane war with first the Dutch, then the Portuguese and then the Spanish. It was, as behooved a set of rulers who were excessively misty-eyed about the memory of the sainted Virgin Queen, the most successful warrior state, especially on the high seas, since the death of Elizabeth, in glaring contrast to the string of military fiascos perpetrated by the hapless Stuarts. Admiral Blake succeeded where Buckingham had failed. Cromwell at his most merciless triumphed where Essex had failed. The republic hammered out an empire not only in Britain (where both James I and Charles I had most pathetically failed) but overseas too, in the North Sea and the Baltic and beyond in the Atlantic, both sides of the equator. It was commercially rapacious and militarily brutal, beery chauvinism erected into a guiding principle of state. So a better guide to this kind of Britain than the execution of its king would be the Navigation Act of 1651, which prohibited any ships other than British or those of the country of origin from bringing cargoes to Britain, thus taking deadly aim at the shipping supremacy of the Dutch. It was a policy to maximize business which (another first) the state was prepared to back up with war if that's what it took. Often it did.

Was this it, then? Was this the reason nearly 200,000 had lost their lives in battle, and far more than that number through disease and misery, just so that Britain could be run by a corporate alliance of county gentry and city merchants? Henry Vane and Arthur Haselrig, and the Rumpers might have said, yes. For it may not be the new Jerusalem but it is no small thing, this liberty of self-interest and of religious conscience. It's a big thing. (And it would seem unquestionably big when making a return appearance at Philadelphia in 1776.) But for Oliver Cromwell, the godly Caesar, it was never,

278

somehow, quite big enough. He was haunted by the thought that this do-as-you-like Britain was too paltry a dividend for all the blood sacrifices that had been made. His long, rambling speeches to the parliaments of the interregnum, which must have been almost as much torture to listen to as they were to give, combed relentlessly through the history of the civil wars in a hopeless effort to define the essential, redeeming meaning of the conflict.

Cromwell could never establish, to his own satisfaction, that clear and unarguable rationale because, just as he was hoping to 'heal and settle' the nation, the civil war was being fought all over again within his own personality. It was the same struggle that continued to frustrate the search for political peace in England: the war between godliness and good order. And the outcome for Cromwell, as for the Commonwealth, was far from clear.

Enough of him belonged to the party of order to respect its strong sense that the Stuarts had been fought so as to keep England the way it was imagined to have been until they came along. That was an England in which monarchs had been bound by the common law and in which there had been no way to tax the people but through parliamentary consent. The country gentleman in Cromwell respected and subscribed to this social conservatism. But anyone who endured his speeches to parliament would have known that there was also a godly zealot inside Cromwell, for whom moral reformation was paramount. For this zealous Cromwell, it made no difference how the war had begun. What mattered was how it must

279

end. 'Religion was not at first the thing contended for but God brought it to that issue at last and at last it proved to be what was most dear to us.' He had worked by indirection, making the Stuart Pharaoh stiff-necked so that his Chosen People might rise and depart. But the vision of the Promised Land was a revelation that no one could have imagined at that setting forth, and it was the task of Cromwell to bring the people to it.

So he was Gideon no more. He was Moses. And the Rumpers seemed to him, more and more, like the worshippers before the Golden Calf. Cromwell looked coldly at the unscrupulous trade in confiscated properties, at the vulgar swagger of republicans such as Henry Marten whom he despised as a drunken libertine, and he was scandalized by the profanation of God's bounteous grace. Cromwell's view of government was essentially pastoral, or, as he would say later, constabular. It was the obligation of men to whom God had given authority and good fortune to provide disinterested justice for their charges. What he saw in the Rump was good law denied to the people so that lawyers might line their pockets. He saw fortunes being amassed in land and trade, and men being sent to fight against the Dutch so that merchants could fill their warehouses and fatten their moneybags. Was it to satisfy such carnal appetites that his troopers had left their limbs behind on the fields of Marston Moor and Dunbar? 'The people were dissatisfied in every corner of the nation,' he would say in a speech in July 1653, justifying the action he took against the Rump, 'at the non-performance of things that had been promised and were of duty to be performed.'

What galled him most was the Rump politicians' air of self-evident indispensability. He, on the other hand, had always considered the regime of 1649 to be provisional, pending the settlement of a proper constitution for the Commonwealth. The time-serving and procrastination, he concluded, had gone on long enough. The Rump needed to expedite plans for its own liquidation. But for a year, at least, Cromwell, who genuinely hated the idea of forcing the issue at sword point, tried, together with colleagues in the army council, to get the Rump leaders themselves to concentrate on the transformation of the Commonwealth into a properly 'settled' form. Much energy and time were spent attempting to reconcile the parties of order and zeal. In early December 1651 Cromwell called a meeting of prominent members of parliament, including Whitelocke, Oliver St John and Speaker William Lenthall, together with senior generals, some of them, like Thomas Harrison, who were becoming impatient to transform the prosaic Commonwealth into something more closely resembling a new Jerusalem. Together they discussed what form the new state should take. Most of the generals said they wanted an 'absolute republic', the MPs a 'mixed monarchy'. But one of the generals—Oliver Cromwell—allowed that some sort of monarchy might suit England best.

A little less than a year later, Bulstrode Whitelocke, the Commissioner of the Great Seal, found out why. As he strolled through St James's Park with Cromwell, the general suddenly asked, 'What if a man should take upon him to be King?' Whitelocke (by his own account) replied with disarming candour, 'I think that remedy would be

281

worse than the disease.' He went on to explain that, since Cromwell already had the 'full Kingly power' without incurring the envy and pomp of the office, why should he do something so impolitic? This dousing of cold water was not what Cromwell wanted to hear. Even less welcome was the home truth that 'most of our Friends have engaged with us upon the hopes of having the Government settled in a Free-State, and to effect that have undergone all their hazards.' While Whitelocke hurried to assure Cromwell that he personally thought them mistaken in their conviction that they would necessarily enjoy more liberty in a Commonwealth than in a properly restrained monarchy, he warned him that the risk of any kind of quasi-monarchy would be to destroy his own power base. 'I thank you that you so *fully* consider my Condition, it is a Testimony of your love to me,' Cromwell replied. But Whitelocke knew that the general was not ready to hear home truths.

> With this the General brake off, and went to other Company, and so into *Whitehall*, seeming by his Countenance and Carriage displeased with what hath been said [especially Whitelocke's advice to make contact with Charles II!]; yet he never objected it against [me] in any publick meeting afterwards.
>
> Only his Carriage towards [me] from that time was altered, and his advising with [me] not so frequent and intimate as before; and it was not long after that he found an Occasion by honourable Imployment [an embassy to Sweden] to send [me] out of the way . . . that [I] might be no obstacle or impediment to his

ambitious designs.

Even if he was not (yet) to be a king, Oliver Cromwell was moving towards an unembarrassed sense of himself as the man chosen by God to settle the political fate of the British nations, to end the 'confusions' of the time. The messiah was coming to dominate the manager. Psalm 110 was much on his mind and his lips: 'The Lord shall send the rod of thy strength out of Zion: rule thou in the midst of thine enemies.' After the deed was done, Cromwell and his officers liked to pretend that the country was desperate to be shot of the Rump. Probably, because of the taxes they had levied to finance the war against the Dutch and the armies in Scotland and Ireland, the parliament and Council of State were indeed unpopular. But that only added to the Rump's own conviction that, once it had got the army off its back, properly reduced and obedient to the civil power, it could lighten the tax load and be seen as the nation's saviour. To the senior army officers, of course, this diagnosis of the Commonwealth's ills was exactly back to front. They and not the Rump were the true guardians of the people's interests. If not the army, then who else could call the oligarchs to account for not properly attending to the plight of the common people, their denial of simple justice, the provision for a sound ministry? In other words, both sides suspected each other of scheming their self-perpetuation on the backs of the citizenry. Both sides saw the precondition for 'settling' the Commonwealth as being rid of the other.

Oliver Cromwell, as usual, would decide the matter, though not exactly in a temper of calm deliberation. He was both soldier and politician, and for some time could see the truth in both sides' assertion that they were the authentic representatives of the people. But by early 1653 he was coming off the fence and down on the side of the troops whose welfare he had so often vowed to defend. In particular he was offended by the Rump's presumption that it could dismiss the soldiers who had given so much to the nation, without adequately attending to their claims of arrears of pay and pensions. He still felt that the parliament could be induced by persuasion, or, if that's what it took, by other means, to go quietly, consenting to its dissolution and making proper arrangements for its elected replacement. But his threshold of suspicion was low. When the Rump leaders such as Thomas Scott, Vane and Haselrig produced a plan for the piecemeal reconstitution of parliament, as and when individual members retired rather than at one fell swoop, Cromwell assumed this was a strategy of shameless self-perpetuation. Worse, he believed the gradual elections would be likely to guarantee an assembly packed with Presbyterians or 'Neuters' hostile to the work of godly reformation that he now thought was the Commonwealth's true justification. Out there in the country, he felt sure, there were pure-hearted Christians who might yet be brought to Westminster to fulfil God's purpose for England. But since the unclean and the powerful stood in their way, they needed help in getting over the stile placed in the way of realizing the republic of the saints. So, at the discussions he convened between parliamentary and army leaders, Cromwell proposed the creation of some sort of executive council to act as steward during the gap between dissolution and new elections—a body which might scrutinize the credentials of those putting themselves forward for the House. Though the Rump, in fact, owed its own preservation to Colonel Pride's Purge in 1648, five years later it was unembarrassed about presenting itself as the guardian of parliamentary freedom against military intimidation.

Still, swords were swords. And the bullies were starting to finger the scabbards. Veiled threats of military intervention were hinted at. It seemed to work. By the evening of 19 April Cromwell evidently believed he was very close to an agreement on a plan for the dissolution and replacement of the Rump. The parliamentary leaders said they would sleep on his proposals and halt discussion on their own plan until they had given them proper consideration.

But on the following morning Cromwell learned that, instead of abandoning their own plan, the Rump leaders were hastily reading it to the House. Always on a short fuse, he now exploded. Reneging on an agreed course of action was final proof, if ever he needed it, that there was no disgraceful subterfuge to which the politicians of the Rump would not stoop if it served their own selfish interests. 'We *did* not believe persons of such quality could do it,' he said in his July 1653 speech narrating the event.

Cromwell stormed down Whitehall escorted by a company of musketeers. Leaving them outside the doors of the parliament house, he took his usual place in the chamber and for a while appeared to respect its conventions, asking the

Speaker's permission to speak, doffing his hat and commending the Rump for its 'care of the public good'. But this was meant as an obituary, not a vote of congratulation, and as Cromwell warmed to his work niceties were thrown aside. Speaking 'with so much passion and discomposure of mind as if he had been distracted', he now turned on the dumbstruck members, barking at them for their indifference to justice and piety; their corrupt machinations on behalf of lawyers (an obsession of Cromwell's); and their wicked flirtation with the Presbyterian friends of tyranny. 'Perhaps you think this is not parliamentary language,' one account has him saying forthrightly. 'I confess it is not, neither are you to expect any such from me.' The hat went back on (always a bad sign), as Cromwell left his seat and marched up and down the centre of the chamber, shouting, according to Ludlow (who was not there but heard the details from Harrison), that 'the Lord had done with them and had chosen other instruments for the carrying on with his work that were more worthy'. Foolhardy attempts were made to stop him in full spate. Sir Peter Wentworth from Warwickshire was brave enough to get to his feet and tell Cromwell that his language was 'unbecoming' and 'the more horrid in that it came from their servant and their servant whom they had so highly trusted and obliged'.

But Cromwell was now in full exterminating angel mode, glaring witheringly at the special objects of his scorn and fury: not just the presumptuous Wentworth, but Henry Vane and Henry Marten, accusing them (though unnamed) of being drunkards and whoremasters. Finally he shouted (again according to Ludlow), 'You are no parliament. I say you are no parliament' and called the musketeers into the chamber. The boots entered noisily, heavily.

The symbols of parliamentary sovereignty were now treated like trash. The Speaker was 'helped' down from his chair by Major-General Thomas Harrison; the mace, carried before him, was called 'the fool's bauble' and taken away by the soldiers on Cromwell's orders. The immunity of members was exposed as a joke. When Alderman Allen tried to persuade Cromwell to clear the chamber of soldiers, he himself, as treasurer of the army, was accused of embezzling funds and put in armed custody. The records of the house were seized, the room emptied, the doors locked.

It was what, in the depressing lexicon of modern politics, we would recognize as a text-book *coup d'état*: the bludgeoning of a representative assembly by armed coercion. In fact it was at this precise moment on the morning of 20 April 1653, when the argument of words gave way to the argument of weapons, that Cromwell himself crossed the line from bullying to despotism. In so doing he undid, at a stroke, the entire legitimacy of the war which he himself had fought against the king's own unparliamentary principles and conduct. When he sent the Rump packing, Cromwell liked to think that he was striking a blow at 'ambition and avarice'. But what he really wounded, and fatally, was the Commonwealth itself, whose authority (if it was not to be grounded on pure Hobbesian force) had to be based on the integrity of parliament. It's true, of course, that the Rump had lost its own virginity five years before when its members allowed themselves to be ushered through Colonel Pride's file of soldiers while their colleagues were barred from the chamber. And Cromwell was certainly right to believe that, if upstanding godliness was the proper qualification for serving in parliament, Marten and his ilk were unworthy of their charge.

But none of this matters a jot besides the indisputable butchery of parliamentary independence that Cromwell perpetrated that April morning, a killing that makes the presence of his statue outside the House of Commons a joke in questionable taste. Was it not to *resist* precisely such assaults on the liberty of the House that in the spring of 1642 parliament had determined to fight King Charles, with Cromwell himself among the most militant in asserting the House's control over its own defences? How was this any different? Had England beheaded one king only to get itself another more ruthless in his indifference to parliament than the Stuarts?

Oh, but this *was* quite different, Cromwell would insist in his speech of 4 July 1653 to the first sitting of the new assembly. His purpose in dismissing the Rump had been not to deliver the *coup de grâce* to parliamentary government, but to give it a new lease of life. His dearest wish was to save the Commonwealth, not kill it. Leaving the Rump to its own devices, he argued, would have done just that, by hastening a parliament full of men fundamentally hostile to the essential causes for which the Republic stood—liberty of conscience and justice for the people. Instead of these saboteurs who would have killed liberty by stealth, there would now sit a gathering of dependably righteous men, appointed rather than elected, who would act as godly stewards for sixteen months while the proper institutions of government were finally 'settled'.

The truth was that, as usual, Cromwell was learning on the job. He really had no clear idea at all what kind of assembly, if any, could or should eventually replace the remnant of the Long Parliament. God for him certainly didn't lie in the details, always too petty to merit his concentrated attention. Instead he spoke in cryptic pieties— 'have a care of the whole flock' (this to the new nominated assembly) . . . 'Love all the sheep, love the lambs, love all, and tender all' . . . 'Jesus Christ is owned this day by your call and you own him by your willingness in appearing here'—none of which was especially helpful when deliberating on the fine print of constitutional arrangements. On the other hand, this kind of parsonical hot air did encourage the most optimistic of the saints, such as the Fifth Monarchist Major-General Harrison along with militant preachers like Christopher Feake, John Rogers and Vavasor Powell, to believe that the long-heralded day of the 'saints' appointment was finally at hand. So they pushed for a 'Sanhedrin' of seventy (all of their godly persuasion) to be summoned to save Britain-Israel. Harrison in particular became very excited by the coming rapture and stalked about in a scarlet coat, his red face coloured by 'such vivacity and alacrity as a man hath when he hath drunk a cup too much'. For a brief, thrilling few weeks it seemed that Cromwell shared their high-temperature elation. Did he not address them as being on 'the edge of . . . promises and prophecies'? Psalm 110 was invoked yet again, as if Cromwell himself was already in the throes of the anticipated rapture: 'Thy people shall be willing in the day of thy power, in the beauties of holiness from the womb of the morning: thou hast the dew of thy youth.'

But this was not Jerusalem. It was England, where rapture and politics seldom cohabit, at least not easily. And when the fervour had abated and Cromwell had calmed down a bit, his political id, the Huntingdonshire country gentleman, leery of disorderly enthusiasm, predictably reasserted itself. And from a glance at the men of the new assembly it was obvious that the Council of Officers had chosen men as impervious to the ecstasies of revelation as any of their parliamentary predecessors; men in fact who resembled squire, rather than preacher, Cromwell. Two-thirds of the 140 were landowners, 115 of them justices of the peace. They included four baronets, four knights of the shire, an aristocrat—Lord Lisle—and the elderly Provost of Eton, Francis Rous, who had been an MP. Most of them bore names like Gilbert, William and Charles, not Adonijah or Hezekiah. So although the assembly became known after its London representative Praisegod Barbon, leather merchant and Separatist, as the 'Barebone's', this was not, for the most part, a gathering of wild-eyed millenarians. What other choice was there? Once the army grandees had turned their back, on both the Leveller programme of expanding the franchise and the hotter Christian sects, the only social group from which the new assembly could be chosen was the same ride-to-hounds class (with perhaps a tad more conspicuous piety) that had always populated the benches at Westminster. Not surprisingly, then, men who would become hardy perennials of the Restoration parliaments—men such as Edward Montagu, Samuel Pepys's patron and later the Earl of Sandwich, and Anthony Ashley Cooper (like Hobbes and Aubrey a Malmesburyite), erstwhile royalist commander in Dorset and later the Earl of Shaftesbury—first made their entry into politics in the assembly which we imagine, wrongly, to have been a temple of Puritanism.

When it became apparent that the vast majority of the Barebone's Parliament were just the usual squires from the shires and would resist the zealots' deeply cherished goals such as the abolition of the tithe, the most fervent of the saints, like Thomas Harrison, departed in high dudgeon. The militant preachers Feake and Powell, who had initially hailed the assembly as the coming reign of Christ, were now left crying in the wilderness, their messianic ambitions reduced to campaigning for the propagation of the gospel in Wales. When the members of Barebone's did manage to agree on dramatic changes, it was in the direction of less religion rather than more, nowhere so dramatically as in the abolition of marriages in church. For three years after 1653, only marriages solemnized before a justice of the peace were considered legal. But this certification by magistrates was not exactly the reborn evangelized Commonwealth that the Fifth Monarchists had anticipated. Unaccountably, too, Cromwell appeared reluctant to prosecute the war against the Dutch with all the ardour they wanted, but seemed to be conniving at a peace. Their dreams frustrated, they took to name-calling, denouncing Cromwell as 'a man of sin' and 'the old dragon' and damning the moderates as the 'unsainted'. Tiring of the rant, and thwarted from the kind of practical government they looked for from the Commonwealth, the leaders of the moderates, including William Sydenham and Anthony Ashley Cooper, came to Cromwell on 12 December 1653 and, in a reversal of what had happened the previous April, voluntarily committed institutional suicide. Resigning their commission on their knees before him, they implored Cromwell to put the miserably captious assembly out of its misery. He was only too happy to oblige.

Barebone's was the closest that Britain (for there were representatives from Ireland, Wales and Scotland in the nominated assembly) ever came to a theocracy: a legislature of Christian mullahs, and it was not very close at all. For all Cromwell's holy thunder about the imminent reign of the righteous, the crackpot frenzy of their matter and manner put him off the saints in a hurry. He seems to have been genuinely horrified by the licence which summoning the godly assembly seemed to have given to every hedgerow messiah to declare his hobbledehoy flock a 'gathered' Church. And he couldn't help noticing that, while the sects were only too happy to avail themselves of the liberty of conscience guaranteed to them by the Commonwealth, they were not inclined to extend that toleration to any of their competitors in the battle for souls. Predictably, then, he became increasingly intolerant of their intolerance. When Christopher Feake and John Rogers made scandalous comparisons between the General and Charles I he had them locked up in the same filthy airless holes in Lambeth Palace where a century before his namesake Thomas Cromwell had incarcerated those who didn't agree with *him*. When Rogers was later dragged out for a show debate with Cromwell, he demanded to know whether he appeared as prisoner or freeman, to which Cromwell responded, with a peculiar mixture of sarcasm and sanctimoniousness, that, since Christ had made us all free, it must be as a freeman. After the charade, the free Christian was dumped back in his cell.

On 16 December 1653, just four days after the gathering of the saints had been dispatched into limbo, Oliver Cromwell was sworn in, at a pompous ceremony in the Court of Chancery, as Lord Protector. The title had last been used by Edward Seymour, Duke of Somerset, during the minority of Edward VI. Given the fact that Somerset ended up on the block, this was not an auspicious precedent. But for the compulsive history-readers of the seventeenth century, the late 1540s meant the hallelujah years of Thomas Cranmer's evangelism, when that first Lord Protector had presided over England's Protestant conversion from Roman error. And Cromwell knew better (at this stage) than to give himself aristocratic airs. On his way to a reception in the Grocers' Hall given by the Lord Mayor he made sure to be seen riding humbly bare-headed through the streets.

There was no need to bother Cromwell with the institutional minutiae of the new regime. Anticipating (not to say expediting) the débâcle of the nominated assembly, the more down-to-earth members of the Council of Officers had a prefabricated 'Instrument of Government' ready and waiting to be put to work. Its principal author was the intelligent and extremely ambitious General John Lambert, who seems to have understood his Cromwell better than anyone since Henry Ireton and to have known when to move him away from prophecy and back to power. Concentrated power and authority were, so Lambert persuaded Cromwell, the best hope of the 'healing and settlement' he was always going on about, and the Instrument of Government would deliver them, he promised, without sacrificing liberty. For the country was to be governed now by 'a single person and parliament'—the formula which became the Protectorate's constitutional mantra for the remainder of Cromwell's life. In fact it was the Lord Protector's Council of State that exercised the day-to-day functions of government. The Council of State was an embryonic cabinet of fifteen to twenty men, many of them drawn from the most managerial figures in the Barebone's assembly including his old comrade and cousin-in-law Oliver St John, Edward Montagu and Anthony Ashley Cooper (until he left the Council in December 1654), along with its secretary and *de facto* chief of security, John Thurloe. But, on paper at any rate, the Protectorate parliaments were not just window-dressing. They were to be elected every three years, to have representatives from all four nations of Britain and to sit for at least five months of each year. In other words they corresponded to the proposals set out by the most advanced parliamentarians of the 1640s, and for that matter to what would actually come to pass after the next round of revolution in 1688–90.

The constitutional blueprint was the easy part. The real problem for the future of the remade kingless state was not its formal design but its political workability. Realistically, as old Hobbes knew, for all the completeness of the apparent victory over the king this new Britain still had trouble in converting passive consent into active allegiance. The problem was compounded by the fact that the closer the Protectorate came to effective and acceptable (if not popular) government, the less distinguishable it became from a monarchy: not perhaps the old Stuart monarchy, but some sort of monarchy none the less, embodied in a virtuous, responsible prince, respectful of the common law and a dependable guarantor of limited religious liberty. This was, in fact, exactly how Cromwell saw himself, and why he had so much trouble thinking up reasons why he should *not* become king—the kind of king parliament had wanted in 1642 and 1647 and which the obtuse, self-destructive Charles Stuart had spurned. This was just the latest of Oliver's convictions about God's intentions for him and for his country. (After all, not all the kings of Israel had descended from the same house. David had not been the son of Saul.) With this conviction lodged in his mind, Cromwell inched towards majesty. His likeness appeared on the Great Seal of the Protectorate. In 1655 his head was superimposed on Van Dyck's equestrian portrait of Charles I. In another engraving he appeared as the armoured Peacemaker in the classic imperial pose between two pillars, decorated with the kingdoms of England, Scotland and Ireland kneeling in grateful supplication while a dove of peace (or the Holy Spirit depending on your theological position) fluttered above his laurel-clad brow.

In that same print Cromwell also features as the modern Ulysses, the Great Navigator who had steered the ship of state safely between the hazards of Scylla and Charybdis. The fact of the matter, though, was that Scylla and Charybdis in the shape of the only two groups on which the Protectorate could base its government—republican zealots and managerial pragmatists (old Cromwellians and new Cromwellians)—still represented opposite and mutually threatening poles of power. If Cromwell steered too close to the pragmatists he risked dangerously alienating the army officers and even the republican politicians of the ousted Rump who had never forgiven him for their expulsion. If he moved more dogmatically towards the zealots, he invited anarchy and the erosion of his own authority as the great, inclusionary Peacemaker.

Ironically, if Cromwell had had a *more* arrogant and dictatorial confidence in his own authority he might have responded to the repeated requests to become king by doing so, thus creating a third way which he could then have presented to the nation as the best way to ensure stability. But the fact was that, for better or worse, Oliver Cromwell was not really cut out to be Leviathan. For almost three years he took a back seat to Lambert and Thurloe in the practical administration of the government, and the political course he steered between the zealots and pragmatists consisted mostly of reactions to whatever had happened to be the most recent threat. In war a famous strategist, in peace Cromwell seldom escaped the trap of tactics. So when the elections to the first Protectorate parliament, which met in September 1654, produced a crop of survivors from the Rump (like

Thomas Scott and Arthur Haselrig) who had no intention of accepting the Instrument of Government, Cromwell's reaction was to authorize yet another purge, evicting anyone not prepared to sign an oath of 'Recognition'. So much for the zealots.

There was one occasion, though, when—providentially, Cromwell might have said—religious conviction and patriotic pragmatism perfectly dovetailed and that was the re-establishment of the community of English Jews. It's not a moment that can be glossed over lightly in the checkered history of Cromwellian England because, however mixed or even confused his motives, Oliver's actions did for once have a measurable and completely benevolent result. For the Jews and their descendants the Protector's title was something more than a formality.

This is not to say that Cromwell's inclination to bring the Jews back to England proceeded from the 'tender-heartedness' optimistically ascribed to him by the chief promoter of the immigration, the scholar and rabbi Menasseh ben Israel, then living in Amsterdam. Like so many of his evangelical contemporaries, Cromwell was responding in the first instance to the messianic timetable which decreed that, only when the Jews had been converted could the decisive destruction of Antichrist get under way. Conversely, Menasseh's cabalistic programme required that only when the Jews had been dispersed among *all* the nations of the earth, would the Messiah appear, his people restored to Zion and the Temple rebuilt. Which was all well and good, but had more pragmatic motives not also nudged Cromwell in that direction the readmission would never have got as far as it did. And those concerns were not about redemption but about money and power.

There had, in fact, been a small community of Marrano (Spanish and Portuguese Jews, supposedly converted to Christianity) living and trading illicitly in the City of London, enough to have founded a secret synagogue in Creechurch Lane. City merchants divided between those who believed the Sephardi Jews, with their network of co-religionists scattered throughout the Hispanic and Netherlandish trading world, were a priceless source of commercial and military intelligence, and those who feared that, if given a foothold, the Jews would drive out the competition. John Thurloe, though, was someone who believed they could only further the ambitious plans to build an English mercantile empire in the Atlantic at the expense of the Spanish, Portuguese and the Dutch. And it was he who encouraged the Jews to take steps to seek readmission. At the beginning of 1655 the proposal was put before the Council of State, where it got a distinctly cool reception. Rumours circulated that Cromwell was about to sell St Paul's to the Jews to be turned into a synagogue, that good English merchants would be driven into poverty by the notoriously rapacious Israelites.

But Cromwell went ahead none the less. In October 1655 he had a personal meeting with Menasseh who was lodged in the Strand near the Protector's house. The encounter was the stuff of the Apocrypha if not the Scriptures. Menasseh thought of Cromwell as a second Cyrus who would further the holy aim of the return to and rebuilding of Jerusalem, and was said, in some of the more

298

self-serving Christian accounts, to have pressed his hands against Cromwell's body to make sure he was, after all, made of mortal stuff. But there were few men of any learning and religious passion in Amsterdam who could withstand the spellbinding mixture of sanctity and intelligence combined in Menasseh's person. It's easy to imagine the two of them exchanging educated opinions on scripture, ancient history, prophecy and science. A momentous sympathy was established. So, although a majority of the Council were against the measure, making it impossible for Cromwell to move to a formal readmission, Oliver used his personal authority both to protect those who were already in London as well as others who might discreetly arrive. It was not what Menasseh had hoped for. Anything short of a public readmission and the prophecy of the full dispersion would fail. Despondent and impoverished, he had to appeal to Cromwell for funds to get himself and the body of his son, who had died in London, back to Amsterdam. He died himself not long after.

But a community had been reborn. In 1656 the outbreak of war with Spain made assets belonging to subjects of the Spanish Crown residing in England subject to forfeiture. One of the affected merchants was Antonio Rodrigues Robles, who petitioned the government to have the seizure annulled on the grounds that he was not a Spaniard but a Jew. When his case was tacitly upheld, it became possible, for the first time for three and a half centuries, for Jews to live, trade and worship openly and, for the most part, untroubled in the City of London. The oak benches on which those Jews first parked their behinds in the little synagogue of Creechurch Lane still exist, moved to the later and much grander temple of Bevis Marks. They are narrow, backless and unforgiving, indistinguishable from the benches of any Puritan chapel—hosts and guests sharing common furniture.

The pragmatic managers of state who, whatever their personal feelings about the readmission of the Jews, understood that it was, after all, in the state's interest, were men whose vision of the world (and of Britain's place in it) was essentially mechanical and commercial rather than evangelical: technicians of power; data-gatherers; calculators of profit, not Christian visionaries. If the goal of the Protectorate was to build the new Jerusalem, then the first thing these men wanted to know was the price of its bricks. We think of these few years as anomalous in British history, but, in this respect at least, king or no king, for good or ill, they mark the true beginning of modern government in these islands. It was at this time that a commercial empire was being created, often by means of unscrupulous military aggression and brutal inhumanity, in the slaving islands of the Atlantic. On the New England seaboard a Commonwealth, at once godly and lucrative, was beginning its spectacular history at Massachusetts Bay. But another empire was being founded too: an empire of knowledge— scientific knowledge that was acquired not just for its own sake but as the raw material of power.

The men who saw a natural continuity between scientifically acquired information and the effective mastery of government would later describe themselves as 'political arithmeticians'. William Petty, who coined the phrase, was himself an astonishing example of the type. The son of a clothier, Petty went to sea only (it was said) to be abandoned by his shipmates with a broken leg on the French coast. Educated first by Jesuits in Caen, subsequently in the rough school of the Royal Navy, Petty revealed himself to be a prodigy at mathematics and natural science—enough of one anyway to be employed in Paris by Thomas Hobbes. Perhaps he was also enough of a Hobbesian to return at the end of the civil war to England, where, still in his twenties, he fell in with the group of scientists who included Robert Boyle, adamant royalist but still more committed 'natural philosopher'. Every such man of science needed a marvel which would command public attention, and Petty, now a qualified physician, got his in 1650 in the shape of Ann Greene, who had been hanged for the murder of her illegitimate child. Rescued in the nick of time from anatomical dissection, Greene, who had been pronounced definitively dead and packed into a coffin, was resuscitated by Petty, who bled her, looked after her and in the end raised a dowry for her marriage. It was the kind of tale that the anecdotalists of the press loved, a relief from the bitter passions of politics. It made Petty famous and it got him elected as a fellow of Brasenose College, Oxford.

It was in Oxford that Petty would first have encountered the nucleus of the company of scientists who, with the Restoration, would be the founders of the Royal Society: Warden John Wilkins of Wadham College, young Christopher Wren and Robert Boyle. They were looked on benevolently by Oliver Cromwell. Boyle may have been a royalist but his brother was Lord Broghill, one of Cromwell's closest friends and advisers. Cromwell himself paid a visit to Wilkins' lodgings where his daughter Elizabeth and her husband, the MP and member of the Committee on Trade, John Claypole, were staying, and took an obviously keen interest in the optical and mechanical devices displayed there. William Petty, though, had ambitions that went beyond the circles of the learned. In 1652 he moved to Ireland as Physician-General to the army (which badly needed medical help), and in the years which followed, applied his acumen for statistics to the business of mapping much of the forfeited land previously identified by the Civil Survey, 1654–6. This was not a matter of disinterested cartography. Petty's land survey was meant to provide Oliver's son Henry, the adversary of the zealot officers, with what, in both senses, was a measured design for the transfer of land from the defeated Irish landowners to the conquering army. He was now the anatomist of the mutilated body of Ireland, working day and night, dictating to short-hand clerks, to complete his assignment. Petty had turned himself, in effect, into the chief scientist of dispossession, but he persuaded himself that his precision was infinitely preferable to the still rougher justice of a chaotic and greedy land grab by the army. He was, after all, not just in the business of eviction but also in that of transplantation, finding land in Connacht on which the displaced Irish could be resettled. When after a year he delivered his immense work to Henry Cromwell, it was a map of population, ownership, land and beasts such as had never been seen before in British history. By mastering the data Petty had become, much to the disgust and dismay of ideological republicans like Ludlow who thought him the Protector's bootblack, the proconsul of Irish colonization. And he was not yet thirty.

For better or worse, men like William Petty were the prototype of the English bureaucrat: as polished in Latin poetry as they were proficient in higher statistics. They gorged on memoranda and got tipsy on the power machine that was the new English state. This was just as well since the scale of business tackled by the Protectorate's Council of State was positively gargantuan. On one, not atypical, day, for instance, the agenda ran to sixty-two items.

But energetic and competent as they might have been in their government offices, the administrators, the 'Yes, Protector' men, knew that all their efforts would come to naught unless they managed to rebuild the old alliance between Whitehall and the counties which had broken down so completely in the 1640s. That meant taking political, as much as administrative, decisions—to restore as justices of the peace the traditional landed gentry who had been roughly supplanted by the county committees appointed during the civil war. So, along with some of the trappings of the monarchy at Whitehall, innumerable, tentative little restorations took place in the counties. Men who had steered clear of, or who had been kept from, the magistracy now came back to pass judgement on drunks and thieves. The calendar of county society began to recover something like its ancient routines. Gentlemen (including the Protector's oldest surviving son Richard, who made no secret of his enjoyment) galloped after stags again. Houses that had been wrecked, plundered or

303

had fallen into neglect during the war were repaired and restored, their parks and farms restocked. Neighbouring landowners could entertain each other again over supper, a pipe and (thanks to the peace with Portugal) a glass of port. Although dancing and theatre were still officially frowned on, music and poetry were again encouraged (not least at Cromwell's own court) as edifying entertainments. The stirrings of pleasure were obscurely sensed. And they were not a good sign for the godly state.

The more republican and zealous members of the Council of State—Lambert himself and his fellow army officers Disbrowe and Charles Fleetwood—looked on the reawakening of the old county communities with misgivings. By encouraging them to come out from beneath the ruins and reseating them in their old places of authority, might not the Protectorate be sowing the seeds of its own undoing? From his perch in Ireland, Lieutenant-General Ludlow was even more incensed at what he took to be craven abdication of republican power to 'time-serving Cavaliers', lawyers and 'corrupt parsons', 'and in the meanwhile such men as are most faithfull to the publique interest for which so much blood hath been spilt . . . such as have been valiant in the field and ventured their lives . . . for the liberties of the people, such as have all along in the greatest revolutions and dangers . . . appeared in their purses and persons for the true interest of the Nation, that these honest men should be thus slighted and undermined' he thought a cause for scandal, contempt and alarm. For such men to come into parliament was to invite back royalism in

304

a Trojan Horse.

In the spring of 1655 their suspicions seemed to have been confirmed when a royalist rising, incompetently led by John Penruddock, broke out in Wiltshire. It was quickly smashed, and was followed by the usual parade of hangings and beheadings, Penruddock's taking place in May. But the sudden threat, together with well-founded fears of assassination, was enough to jolt Cromwell out of complacency. He was also badly shaken by the disastrous outcome of an expedition against the Spanish in the Caribbean, an unaccustomed military fiasco which he took as God's verdict on the sinfulness of the nation. Statistics weren't everything, it seemed.

Time, then, for contrition. Time for repentance. Time for a heavy dose of zeal. For about a year and a half from July 1655 Cromwell let the outriders of righteousness, the major-generals, have their head, inflicting on England a coercive military regime the like of which had not been seen since the security states of Walsingham and Thomas Cromwell. Over the reassuring map of the counties were laid twelve military cantons, each governed by a major-general. Their mission was, in the first instance, a police action, dismantling the embryonic county militias and replacing them by rock-solid loyal cavalry financed by a 'decimation'—collecting a tenth of the value of royalist or suspected royalist estates. Security and pre-emptive deterrence were thus economically combined. But Cromwell, and to an even greater degree his generals, were also convinced that a true pacification meant tackling the task which so often had been shirked or postponed in the name of reconciliation: the rigorous conversion of profane, carnal England to a state of godly submission. In the name of the decimation, gentry like Sir Ralph Verney, who had returned to England but whose record as a supporter of parliament in 1642 was not enough to clear him of suspicion, were summoned to appear before the generals and their assessors and give security for their levies. Failure to pay meant confiscation or imprisonment.

Very quickly the major-generals became a flying squad for righteousness. Quixotic though it was, this was a crusade that the Puritan zealots had been fighting since the beginning of the civil war, when James I's permissive *Book of Sports* had been burned by the Common Hangman and edicts published to make sure pleasure never happened on a Sunday; now once more 'no persons shall hereafter exercise or keep maintain or be present at any wrestling, shooting, Bowling, ringing of bells . . . masque, Wake, otherwise called feasts, church-ales, dancing and games'. Away too with cock-fights, cock-running, horse-races and bear-baiting. Woe betide anyone caught putting up a maypole, working on the Sabbath or furtively celebrating Christmas. Alehouses were to come under vigilant licensing and inspection and were to be purged of fiddlers and gamblers. The Swearing and Cursing Act punished anyone caught uttering a profanity with a fine according to their status (more for gents than commoners). Children under twelve heard saying something filthy were to be whipped. Convicted fornicators were to spend three months in prison, adulterers to suffer the death penalty.

This is the stereotypical image we have of Cromwell's England: a dour Puritan Sparta where the military was mobilized to wipe out fun. And as far as the ambitions of the major-generals go, it's not altogether wide of the mark. But, needless to say, the experiment in enforced virtue was a dismal flop, not least because of the impossibility of supplying the manpower to police it. Lacking their own Enforcers for Christ, the major-generals had no option but to fall back on the constables and justices who were already in place. And they were very unlikely to be sympathetic to the great work. On the contrary, the records of local magistrates are full of malefactors who paid no attention whatsoever to the morals police. Punishment, when it was meted out, was often an elaborate joke. When John Witcombe of Barton St David in Somerset was put in the stocks for swearing, his own minister, protesting the illegality of the law, brought him ale to keep his spirits up. In Cheshire, a servant girl who had been denounced as flagrantly violating the Sabbath by working on a Sunday was (incorrectly) judged a minor so that, instead of being fined, she could be 'corrected' by her master. In the presence of the local constable her punishment was 'turned all into a jest. The master plucked off a small branch of heath from a turf and therewith gave her two or three such gentle touches on her cloathes as would have not hurt an infant two days old.'

In many places this must have been as deep as the bite of 'Cromwell's mastiffs' reached. Secretary Thurloe's papers are full of their bitter complaints at the hopelessness of their task. 'I am much troubled with these market towns,' Major-General Berry wrote from Monmouth, 'everywhere vice abounding and the magistrates fast asleep.' But if their attempt to impose godliness on horseback was a failure, they did alienate enough of the people whom the Protectorate needed to survive—the county gentry—to give Cromwell serious pause. Although the military regime did its best to intimidate during the elections of 1656, the results produced a majority which swept parliament clean of their supporters and dismantled their entire structure of power. Prodded by the pragmatists on the Council, Cromwell now swung back—permanently this time—to a conservative regime of 'settling'.

In the summer of 1657 he accepted the 'Humble Petition and Advice' and a government that was virtually the same as the reformed monarchy envisioned by the Long Parliament, the one critical difference being the commitment to protect liberty of conscience. But even this commitment was beginning to wobble, as the threshold of censure on Christian sects deemed scandalous became much lower. Despite assuring Cromwell (he could not take an oath) in a face-to-face interview that he submitted to the powers that be, the Quaker leader George Fox was still repeatedly locked up in conditions of nightmarish filth and squalor as a menace to the public peace. When he attempted to warm himself by lighting straw in one of his cells, his gaolor pissed on the fire to put it out and threw shit on the prisoner from a gallery above. Horrible though these trials were, they were nothing compared to the fate of Fox's maverick protégé James Nayler, tried for blasphemy by parliament and the Council of State in the late autumn of 1656. Nayler's crime had been to ride through Bristol in imitation of the

Saviour (pretending that he *was* Christ, said his prosecutors), his few disciples crying hosanna as he trotted through the rain-soaked streets. For his deranged temerity Nayler was pilloried for two hours, his forehead branded with a 'B' for blasphemer, his tongue bored through with a hot iron, and flogged through the streets of London— and then taken to Bristol to be flogged all over again before being incarcerated. He endured the excruciating torment with astonishing fortitude, but died four years later still suffering from its after-effects.

To his credit, Cromwell seemed as disturbed as anyone by the punitive overkill of the House and actually questioned the legitimacy of the trial. Afterwards he seemed to want to moderate the power of a single House and so became open to the restoration of a second, upper chamber, designated unimaginatively as 'the Other House'. Bulstrode Whitelocke was installed there as Viscount Henley, alongside Cromwell's two new sons-in-law, Viscount Fauconberg and Robert Rich, the Earl of Warwick. History seemed to be on fast rewind to 1642, with Cromwell playing the part of the king-who-might-have-been. As John Pym had wanted, parliament now had the authority to approve or veto appointments to the high offices of state. No taxes could be raised or declarations of war or peace made without its consent. In fact, the constitution of 1657 was so close to being the responsible monarchy, constrained by the common law, which the civil war had been fought for that it seemed only logical to cap it with a responsible king. Whitelocke, who had been against the idea five years earlier, had now evidently changed his mind, personally urging it on Cromwell as the best way to stabilize the future of the reformed state of Britain.

But though he was tempted, in the end Cromwell could not manage to turn himself into King Oliver I. Political reasons certainly weighed in his decision to reject the offer (provided he could none the less name his successor as Protector), for generals Lambert and Fleetwood all but threatened a major mutiny in the army should he dare to mount the throne. But Cromwell showed he could handle the army by abruptly cashiering Lambert and purging the officer corps of any he thought disloyal to his regime. The most serious restraint came, rather, from his own exacting conscience: his deeply felt certainty that, since God had decreed the 'extirpation' of the monarchy in England, it was not for him to overturn that decision. If a new sign came from Providence that he should indeed be a king unto Israel that would be different. But the Almighty fought shy of direct communication in 1657 and the brow of the Protector remained unanointed.

Oliver Cromwell would, in fact, get to wear the crown, but only once he was dead. On 3 September 1658, the anniversary of the battles of both Dunbar and Worcester, he passed away. While he was breathing his last a tornado-like tempest bore down on England, ripping out trees and sending church steeples (with their unused belfries) crashing to the ground. To the omen-conscious (which meant virtually everyone), this was no coincidence. It was the Devil coming to get his due, for an old story had circulated that after the battle of Worcester Oliver had sold his soul for supreme power. There were other dire portents. Although 1658 was a rare year free of battles, won or lost, the shadow of mortality still seemed to fall heavily over the nation. The winter had been brutal. Crows were found with their feet frozen to branches. Trade stopped. Grain prices went through the roof. An epidemic of the 'quartan' fever (probably some form of influenza) held in its deadly grip a country already weakened by plague. Poor John Evelyn had his darling five-year-old prodigy son die in late January, and a second child perish barely two weeks later. 'Here ends the joy of my life,' he wrote later, 'for which I go even mourning to my grave.' Terrified survivors in the cities abstained from fish and flesh and ate nothing 'but sage posset and pancake or eggs or now and then a turnip or carrot'. Whatever she ate, fever and cancer carried off Cromwell's favourite daughter in August. The Protector fell into a distraction of sorrow and then seemed to go under with the sickness himself. At Greenwich John Evelyn joined the crowds watching a beached whale thrash its flukes hopelessly on the mudflats, blood pouring from its wounded spout. Even reasonable men were mindful of the portent. *Leviathan* was in its death throes.

By the time the leaves were on the turn Oliver was dead, though not quite gone. There had been a botched embalming. The regime, which wanted to preserve the Protectorate, had started by failing to preserve the Protector. But before the inevitable atrophy, an effigy had been cast from the body. It was then exposed for a lying-in-state at Somerset House, in the manner of the medieval kings, robed in imperial purple, the shrine lit by a great incandescence of candles. But then it was decided that he should be winched upright, and there he stood for another two months, stiffly erect like a mannikin, crown on head, sceptre and orb in his hand, king at last. On 23 November there was a massive state funeral which ended in ignominious fiasco. According to the French ambassador (who was not exactly innocent in the débâcle), altercations about diplomatic precedent and protocol delayed the beginning of the enormous procession, which took seven hours to file through London. By the time it finally got to Westminster Abbey it was nearly pitch dark, and the inadequate supply of candles inside the church made it impossible for the ceremonies to be prolonged. So for the ruler who, above all others, had most loved sermons, and who relentlessly meditated out loud on God's purpose in history, there were no funeral orations, no prayers, no preaching. Just a few short sharp blasts on the trumpets before the effigy was bundled into a waiting tomb. But not before little Robert Uvedale, one of the Westminster school boys summoned to attend, had made his way through the chaotically exiting crowd and stolen away with a souvenir, the 'Majesty Scutcheon' on which the arms of the British nations were figured on a flag of white satin.

Had Cromwell been able to write his own funeral eulogy, what would he have wanted to say about his extraordinary career? Certainly not its trajectory from obscurity to supreme power, because, avidly as he embraced it, there was always a side of Cromwell which was deeply disgusted by it. When, not long before he died, he protested that he 'would have been glad to have been living under a woodside, to have kept a flock of sheep rather than to have undertaken such a place as this was', the confession seemed, and was, perfectly genuine. His was, in fact, the classic case of great power falling to the very person who least wanted it, and precisely for that reason. The only hero of the civil wars who wanted it even less was Thomas Fairfax, who never quite recovered from the trauma of the trial and execution of the king—and who would re-emerge from his Yorkshire obscurity to help put Charles I's son back on the throne. Cromwell could never be that self-effacing because he had, like Moses, gone through an experience of the Call, just as surely as if he had heard a voice coming from the Burning Bush, and believed that his life thereafter was devoted to the execution of God's design for the nation.

Ironically, it was just because that design seemed to be a work-in-progress for Jehovah who only vouchsafed glimpses of it now and then, even to a servant as doggedly devoted as Cromwell, that he never much felt the need to work out a consistent strategy for the republic, nor a policy which might have been able to reconcile the self-evidently conflicting claims of parliamentary liberty and Christian godliness. Nor did he even bother to arbitrate in any consistent way between zeal and freedom. Rather he let God show him the way. And if God changed his mind every so often, well that was His privilege.

Buried amid the immense screed of Cromwell's pious circumlocutions to parliament was, however, a genuine statement of what he wanted for England, if circumstances would ever permit. (That he could *make* the circumstances permit, nudge

God along a bit, was a thought he dismissed as sacrilegious.) It turns out that the vision of this angry, ruthless, overbearing, self-torturing man was a thing of consummate sweetness, humanity and intelligence. More astonishingly still, the most deeply felt principle of the man who created the matrix of the modern English state was, in its essence, liberal. For at the heart of that conviction lay tolerance: the unforced hope that men (provided they were not Catholic) might be allowed to be left alone to receive Christ in any way they wished; to hoe their few acres and keep their pigs, untroubled by the rude intrusions of the state—always provided they did not conspire against the freedom of others. After all his slaughters, his marches and his red-faced fits of shouting, what Oliver Cromwell really wanted, for everyone, was a quiet life: 'a free and uninterrupted Passage of the Gospel running through the midst of us and Liberty for all to hold forth and profess with sobriety their Light and Knowledge therein, according as the Lord in his rich Grace and Wisdom hath dispensed to every man and with the same freedom to practice and exercise the Faith of the Gospel and lead quiet and peaceable lives in all Godliness and Honesty without any Interruption from the Powers God hath set over this Commonwealth.'

It would be perhaps another two and a half centuries before anything like this dream could be realized. And by then, really, no one much cared.